Finger-Licking Good

Finger-Licking Good

The Ins and Outs of Lesbian Sex

Tamsin Wilton

With cartoons by the author

CASSELL

For a catalogue of related titles in our
Sexual Politics/Global Issues list please write to us
at the address below.

Cassell
Wellington House
125 Strand
London WC2R 0BB

127 West 24th Street
New York, NY 10011

First published 1996

British Library Cataloguing-in-Publication Data
A catalogue record for this book is available from the British Library.

ISBN 0–304–33257–7 (hardback)
      0–304–33259–3 (paperback)

Typeset by Ben Cracknell Studios
Printed and bound in Great Britain by Biddles Ltd
of Guildford and King's Lynn

Contents

Acknowledgements

I have been wanting to write this book for years, but could never think of a publisher brave enough to publish it. I could hardly believe my ears when Roz Hopkins gave the proposal the Cassell thumbs up. So huge thanks to her for her faith in the idea, and for being supportive and interested all the way along. Far too many of my friends have had to put up with helping me thrash out (so to speak) my ideas about lesbian sexuality at every stage from the decidedly half-baked to the over-cooked. For this I must thank Norma Daykin, Lorraine Ayensu, Hilary Lindsay, Dede Liss, Mandy Kidd, Cécile Velu, Keiko Ishimaru and (especially) Lisa Adkins, whose gift for remaining lucid after the clubs have closed is extraordinary! Thanks, too, to the students on my 'Lesbian Culture and Society' course in 1995, who engaged so enthusiastically in heated but never acrimonious debate, and to Fiona Stewart, Susan Kippax and Marg Hay for taking the trouble to send me material I would otherwise never have come across.

Thanks to Tee Corrine, Della Grace, Kiss and Tell, Lawrence Jangey-Paget and Laura MacGregor for permission to reproduce their photographs. Thanks to Dave Watkins for technical support.

Needless to say, final responsibility for the resulting book, warts and all, is mine.

This one's for the dykes!

Introduction:
Of Battles Lost and Won, or Why We Need Another Book on Lesbian Sexual Politics

Half way through researching this book I spent a pleasant evening at Kitty Lips, the 'in' club for lesbians and their friends in London. As often happens to me nowadays in dyke clubs, I found myself in a kind of time warp. The light show and the decor, with its huge copies of Warhol portraits of camp goddesses – Taylor, Minnelli, Monroe (together with a clumsy attempt to 'do' Sandra Bernhardt in the same style) – reminded me forcefully of the days of my misspent youth in the 1960s. So too, of course, did the 'loved-up' club drug culture of ecstasy. Great. I loved it, it made me feel right at home. But that was the only thing which was familiar. By the end of the night I was forced to admit that I was completely out of my cultural depth. Fortunately, the baby butch chum I was hanging out with was a fellow sociologist, and quite content to put up with my on-the-spot ethnographic theorizing.

Kitty Lips was swarming with young women in Beth-of-Brookside drag. Clad in cute angora cut-off tops or satin skirts, they simply were not giving off any semiotic signals which said 'dyke' to me. Hardened pervert that I am, the sight of fluffy, angelic girl couples entwined in erotic abandon succeeded in shocking me. Moreover, some of the cute girls were boys. Not only were the semiotics unfamiliar, so too were the sexual interactions. There was the familiar mix of lesbians, gay boys and curious hets (recognizeable by the anxiety with which the man kept hold of his woman). There were also several triads, of two men and one woman, engaged in preliminary sex play of various kinds. Nobody (except the author of the current work) turned a hair. I was recalling my own hippy adolescence, and how I laughed at the adults who complained that they couldn't tell the boys from the girls. Suddenly, I was on the wrong side of the generation gap, with no idea how I had got there.

This, then, is postmodern, postfeminist, *postqueer* lesbian sexuality. It seems in many ways utopian. Here are young women who are so safe and secure in their lesbianism (at least, in this relatively protected space) that they can wear what they want. They don't have to make the effort to engage with any bullshit about lesbians being masculine or wanting to be men; they can perform 'femme' to the fluffy hilt without signalling that they are out looking for a butch; they can be as polymorphous-perverse as they want without fear of being thrown out of the sisterhood. This is sure as hell political, but not within the traditional paradigm of feminism or gay liberation.

Of course, much of this reflects nothing more radical than fashion. I can trace an historical circular movement around the twin poles of gender. In the 1960s, when androgyny was coded feminine, both sexes wore flowing locks, loose brightly coloured clothing in crushed velvet, corduroy, satin and suede, adorned with glittering mirrors and chains, and moved in a sensual cloud of incense and the tinkle of many bells. In the 1980s and early 1990s, androgyny became masculine, with both sexes sporting flat tops or Ripley-style crops, designer jeans, Doc Martens or Timberland boots, chinos, crisply styled jackets or sports wear. Now we seem to be back with androgyny-as-feminine: the emphasis for both sexes is on sensual fabrics – washed corduroy, brushed or sueded cotton, satin and angora, and Jean-Paul even got the boys to wear kilts and crop tops (the height of gender-fuck on bodies sculpted into butch excess down at the gym). But fashion itself is a barometer of social change, albeit a crude one, and the androgyny of the high street now contains distinct references to the gender-fuck of queer.

I, meanwhile, had just returned from a conference in Melbourne, where I had picked up a copy of *the Journal of Australian Lesbian Feminist Studies* containing an approbatory review of revolutionary feminist Sheila Jeffreys's latest book *The Lesbian Heresy*, in which she systematically attacks the shift towards the erotic which she sees as depoliticizing lesbianism. The cultural dissonance was just too great. Jeffreys was simply (and rightly) irrelevant in the context of Kitty Lips. The sex wars, it appears, have not been won or lost; they have simply become unimportant.

Casualties of the forgotten war?

If the sex wars are now irrelevant, then so is this book. Clearly, I would not put myself through the stress of writing it (the hours poring over lesbian porn magazines, the unpleasant necessity of stocking my bookshelves with lesbian erotica, the hands-on research with sex toys ... you can imagine how hard it was) if I thought the task was pointless. Indeed, many lesbian writers have confidently declared the all-clear, speaking of the hostilities over lesbian sexuality in the past tense. For example, Susie Bright (aka Susie Sexpert) proclaims that 'the dildo wars are over',[1] and announces that 'Lesbians are the vanguard of cross-pornographic pollination'.[2] Yet Bright herself has been caught in the crossfire more than once, and every lesbian who produces erotic texts (whether in the form of images or writing), or who publicly supports the open exploration of lesbian sexuality, has a tale to tell of being trashed, censored or subjected to verbal abuse.

The phrase 'sex wars' refers to an exchange of hostilities within the context of feminism, but the silencing of lesbian sexuality takes place at the hands of other, far more powerful, forces as well. As Canadian dyke sex artist Persimmon Blackbridge reminds us, feminists have never been the most important controlling force in lesbian sexuality. She writes: 'Let's be clear about this: it wasn't feminists who taught me sexual shame. I learned it long before, under harder hands.'[3]

Lesbian sexuality – desire, sexual activity, sexual pleasure, sexual identity – is everywhere under attack. Right-wing politicians and governments, religious fundamentalists, straightforward bigots, sexists and homophobes, moral entrepreneurs of all kinds, all devote frightening amounts of energy and money in an attempt to eradicate us and our pleasures. We cannot afford to lose sight of that threat, nor must we stop evolving strategies of resistance. Disturbingly, those feminists who also seek to police lesbian sexuality have not merely relented, taken out a subscription for *On Our Backs* and sent off for their very own sex toys. *That* would indicate that the sex wars had, indeed, been won, within feminism if not on the wider battlefield. Such is not the case, however, as my own experience shows.

I am involved with lesbian sexuality on many levels (stop giggling at the back!). As an academic I teach about lesbian sexuality at my university, both in open-access Lesbian Studies courses and in a

'Feminist Approaches to Sexuality' course on a Master's programme in Women's Studies. As someone working in the field of HIV/AIDS, I have argued for explicit safer sex materials for women, both lesbian and non-lesbian, and have criticized the failure of the AIDS community to provide these materials. As a lesbian and a member of the wider lesbian and feminist 'communities', I have taken part in debate and discussion about many issues surrounding lesbian sexuality, and I have also had lots of lesbian sex – believing that theory and practice must go hand in glove (so to speak).

All this activity has been very low-key, but despite this, every aspect of my involvement in lesbian sexuality has elicited hostility from other feminists, either directly or indirectly, as well as attempts at censorship from outside feminism altogether. Angry students have tried to get a number of books for my courses banned from the university library on the grounds that they 'promote violence against women'; male academics from another faculty have also exerted pressure on the library to remove *Gay Times* from its shelves because they found it offensive; and the local community bookshop refuses to stock some of the books on my reading lists because they are 'pornographic'. The British radical feminist journal *Trouble and Strife* asked me to submit an article on lesbian photographer Della Grace, but when the finished

4

article turned out to be supportive of not only Grace but gay photographer Robert Mapplethorpe, they refused to publish it without substantial changes (which I was not prepared to make). The same journal, having commissioned me to illustrate an article (for free), censored one of the cartoons I sent in. Without thinking it necessary to consult me, they chopped it in half, removing not only the rude punchline but the whole point of the joke.

It is important, however, to set *feminist* attempts at censorship in context. It was not feminists who attacked the university library for stocking *Gay Times*. Moreover, the institutional power of feminism is not great. If a feminist journal will not publish an article, a non-feminist journal will. Potentially the most damaging brush with censorship that I have experienced was from a mainstream academic publisher who, when I delivered the manuscript of a book on safer-sex representation, refused to publish the accompanying illustrations, informing me that 'we certainly cannot publish any of the proposed illustrations depicting nudity and various sex acts'. So resolute was their refusal to allow these images to take the public stage under their name that they were prepared to release me from my contract and lose the book from their production schedule.[4]

I am not alone in my experiences of censorship and attempted censorship. But my work is not especially outrageous and is largely confined to fairly narrow circles – the AIDS fraternity, local lesbian communities and fellow academics. That even such tame stuff as this should spark off attempts at silencing and censure indicates just how ubiquitous is the hostility to queer sexuality in general and lesbian sexuality in particular. The sex wars are not over. If anything, the opposing camps have simply become entrenched.

On power, sex and the lesbian thought prefects

I wrote this book for many reasons, some of which I am probably not aware of myself. The most important reason is that there are people out there who clearly believe that they have the right to judge, to criticize and to attempt to control (or, indeed, to prevent) what I and other lesbians do in bed. What is more, many of them see it as their duty to save me, in one way or another, from perdition. My sexual behaviour apparently puts me at risk of any number of fates worse than death, from eternally cooking in the fires of hell to becoming male-identified, a lesbian heretic or a snool.[5] As the survivor of a stringent religious upbringing, I know at first hand the harm that priests and prophets can do to a human being, and I am no more inclined to be 'saved' by the prophets of revolutionary feminism than by the vicar of my childhood parish (who, incidentally, got his kicks out of pulling little girls' panties down and giving them a good spanking). This book is an act of resistance.

I am many things – writer, lesbian, lone mother, activist, teacher, sociologist, cat lover, carnivore – and included in this long list of 'things' that I am is the word 'academic'. The fact that I am an academic has specific implications for the way I approach the act of writing a book about lesbian sex. Firstly, it means that I have access to an enormous body of information about sexual behaviour, sexual identity and sexuality, and that I can integrate that into my thinking and writing (and, if I so choose, into my fucking). Secondly, it is noted on a fairly regular basis that academics have an unfortunate tendency to believe that the intellectual skills which they have acquired mean that their utterances are more objective (and hence somehow more 'truthful') than those of non-academics. Critics – as a rule, speaking from a position of commitment to the rights of people who have the 'wrong' genitals, colour, class, dis/ability, sexual orientation, language or age and whose access to the academy is consequently restricted or resisted – point out that 'objectivity' is always in some way ideological. Until very recently, 'objective truth' more often than not consisted of those sets of beliefs and assertions which coincided with the interests of white, heterosexual men, members of a ruling-class who controlled the entire academic enterprise. 'Scientific objectivity' has been manufactured, manipulated and deployed to justify everything from the slave trade and the Final Solution to withholding suffrage from women and castrating gay men[6]. As an uneasy inhabitant of the academy, I am constantly aware of the need to speak from my own position, that of a white queer woman of working-class origin, rather than some illusory position of 'expert'.

My thinking about lesbian sexuality is (of course) deeply rooted in my own experience[7] of sex with women and with men, and owes at least as much to those experiences as to academic research. In reflecting on this, I am following an honourable lesbian tradition. The writers on

6

lesbian sex whose work I most respect – Joan Nestle, Lizard Jones, Persimmon Blackbridge, Audre Lorde, Dorothy Allison, Susan Stewart and Pat Califia are among the names that spring to mind – have all produced theoretical or political writings which are inseparably inter-woven with accounts of their own sexual lives and selves.[8] Let me begin this exploration of lesbian sex with a personal anecdote.

There's someone in my head telling me what to do

Come and be a voyeuse on a scene from my lesbian past which might be familiar to you. I'm in bed with my first Real Lesbian Lover. We're at that delightful and anxious stage of recognizing that this is going to be More Than Just Sex; we're on the threshold of A Relationship. But it's all still deliciously fluid and unformed, and hasn't yet solidified into familiarity or power games or being invited everywhere as a single unit.

It's brunchtime – about three in the afternoon. We've spent all night and all morning fucking like bunnies, and now we're catching up on each other's sexual histories in a lazy, curious exchange. We're both idiotically secure in the certainty that no one can *possibly*, *ever*, have had such wonderful sex before. Only this is *slightly* different, because all my previous lovers up until this point have been men or straight women. There's a tacit assumption that they don't count, that I was some kind of virgin when I met her. So I'm just a tad nervous hearing about all *her* previous lovers. She's much younger than me and seems to have got through half the dykes in the city. My nervousness increases. But she reassures me that this is far and away The Best Sex She Has Ever Had, and begins to draw little circles on my skin with a wet fingertip while she tells me about the Lesbian Sex Police.

The Lesbian Sex Police are a manifestation of the way she (and most of her previous lovers) internalized the proscriptions of a peculiarly narrow and punitive version of lesbian feminism. They may not have been real women, but their influence on her sexuality has been very real indeed. She recites the list of prohibited (because male-identified) behavi-ours: looking at a woman with desire (offence – sexual objectification); gazing at, adoring or touching her breasts (offence – colluding with the fetishizing of women's body parts); lying on top of or underneath a woman (offence – replicating the power inequalities of heterosex); touching her buttocks or her cunt (offence – fragmenting her body);

telling her (or even thinking) that she is 'beautiful' (offence – resorting to an oppressive patriarchal concept); caring whether either of you has an orgasm (offence – being goal-orientated in an inherently masculinist way); or doing it with the light on so you can watch each other (sexual objectification again). The idea of penetrating a woman's vagina, even with a fingertip, was regarded as such an overwhelmingly patriarchal act that it was unthinkable, while sex toys belonged in some padlocked chamber of horrors along with iron maidens, thumbscrews and racks. These rules severely limited the amount of sexual pleasure she was able to share with her similarly haunted partners. Then I turned up.

I was an improper lesbian feminist. Innocent (at that time) of the gospel of revolutionary 1970s lesbian feminism, uninformed about the horrors of male-identification, overwhelmed with delight and excitement at being able to put my hands on a woman, I hadn't been properly socialized into this subculture (which, as she spoke, increasingly began to feel like a sect). And, just as the devil is supposed to do to the unwary, I had led her into temptation. She was letting her fingers do the walking even as we spoke, and the theoretical/political aspects of our conversation didn't develop much further that day. But her painful revelation made a deep impression on me.

You're a cad, Angela

Since then, I have discussed this question with many lesbians, and read the accounts of many more. Some speak of the Lesbian Sex Police, some of the Lesbian Thought Police. All agree that a small and angry group of women have had an extraordinarily powerful effect on the beliefs, self-esteem and sexual activities of large numbers of lesbian feminists.

I am unhappy with the word 'police' in this context. The police have very real power, backed up by the patriarchal machinery of the state. However angry and vocal a bunch of lesbians might be, they have really very little power. They are not about to knock on your door in the middle of the night, arrest you for possessing a cucumber with intent, and drag you off to languish in the nick. To refer to them as lesbian police is to exaggerate their power. This is politically worrying on two counts. Firstly, because it tends to make us forget that, as Leonore Tiefer reminds us, 'the differences among feminists pale in comparison with the differences between those committed to the elimination of oppression against women and those committed to maintaining the status quo'.[9] Secondly, because the idea of 'lesbian police' trivializes the very real powers of the state police. The power which such women have is given to them by the lesbian and feminist communities, not by governments and the machinery of law. As cases such as *Bowers* v. *Hardwick* in the USA, or Operation Spanner in the UK demonstrate all too clearly, the *real* police have *real* power to invade the privacy of your sex life and destroy it.[10]

Lacking legislative power or formally sanctioned authority, lesbians who attempt to control how other lesbians have sex, or how they speak about lesbian sex in words and pictures, do have a significant amount of community power. As has already been demonstrated, they can restrict other lesbians' access to books, can prevent their work being published in feminist or community publications, can encourage local lesbian communities to exclude certain women, and can make some women's lives miserable by labelling them pornographers, fascists or supporters of violence against women. It is damaging to anyone to be excluded from a community which is important to them. For lesbians, faced with a wider society which refuses to recognize our existence, or which is directly hostile, to lose the support of our local lesbian community can be devastating. This is especially true for lesbians who are young and still exploring their identity, for older lesbians, for lesbians who are disabled, ill or living in institutions, minority lesbians, homeless lesbians, lesbians living in poverty or lesbians who live outside the major urban centres. It is no small matter to attempt to police 'the lesbian community' by excluding those women who do not conform to a limited model of feminist political correctness. And, as many lesbians have made clear, this experience of exclusion can be very hurtful:

> when the women's movement started, I said, hot diggity, that's great. And I really feel like over the years the most hurtful and cutting rejections I've had have come from my sisters, primarily in the women's movement and later in the PC [politically correct] lesbian movement.[11]

Given that the power wielded by the 'sex police' is located in the community itself, they more closely resemble prefects than police. Prefects, those conformist pupils chosen by adult teachers to police the behaviour of their peers within the school regime, become traitors to and controllers of their peer culture without acquiring the real power of adults. This is pretty much how the lesbian sex prefects behave. It is also important not to lose sight of the secondary function of prefects, which is to deflect disobedience and dissent away from the real source of authority. This too is useful when considering the lesbian sex prefects: because feminism is *not* the enemy. Without thirty years of feminist activism Kitty Lips would not be possible. Without thirty years of feminist theory, the cutting-edge firework display of Queer Theory would not have emerged.

Many of the most important defenders of lesbian sexuality, many of the most productive makers of lesbian erotica and/or representations of lesbian sex, are feminists. It was the rise of the Women's Liberation Movement (WLM), the second wave of feminist political activism, which first enabled lesbians to claim a proud and transgressive identity. I am not attempting a wholesale recuperation of feminism here, just pointing out that feminism has been of immeasurable importance to the development of our lesbian and/or queer communities. The relationship between feminist politics/ideology and lesbian sexuality has been a complex and contradictory one, but mostly positive nevertheless, as Persimmon Blackbridge recounts:

> The feminist movement gave me far more than its faults. It gave me hope, pride, work, a place to stand. But sometimes it seemed no different from where I grew up. You had to pretend and not notice you were pretending. You had to shut up and swallow it. So I went to those meetings and kept my mouth shut when some of the bad pictures in the anti-porn slide shows turned me on.[12]

The lesbian sex prefects somehow became the loudest voice in lesbian feminism (indeed, in radical feminism[13]). For lesbianism was important to feminism. Despite widespread anti-lesbianism within the WLM in its early days,[14] the lesbian soon came to represent, for many women, a radical-feminist ideal. In the words of Sydney Abbott and Barbara Love, 'The startling fact is that Lesbians already meet the criteria that Women's Liberation has set up to describe the liberated woman ... Lesbians live what Feminists theorize about; they embody Feminism.'[15]

But feminists did not make any attempt to understand lesbian culture – which, after all, predated the WLM. Rather, the *idea* of lesbianism was co-opted into a very specific political agenda. To be a lesbian was to occupy some utopian safe space outside the troubled realm of male-dominated heterosexuality. It was to refuse male control, to challenge male supremacy at what radical feminism identified as its very heart – sexuality. This position was famously summed up by the American breakaway group Radicalesbians in 1970: 'A lesbian is the rage of all women condensed to the point of explosion.'[16] As the representatives and guardians of the feminist utopia, it was simply intolerable that lesbians should appear to be or do anything which was associated with men and male power. And as the feminist deconstruction of male supremacy and patriarchal heterosex developed, more and more behaviours became identified as male supremacist power play: butch and femme, sadomasochism (S/M), using 'pornography', etc. etc. Having initially offered lesbians *for the first time* a political and social framework within which they could be proud of being lesbians rather than apologetically assimilationist, feminism swiftly went on to reject almost every aspect of traditional lesbian culture.

The irony in this is profound. Lesbians were trashed for any behaviour which could be labelled male-identified, from political activism with gay men to commenting on another woman's attractiveness. Yet the radical feminist idea of the lesbian was entirely governed by masculinity. If a lesbian is 'the rage of all women', who is that rage directed against? Men. If lesbianism represents a separatist safe space, who or what is it separating from? Men. If lesbians must control their sexual behaviour to avoid doing anything which a man might do, or which expresses something like male power, who does that leave safely in charge of the greater part of sexuality? Men.

This book is in part an attempt to reclaim lesbian sexual culture *for lesbians*. Not for male voyeurism, not for feminist politics, not for appropriation by het capitalists or for exploitation by religious or right-wing moral entrepreneurs, but for lesbians. It is an act of tom-catting around the whole field of sex, marking out lesbian territory. For sex is important to lesbians on many levels, and our lesbian sexual culture is rich, exciting and various. Nor is this simply sexual libertarianism, because sex and sexuality are always unavoidably *political*, and sexual 'identity' is always a social and cultural construct (and, hence, always political too).

The sex wars are not over, the dildo wars are not over, the porn wars are not over; it's tempting to suggest that perhaps it's time to make love, not war! But this is too simplistic, and fails to resolve anything. What I've tried to do instead is to stand back from the heated arguments *within* lesbian communities and develop a fresh perspective on each of them, drawing attention to the disturbing strand of politico-moralistic dogmatism which runs through pro-censorship feminism and celebrating the strength and vitality of lesbian sexual culture. There is some nasty stuff in these pages: the chapters on pornography and sadomasochism contain material which is both disturbing and offensive. But it is not porn or s/m which disturb and offend, but the anti-porn and anti-s/m tactics of the four-legs-good-two-legs-bad[17] school of feminism. It is distressing to recognize the extent to which the lesbian prefects, a handful of misguided and vocal women, have attempted to control the sexual behaviour of other women, and the horrific strategies which they have been prepared to use. It is this legacy of the 'sex wars' which has been a profoundly damaging influence on some lesbian communities and has done much harm.

I need to make absolutely clear my own allegiance to radical feminism, and my anger that the actions of a minority have made it so easy to dismiss radical feminism as erotophobic, man-hating or anti-lesbian. I have, therefore, tried to be as specific as possible about the particular political perspectives *within* feminism that I am discussing. The oversimplistic division into 'radical feminism, socialist feminism, liberal feminism', which unhappily remains the staple of too many Women's Studies courses, is really not very useful. So I refer to revolutionary feminists (by which I mean feminists who support the political approach exemplified by Sheila Jeffreys and the Leeds Revolutionary Feminist Group), political lesbians (i.e. women who define lesbianism as a refusal to have sex with *men*, not as anything to do with sexuality between women), pro-censorship feminists and, when speaking of a political trend which includes all of these groups, orthodox lesbian feminism. I hope this will help to highlight the fact that it is a minority of women within feminism who hold these views, and that they are not representative of feminism, or even of 'radical feminism'.

The state in our bedroom

Although this book is primarily an exploration of political struggles around sex *within* lesbian communities, it is set against a background of wider struggle. The resurgence of the right wing, the revival of religious fundamentalism, the increase in fascist activity and the construction of 'family values' as a political and social totem, together constitute a frighteningly powerful force anxious to eradicate lesbians and lesbian sex in particular. The shameful spectacle of these groups making political capital out of the HIV pandemic makes it clear that they will stoop very low indeed to achieve their goals. Queer sex is in the public eye as never before, with the in-your-face tactics of the new breed of activism engendered by these threats to our wellbeing and survival. Many of the codes and ideas of the queer subculture have been assimilated into a mainstream culture long accustomed to parasitizing on dyke and fag energy.[18] Yet this increased visibility is both the product and the potential target of homophobic and anti-lesbian hostility.

Being a lesbian may be 'cool' between the pages of liberal newspapers or trendy fashion magazines; it is still dangerous out in the real world. Lesbians continue to be harmed just for being lesbian. Many of us risk losing our jobs, our homes, our children, access to our sick lovers, our liberty or even our lives if our sexuality is known. Even those of us with the good fortune to work in places where our sexuality is superficially tolerated (such as most British or American universities) work in an atmosphere of unspoken antagonism and obscured homophobia which is continually draining.

The public face of lesbianism in mainstream culture is, importantly, a young, white, privileged face. Black and minority lesbians, working-class lesbians and older lesbians are all hidden in the mainstream co-option of lesbian images. The same has happened in feminism. The universal image of 'the lesbian' is far from truly representative of the diversity of lesbian communities, nor does it reflect the nuances of race, class, age and dis/ability which are present in *all* sexual desires, encounters, behaviours and cultures, not only lesbian ones. Clearly, lesbianism is co-opted by many different groups in the service of many different political agendas, and is in addition co-opted for purely commercial reasons by postindustrial capitalism, as Julia Epstein and Kristina Straub suggest:

> gender ambiguity, in and of itself, answers to many political masters ... capitalism allows marginalized or stigmatized forms of sexual behaviour and identity to filter into contemporary consumer culture

packaged in disguised forms which take away the edge of political threat posed by those sexualities.[19]

However, the exploitation of queer culture by capitalism is not exclusively negative. Were there no capitalist interest in exploiting queer markets, you would not be holding this (commercially published) queer book in your hands. The exploitation can, to a certain extent, be a two-way process, although we queers attempt to ride the monster of capitalism at our peril. This book represents my five minutes in the saddle. It is for dykes.

Notes

1. Susie Bright *Susie Sexpert's Lesbian Sex World* (San Francisco: Cleis Press, 1990), p.137. For more on the dildo wars, see Chapter 7.

2. *Ibid*. p. 140.

3. Kiss and Tell, *Her Tongue on My Theory: Images, Essays and Fantasies* (Vancouver: Press Gang, 1994), p. 7.

4. To satisfy your curiosity, the illustrations in question included a photograph from a safer-sex booklet for gay men produced by the Terrence Higgins Trust, a telephone sex-line advert from a heterosexual women's soft porn magazine and a cartoon version of Leonardo da Vinci's drawing of Vesalian Man which simply turned him into a woman. All of them are freely available in the public domain, and all were subsequently published by the *Times Higher Educational Supplement* (23 June 1995) to accompany an article I wrote about the episode.

5. 'Snool', for the uninitiated, is Daly-speak for 'normal inhabitant of sado-society, characterized by sadism and masochism combined'. From Mary Daly and Jane Caputi, *Webster's First New Intergalactic Wickedary of the English Language* (London: Women's Press, 1987), p. 227.

6. For an account of the role of science in the construction of racism, see Robert Miles, *Racism* (London: Routledge, 1989).

7. If only heterosexual writers were as conscious of the personal and partial nature of their own views on sex! Sadly, heterosexuality is so thoroughly dominant and so naturalized that straight commentators are generally completely unreflexive in their assertions about sex and sexuality. A good example is Roger Scruton's *Sexual Desire: A Philosophical Investigation* (London: Weidenfeld & Nicolson, 1986), which, while laying claim to philosophical rigour, is crammed with romantic nonsense about the complementarity of femininity and masculinity, the languishing feminine frustrations of lesbians, etc. Although it is rather touchingly naive from a queer perspective (or a feminist perspective, or a sociological perspective), Scruton's academic status means that the book has dangerous implications.

8. This is not entirely restricted to lesbian writers. Some straight feminist writers – Lynne Segal is a good example – have foregrounded their own sexuality in this way.

9. Leonore Tiefer, *Sex Is Not a Natural*

Act and Other Essays (Oxford: Westview Press, 1995), p. 113.

10. For more discussion of the law and queers, see the editors of the Harvard Law Review, *Sexual Orientation and the Law* (Cambridge, MA.: Harvard University Press, 1990 for the US) or the now somewhat out of date, Paul Crane, *Gays and the Law* (London: Pluto Press, 1980). For a fairly current overview of the legal position of lesbians and gay men in Europe, including the UK, see Peter Tatchell, *Out in Europe: A Guide to Lesbian and Gay Rights in 30 European Countries* (London: Channel 4 *Rouge* Magazine, 1990).

11. Debbie Bender in Lily Burana, Roxxie and Linnea Due (eds.) *Dagger: On Butch Women* (San Francisco: Cleis Press, 1994), p. 106.

12. Kiss and Tell, *Her Tongue on My Theory*, p. 7.

13. Lesbian feminism and radical feminism are *not* the same thing. Nor is lesbian feminism necessarily revolutionary feminism, separatist feminism or pro-censorship feminism.

14. By the WLM, I mean the so-called 'second wave' of feminist activism which swept across the USA and the rest of the 'first world' in the 1960s. For an account of anti-lesbianism in feminism at that time, see Sydney Abbott and Barbara Love, *Sappho Was a Right-On Woman: A Liberated View of Lesbianism* (New York: Stein & Day, 1972), or Tamsin Wilton *Lesbian Studies: Setting an Agenda* (London: Routledge, 1995).

15. Abbott and Love, p. 136.

16. Cited in Wilton, *Lesbian Studies*, p. 38.

17. Apologies to George Orwell for stealing this from *Animal Farm*.

18. For a discussion of the tendency of straight mainstream culture to scavenge off queer culture, see essays in Moe Meyer (ed.) *The Politics and Poetics of Camp* (London: Routledge, 1994).

19. Julia Epstein and Kristina Straub (eds.) *Body Guards: The Cultural Politics of Gender Ambiguity* (London: Routledge, 1991), p. 10.

What Do Lesbians Have to Do with Sex?

Lesbians and sex: never the twain shall meet?

'What do lesbians have to do with sex?' may seem at first sight a fairly pointless question. Lesbianism has generally been understood, at least since the nineteenth century, as one of the 'sexual perversions', and 'lesbian' is commonly spoken of as a *sexual* identity. My 1976 edition of the *Concise Oxford Dictionary* defines lesbian as 'a female homosexual', and homosexual as 'being sexually attracted only by persons of one's own sex'. Yet in the 1970s Robin Morgan insisted on the right to call herself a lesbian even though she was in a committed heterosexual marriage, and even though she did not have sex with women[1] while Marilyn Frye suggested, a decade later, that 'the term "sex" is an inappropriate term for what lesbians do'.[2] On the one hand, Ginny Berson, a member of the radical-feminist lesbian group the Furies, declares that 'Lesbianism is not a matter of sexual preference',[3] while on the other (and twenty years later), Judith Stelboum insists that 'When I talk about myself as a lesbian I openly declare my sexual preference ... there is one aspect of my life that is a constant. The truth of loving women. Defining myself as a lesbian means declaring myself in a sexual context.'[4] Such contradictory statements indicate more than confusion or uncertainty about the relationship between lesbians and sex; they suggest out and out conflict. These women are not intent on clarifying the finer points of the relationship between lesbian identity and lesbian sex; they are clashing head on about whether sex has *anything at all* to do with calling yourself a lesbian.

These particular arguments are the result of feminist interventions in the question of lesbianism, and they are probably the most familiar to lesbians today. They gave rise to an extraordinary degree of hostility, often setting lesbian against lesbian and splitting communities down the middle, both in the USA and the UK.

To anyone casting a casual eye over the lesbian cultural scene today, it appears that this particular rift has been healed. Arlene Stein writes that 'the fiery battles have flickered out ... the ideological debates and emotional clashes of the past have faded to a distant memory'.[5] Yet a closer look from a different vantage point reveals the stubborn and continuing presence of the so-called 'anti-sex' tendency within lesbian feminism,[6] and its influence among significant groups of lesbians. There has been a warm welcome in many lesbian communities for Sheila Jeffreys's book *The Lesbian Heresy*,[7] in which she attacks

> the development of a lesbian sex industry which reinforces the idea that lesbianism is just about sex, the re-emergence of a lesbian sexuality based on dominance and submission – butch and femme, sadomasochism, lesbian pornography, sex therapy, fashionable post modernist theory which de-politicises *everything*, queer politics in which lesbians are subsumed into 'gayness' as if we have the same political concerns, interests and sexual obsessions as gay men...[8]

(To which it is instructive to counterpose Della Grace's self-consciously provocative assertion that 'lesbians even have "gay male" sex'.[9]) Even Stein, while representing the 'fiery battles' as things of the past, admits that 'some stalwart feminist bookstores still refuse to carry lesbian porn'.[10] This is not the trivial matter Stein's casualness implies. For a lesbian living in a large city, the refusal of one bookshop to stock 'lesbian porn' simply means the inconvenience of travelling to another which will, or – increasingly – simply walking in to the nearest branch of one of the large commercial bookshop franchises (for example, Waterstones in the UK), whose lesbian and gay sections are now established and well stocked. For lesbians living in smaller cities or towns, there is no Waterstones, and it is unlikely that more than one bookshop will stock lesbian texts at all.

Lesbians living outside the major conurbations, lacking access to the social and commercial resources of big-city queer life, are likely to be more isolated, subject to a greater degree of stigma and hostility from their wider (non-lesbian) community and to be less well off than their city cousins. The lesbian 'scene' in major cities such as New York, London, Manchester, San Francisco, Sydney or Melbourne is generally perceived as 'lesbian culture', or 'the lesbian community', whereas in fact the majority of lesbians, who do not live in such centres of queer urban coolth, often inhabit a very different milieu. For these women, the refusal of their local bookshop to stock 'lesbian porn'[11] may impose severe restrictions on their ability to make informed political, social and sexual choices.

It is not, however, only feminists who have attempted to sever the link between 'lesbian' and 'sex'. This chapter outlines a variety of political and ideological attempts to stamp out lesbian sex, and argues that to allow the word 'lesbian' to be used to describe anything other than a *sexual* entity is offensive, oppressive and (ironically) anti-feminist as well as anti-lesbian.

The lesbian who ate Chicago: scarey dykes and frightened boys

It is easy to forget that the very idea of women writing about women – let alone lesbians writing about lesbians – represents an extraordinary revolution. It is also very new; most of this revolution has taken place in my lifetime. Before this, things were very different. From the invention of the printing press to the late 1970s the 'truth' about the world was thought up, written, printed, published and distributed by men, whose absolute control over the process is now hard for us to imagine. So the 'truth' about lesbians has, until the beginning of the 1970s, been men's truth. The Radicalesbians, a group of lesbian feminists which broke away from the WLM in response to the movement's hostility towards lesbians, recognized the implications of this in 1970 when they wrote:

> Lesbianism ... is a category of behaviour possible only in a sexist society characterized by rigid sex roles and dominated by male supremacy. ... In a society in which men do not oppress women, and sexual expression is allowed to follow feelings, the categories of homosexuality and heterosexuality would disappear. 'Lesbian' is one of the sexual categories by which men have divided up humanity.[12]

'Lesbian', then, is a word invented and given meaning by men. Why did men find it necessary to invent this category, and what meanings have they given it?

It is instructive to read what male 'experts' have written about lesbians. Two themes emerge strongly in this literature: the idea that lesbians are in some way *masculinized* – they are either intrinsically masculine or they long to become men – and the idea that lesbians do not and cannot have 'real' sex, because sex *is*, on many levels, a male activity and (ironically because they are *feminine)* this excludes lesbians by definition. Both sets of beliefs are quite clearly driven by an intense male anxiety provoked by these women who do not obey the supposedly 'natural' laws of desire. After all, the desire and sexual pleasure which is engendered between two women makes men and their penises utterly irrelevant. In societies structured around the power and importance of masculinity, a power symbolized by the phallus,[13] it is intolerable that any individual who lacks a penis (for this is how women are defined) should appear to be so completely indifferent to penises and the people who own them. So intolerable is this possibility that it must be denied, erased, silenced so that desire and sexual activity between women may be represented as 'really' desire for the phallus. Within this paranoid masculinist discourse, both 'butch' and 'femme' lesbians[14] may be dismissed as rather pathetic creatures: the butch because, try as she might, she can never be a 'real' man and the femme because she can never get 'properly' fucked.

So the nineteenth-century sexologist Krafft-Ebing describes lesbians as unable to be women, striving unsuccessfully to be men:

> For female employments there is manifested not merely a lack of taste, but often unskillfulness in them. ... Instead of an inclination for the arts, there is manifested an inclination and taste for the sciences. Occasionally there may be attempts to drink and smoke.[15]

This is rather transparently bound up with a political agenda, the need to dismiss women who may be interested in 'the sciences' as suffering from sexual psychopathology, but the main drift of his argument is that lesbians are imitation men. As Diane Richardson points out, this widespread heterosexual fantasy can have important negative consequences for lesbians:

> At an individual level, such stereotyping can create anxieties in some lesbians about imitating heterosexuality. This may discourage them from engaging in certain kinds of sex: for example, lying on top of a woman and gaining sexual pleasure by rubbing against her body, or putting fingers or an object into the vagina of another woman, or having that done to themselves. As one woman said, 'If I want that I might as well go with a man'.[16]

At the height of the sexual revolution of the 1960s, David Reuben was mockingly dismissive of lesbian sex, on the grounds that 'One vagina plus another vagina equals zero',[17] an even more explicit attempt to reinsert the dethroned phallus into lesbian sexuality. Interestingly, the supposed arch-guru of hetero-feminist lust, Germaine Greer, agreed with Reuben's position, dismissing lesbianism in *The Female Eunuch* on the grounds that 'a clitoral orgasm with a full vagina is nicer than a clitoral orgasm with an empty one'.[18]

This somewhat desperate desexualization of lesbian sex remains the strategy most frequently resorted to by nervous men whose sexuality is threatened. Right-wing philosopher Roger Scruton, who clings to an archaic (and in any case historically and culturally specific) belief in heterosexual complementarity whereby the timid passivity of woman reins in the animal energies of man, lets his heated imagination lead him to beds of lesbian lust, where he finds

> there is an extremely poignant, often helpless, sense of being at another's mercy. The lesbian knows that she desires someone who will not typically make those advances that are characteristic of a man, even if she wants to. ... She can only wait, and wish, and pray to the gods with the troubled fervour captured by Sappho in her hymn to Aphrodite: *poikilothron athanat' Aphrodite.*[19]

Psychologist Anthony Storr, on the other hand, is smugly convinced that he knows something we don't:

> Lesbians who protest that, for them, this kind of relationship is better than any possible intimacy with a man do not know what they are missing. There is no doubt that for women who, for whatever reason, have been unable to get married, a homosexual partnership may be a happier way of life than a frustrated loneliness, but this is not to say that it can ever satisfy.[20]

This strategy reduces lesbian sex to something trivial and childish, an inadequate make-believe. Real sex is only possible between a man and a woman, because real sex means using a penis (not a finger or a hand or a tongue or a dildo or something enticing from the vegetable basket in the kitchen) to penetrate a vagina. As Diane Richardson points out, this generally accepted model of what sex *is* turns 'lesbian sex' into an oxymoron:

> This view of sex as penis in vagina, as something done to a woman by a man, implies that lesbians don't really have sex, they have 'foreplay'. ... Lesbian sex has often been conceptualised as immature, not as satisfying as intercourse, second-best sex.[21]

Richardson identifies four factors which work to 'desex' lesbianism: psychologists, historians, feminists and the general stereotype which insists that lesbians want to be men. Psychoanalytic accounts tend to interpret lesbian desire in terms of mother-fixation, leading to the assertion that 'lesbian relationships [are] primarily emotional rather than sexual'. In addition, it is assumed that women are generally successfully conditioned or socialized into the passivity and responsiveness mandated by their gender role. Such assumptions, as Richardson points out, are often shared by lesbians themselves. She cites Margaret Nichols: 'Two women together, each primed to respond sexually only to a request from another, may rarely even experience desire, much less engage in sexual activity'.[22] Perhaps Margaret Nichols and Roger Scruton move in the same circles!

Richardson is not alone in her concern that historians, such as Lillian Faderman in her influential book *Surpassing the Love of Men* (1981), have desexualized the 'lesbians' of previous generations. Certainly Faderman's research into 'romantic friendships' downplayed the significance of sexual activity between women. However, it is difficult for historians to do anything else. Evidence of sexual activity is circumstantial at the best of times, and when that sexual activity is stigmatized, discredited or criminal, women are likely to have done everything possible to ensure that it remained secret. Moreover, documentation presents a serious problem in this context: it is hard to imagine that receipts for dildos, in elegant copperplate handwriting, would be found among the papers of your average Victorian lesbian! Add to this the fact that women's lives have generally left only the faintest traces in the historical record, and it becomes clear that the search for 'hard' evidence of lesbian sexual activity is likely to be in vain.

In addition to the psychologists and the historians, lesbian sexuality is erased in official discourse and in mainstream popular and medical discourse about sexuality. Anna Marie Smith identifies the desexualization of lesbianism which has taken place during official debates on legislation in the British Parliament, and in official HIV/AIDS discourse in the USA: 'When asked why the Center for Disease Control has not carried out any research on woman-to-woman transmission of the virus, an official replied, "Lesbians don't have much sex".'[23] Smith goes on to warn that 'the exclusion of lesbian sexuality from official discourse on homosexuality constitutes a thoroughly anti-lesbian strategy ... the reduction of lesbian-ness to harmlessness is a subtle and extremely effective attack on our hard-won presence'.[24]

It is becoming clear that lesbian sexuality is simply absent from mainstream discourse. The great flow of words which maps out social and cultural 'reality' is silent about the subject of lesbian desire and lesbian sexual activity. This silence circulates from medicine to government, from psychology to history, from philosophy to popular sex manuals, each category of 'expert' reinforcing the 'truth' of lesbian sexlessness. It is even present in academic textbooks on human sexuality:

> Virtually every book on human sexuality (those used as textbooks by medical schools and many other professional schools) still proclaims the un-fact that Lesbians are really not so much interested in sex or orgasm as they are in hugging and kissing a lot.[25]

As Phyllis Lyon comments, 'This kind of misinformation is an attack on all women's sexuality'. Anna Marie Smith, too, is clear that 'the erasure of lesbian sexuality in official discourse is not a random strategy but the product of sexism'.[26] This perspective suggests that we should look to feminism for a radical strategy in affirmation of lesbian sexuality and in opposition to this sexist erasure. Yet 'feminism' is all too often cited by lesbians as condoning or colluding with the desexualization of lesbianism. Indeed, the struggle to reinscribe the erotic onto the harmless, cuddlesome 'lesbian' of patriarchal discourse has been fought with the greatest energy on the terrain of feminism itself. How may we begin to understand this conflict?

Nice feminists don't? The unsexing of lesbian feminism

The various ways in which male experts co-opted lesbian sexuality, in order to prop up the patriarchal system which desire between women threatens to undermine, set the terms of engagement around lesbian sexuality for the WLM. Moreover, after a brief, heady few years in which celebrating and 'freeing' female sexuality seemed like an unproblematic part of the feminist movement, years in which Greer could declare that 'what is certain ... is that the patriarchal state could never survive the re-conquest by women of their own sexuality',[27] feminist researchers began to reveal the extent of male sexual violence against women.[28] As the commonplace horrors of sexual violence started to emerge, it was no longer possible to believe that the feminist 're-conquest' of sexuality would be easy, nor that it would result in the overthrow of patriarchy.

The final attempt by jittery men to bring lesbian sex safely into the patriarchal fold is to reinscribe it into heterosexual pornography (see Plate 2) where it becomes nothing more than a titillating hors-d'oeuvre to the main course (i.e. *real* sex, with a *real* penis). Many lesbians have commented on this 'theft' of lesbian sexuality in the interests of the male porn industry,[29] and how difficult it then becomes for lesbians to make our sexuality visible in an assertive way. Importantly, it also set up a confusing association between explicit representations of sex between women and the entire genre of pornography which many pro-censorship feminists – including Andrea Dworkin, Catherine MacKinnon, Sheila Jeffreys and others – see as a cornerstone of male power and women's subordination.

Faced with these problems, namely a profoundly problematic 'sex' which was interwoven with fear, hatred and dismissal of women and with physical and emotional violence, it is perhaps unsurprising that feminists reacted by de-emphasizing the sexual aspect of lesbianism, or indeed by rejecting sex altogether. Within the terms of one kind of radical-feminist political discourse, lesbianism became constructed as an *escape*, not just from sex with men but from sexuality *per se*.

It is important to put the anti-sex tendency within radical feminism into perspective. It should not be forgotten that lesbians owe a great deal to feminism and to the WLM. It was, after all, the feminist politicization of lesbianism which set the stage for the construction of a proud, assertive lesbian identity and which catalysed the growth of an international network of lesbian communities. As Margaret Cruikshank writes in her history of lesbian and gay liberation in the USA, 'Lesbianism existed but could not flourish before women's liberation'.[30] Countless autobiographical accounts written by lesbians who grew up before 1980 acknowledge the liberating impact of feminism on their lives:

> Feminism healed the core contradictions of my life. Feminism said I was clearly a woman, but that I could be any kind of woman I wanted to be, and that in fact I was 'an amazon', a kind of proud, free woman who refused to be defined by the rules of the patriarchy.[31]

Many sex-radical lesbians, including Pat Califia, Dorothy Allison and Joan Nestle, refer to themselves as feminists, and acknowledge the transformative effect which feminism has had on them. Califia's account is fairly typical 'When I left my parent's home to attend college, I met other feminists for the first time. I also met other lesbians. When I realized that this was a choice available to me, I felt an immediate rush of relief.'[32] Dorothy Allison goes further: 'It was a miracle that I discovered feminism and found that I did not have to be ashamed of who I was.' Yet, as all too often in such recollections, the memory of being inspired by feminism is closely followed by recollctions of being let down, rejected, betrayed: 'I have to tell you it was a miracle I did not kill myself out of sheer despair when I was told I was too lesbian for feminism, too reformist for radical lesbianism, too sexually perverse for respectable lesbianism.'[33] What form did this betrayal take? Within the development of radical feminism there appear to be three related strategies hostile to the notion of lesbianism as a *sexual* identity: the representation of lesbianism as about 'more than' sex; the rejection of certain aspects of sexuality as intrinsically masculine; and the construction of the notion of 'political lesbianism' as a *non-sexual* lesbian identity. These strategies must be mapped onto the ignorance and hostility which the wider feminist movement demonstrated towards the issue of lesbianism, for there was, and continues to be, much straightforward anti-lesbianism among straight feminists.[34]

From its beginnings, the politically innovative phenomenon of lesbian feminism was the property of women who were keen to downplay questions of desire and sexual practice and to foreground politics. For example, the 1978 lesbian anthology *Our Right to Love*[35] contains four articles on sexuality and fourteen on lesbian activism. Leading lesbian writers insisted that lesbianism should not be 'reduced to' sex. 'Men who are obsessed with sex are convinced that lesbians are obsessed with sex,' wrote Judy Grahn. 'Actually, like other women, lesbians are obsessed with love and fidelity'.[36] Some women painted what seems to us today to be a hopelessly naive and romantic vision of lesbian love, claiming 'love' as an intrinsically female quality and rejecting 'lust' as intrinsically male. Rita Laporte, one-time contributor to the ground-breaking lesbian magazine *The Ladder,* wrote that 'Your males, arrested at the primitive level of genital sexuality, have little or no notion of what love means. Only your lesbians know the meaning of true love, that mature dedication to another that transcends animal lust.'[37] While, in a similar vein, Robin Morgan too declared that women were simply too refined and sensitive for the coarseness of physical passion:

> Every woman knows in her gut the vast differences between her sexuality and that of any patriarchally trained male's, gay or straight ... that the emphasis on genital sexuality, objectification, promiscuity, emotional non-involvement and coarse invulnerability was the *male style* and that we, as women, placed greater trust in love, humour, tenderness, commitment.[38]

This outright rejection of lust in the name of the 'higher nature' of women was not invented during the second wave of the WLM. It parallels similar protestations made by early 'first wave' feminists, many of whom supported social reform movements promoting social purity, temperance and chastity. The struggle over sexual liberalism has marked many of the revolutionary struggles of the modern era, and sexuality carried a quite specific set of meanings during and after the sexual revolution of the 1960s. Elizabeth Wilson suggests that 'feminism took over from established revolutionary movements a moralism about the meaning of sexual behaviour in relation to politics' and furthermore that 'Feminists de-emphasised sex and the erotic, whether intentionally or not, partly perhaps in reaction against the "swinging sixties" and the insistence of that period on male-defined sex with no strings attached.'[39]

Whatever the reasons, feminist political discourse constructed 'love' and 'sex' in a way which was not only quite extraordinarily polarized but also gendered to the point of essentialism: 'Feminists were talking about a Manichean struggle between the hell of wrong desires and the heaven of a love devoid of pain.'[40] It was only a short step from privileging love and affection over lust and desire to Ti-Grace Atkinson's uncompromisingly anti-lesbian, anti-sex position:

> lesbianism is based ideologically on the very premise of male oppression: the dynamic of sexual intercourse. Lesbians, by definition, accept that human beings are primarily sexual beings. ... A case could be made that lesbianism, in fact *all* sex, is reactionary, and that feminism is revolutionary.[41]

Although this extreme erotophobic anti-lesbianism was always a minority position within feminism, it did set an agenda against which lesbians were forced to react, and some responded by agreeing that 'sex is reactionary', and detaching lesbian identity from sexuality altogether. As Kathryn Harriss puts it, 'Lesbianism was ... torn away from its "limited" patriarchal association with sex and made synonymous with any bonding between women which showed women's solidarity with one another or any networks which ... resisted male power.'[42]

This idea of the lesbian as a superior creature who rises above sex continues to inform some lesbian-feminist thinking today. Gillian Hanscombe declared in 1991 that 'It's passion, not mere sex, that is the sure foundation of lesbian identity'. She continues:

> Some of us ... now need to stand up and be counted and to say clearly what we think decent lesbian sex is really about: decent meaning satisfying; and decent also meaning ethically defensible. ... Sex as outlined by enthusiasts for sadomasochism (empty-headed, wrong-headed, disreputable, disrespectful, decadent), or as recommended by exponents of half-baked therapies, is not what most of us ever went to the barricades for ...[43]

Whatever else it may be, this passage is as profoundly disrespectful of lesbians as anything a man ever wrote. My own response, when I read the words 'empty-headed, wrong-headed, disreputable' directed by one lesbian against others whose desire differs from hers, is anger at that thoughtless sense of entitlement. How dare she? Just what is it that leads Hanscombe to believe that her dismissive rudeness is acceptable? It is a reaction shared by many lesbians in response to feminists speaking out against lesbian sexuality.

Biting back: reclaiming lesbian sex

It was the Leeds Revolutionary Feminist Group who summed up the notion of political lesbianism, making explicit its complete rupture from sexual desire, pleasure or activity: 'a political lesbian is a woman-identified woman who does not fuck men. It does not mean compulsory sexual activity with a woman.'[44] For many lesbians this forceful erasure of lesbian desire, a desire so closely linked to their discovery of feminism as something which made it possible for the first time to be out, proud and self-defined, cut to the bone. As a consequence, many angry and bitter rejections of political lesbianism followed, as lesbians began the process of reasserting the centrality of sex to lesbian identity. Many described the lesbian-feminist vision of lesbian sexuality in mocking tones. Pat Califia's account is typical of her acerbic style:

> I am obviously a sex pervert, and good, real true lesbians are not sex perverts. They are the high priestesses of feminism, conjuring up the 'wimmin's' revolution. As I understand it, after the wimmin's revolution, sex will consist of wimmin holding hands, taking their shirts off and dancing in a circle.[45]

This Disney vision, although from the satiric perspective of an avowed sex-radical, is not too far removed from the way in which lesbian feminists represented lesbian sexuality. It is also uncomfortably close to the sanitized lesbianism of mainstream patriarchal mythology. Carole Vance's account of the liberal sex-educational films shown at a conference on 'sex research' in the early 1980s makes this quite clear:

> in contrast with the films on heterosex and gay men's sex, lesbian sex occurred in a field of daisies, chronicled by discontinuous jump cuts.

Sexual activity, never genital, consisted of running in slow motion through sun-dappled fields, hand holding and mutual hair-combing.[46]

Lesbians who had been politically active before the second wave of the WLM recognized fairly swiftly the need to struggle against the desexualization which seemed to be inherent in the feminist co-option of lesbian 'identity'. 'We Lesbians from the fifties', wrote Joan Nestle, 'made a mistake in the early seventies: we allowed our lives to be trivialized and reinterpreted by feminists who did not share our culture.'[47] Nor was the clash a straightforward one between conflicting lesbian-feminist ideologies; important questions of class and 'race' were deeply implicated in the political lesbian/sex radical divide.

The question of class seems to have been particularly significant in this instance, although it is neither possible nor useful to disentangle class from racism. It is no coincidence that so many of the most important lesbian sex-radical writers – Pat Califia, Joan Nestle, Dorothy Allison – are working class, nor that feminism was perceived throughout the 1970s and 1980s as a largely white middle-class movement. Nestle 'quickly got the message in my first Lesbian-feminist CR [consciousness raising] group that such topics as butch-femme relationships and the use of dildoes [sic] were lower class',[48] while Dorothy Allison is quite clear that class is central to her lesbianism and her relationship to feminism:

> I know that I have been hated as a lesbian ... by 'society' ... but I have also been hated or held in contempt (which is in some ways more debilitating and slippery than hatred) by lesbians for behaviour and sexual practices shaped in large part by class. My sexual identity is intimately constructed by my class and regional background, and much of the hatred directed at my sexual preferences is class hatred – however much people, feminists in particular, like to pretend this is not a factor.[49]

To the extent that the mainstream of 'second wave' feminism has been criticized for its neglect of class and racism, women who fall outside the boundaries of class and race advantage have been able to construct a more sophisticated model of sexuality than their privileged sisters, a model mapped onto a network of power relations structured by socio-economic relations and by racism. 'What I know for sure,' writes Allison, 'is that class, gender, sexual preference, and prejudice – racial, ethnic and religious – form an intricate lattice that restricts and shapes our lives, and that resistance to hatred is not a simple act.'[50] Discussing the case of Jennifer Saunders (a young, working-class white British lesbian imprisoned for supposedly passing as a man in order to have sex with her girlfriends), Anna Marie Smith writes:

> The conflation of gender and sexuality in sexist discourse is also structured in terms of race and class differences. ... The upper-class white woman possesses exemplary femininity for sexist discourse since its very notion of femininity is in essence a racist and bourgeois construct which passes as a universal category. ... Lesbians who are ... working class, black and/or delinquent acquire much more visibility because they are women who, by their racial, class and criminal status, cannot possess exemplary forms of femininity.[51]

The construction of 'lesbians' as women who rise above mere lust is revealed in this more sophisticated critique as a racist, classist construction which colludes with the sexist reduction of female desire and agency to dancing through the daisies. Once other relations of power are reincorporated into the feminist critique, 'political lesbianism' begins to appear more like 'apolitical lesbianism' or even 'patriarchal lesbianism'. It becomes startlingly obvious that a non-sexual, sisterly, anti-erotic 'lesbianism' is not only anti-lesbian, it is anti-feminist into the bargain.

Beyond the daisy field: lesbian lust ascendant?

The notion of the lustful dyke as the most effective agent in the feminist struggle is not universally accepted among lesbian feminists, although it is joyfully and playfully celebrated by many lesbians, some of whom identify as feminists but many of whom (in reaction against the erotophobia of much feminist discourse) do not. Vera Whisman, charting the resurgence of the sexual lesbian, cites a reader's letter to the American magazine *Out/Look*:

> Lesbians are doing and talking about things we have never done or talked about before.[52] We are moving beyond the realm of Sisterhood into the world of the nasty, the tasty, and the sexy ... we are finally

29

able to voice certain questions about desires that the self-righteous atmosphere of political correctitude and erotophobia we called lesbian-feminism kept us from uttering.[13]

Dorothy Allison's strategy for reaffirming lesbian sexuality in the face of the sexless political lesbian is to chart the history of the process of desexualization *as a problem for lesbians*. She wittily marks out the traces of the non-sexual feminist lesbian through three decades and three different varieties of dyke, starting with the political lesbian:

> Political lesbians made the concepts of lust, sexual need and passionate desire ... detached from the definition of lesbian. The notion that lesbians might actually be interested in having orgasms with other lesbians, that lesbians might like to fuck and suck and screw around ... became anathema.

... moving on through the mystic world of the spiritual lesbian:

> By the late seventies I was tracking the progress of the spiritual lesbian, a close cousin of the political lesbian, perfectly woman-identified and adamant about what was and was not acceptable practice for the rest of us.

... and finally casting a critical eye on that favoured creature of deconstruction, the theoretical lesbian:

The theoretical lesbian was everywhere all through the eighties, and a lot of times I could have sworn she was straight. ... The lesbian was the advanced feminist, that rare and special being endowed with social insight and political grace.[54]

Allison concludes that 'The lesbian you're talking about ... is the rage of all women, perhaps, but the lust of a few.' And it is that reinsertion of 'lust' into the idea of lesbianism which rescues 'lesbian' from the sexless daisy field and obsessive hair-combing of male anxiety and feminist erotophobia/moralism.

Other lesbians have pointed out that the desexualization of lesbianism is particularly problematic for disabled lesbians, since it does not (and cannot) respect and support their struggle to be accepted as sexual, desiring and desirable. 'We [disabled lesbians] are generally not taken seriously,' writes Kirsten Hearn, 'since we are not supposed to have any sexual feelings whatsoever, let alone the ability to carry them out.'[55] Some black lesbians, too, reject politically correct lesbianism, pointing out that the issue of sexuality for lesbians of colour is very different from that experienced by white lesbians: 'My everyday life as a Black lesbian writer is marked by the struggle to be a (sexual) black lesbian, the struggle for the language of sexuality'.[56] Karen/Miranda Augustine rightly locates the refusal to recognize racism as relevant to sexuality in the queer community as much as in feminism:

As a queer-identified Black woman, I have felt unsatisfied by the sexual liberation rhetoric firmly anchored within lesbian and gay spaces ... this cornucopia of women's sexual practice within the mainstream of the lesbian, gay and bisexual communities has conveniently disregarded the very complex issue of race – and where it all fits.

She concludes by naming the kind of damage which political correctness can do:

I'm not big on sexuality theories because the very things that swell my clit, when thrown into the whirlwind of lezzie political correctness, just don't figure. And depending on how strong I'm feeling, shame is often the outcome, if what's turning me on is deemed degrading to my sex by the progressive elite.[57]

The reinstatement of a proudly and explicitly sexual element in lesbian identity and politics is, as such statements show, more than the simple Oedipal rebellion against 'mummy feminism' which some older feminists represent (or dismiss) it as. It incorporates elements of resistance against the marginalization and oppression *within* both feminist and queer movements of black, disabled and working-class lesbians. As such, lesbian lechery is an important activist strategy.

Not all lesbians have welcomed this newly reborn lecherous lesbianism. Some lesbian feminists in particular have been quick to reject lesbian sex-radicalism, although the arguments put forward against it look increasingly suspect. Julia Penelope complains that 'These days, it seems that Lesbian political activism has been replaced by quick-fix Lesbian sex', and goes on to warn how; 'Some Lesbians have chosen, I fear, beds to lie down on that delude them, and they rise up, not empowered, but oblivious to the work we must yet do'.[58] There are two problems with this representation of sex-radical lesbians, however much one may agree with Penelope's political position. Firstly, her phrase 'the work we must yet do'. Who is she including in this 'we', and what 'work' does she mean? Although Penelope's meaning for 'work' remains unexplained throughout the piece, and is impossible to define even from contextual clues, it is clear that by 'we' she means *all* lesbians, and that her meaning for 'lesbian' is a highly specific lesbian-feminist one. The 'work', it is perhaps safe to conclude, consists of the struggle to realize Julia Penelope's social and political vision. It is ironic that Penelope's language is so veiled and her meanings so covert, since the piece in question is concerned with language and the politics of meaning! It seems to me both naive and offensive to presume that all lesbians can be roped into this 'we', with no discussion of the important social and political issues which differentiate us.

The second problem lies in her evocative image of lesbians lying down on and rising up from beds 'that delude them'. This entire metaphor (setting to one side the farcical notion of wilfully deceptive furniture) is saturated with the assumption that the writer has a privileged perspective that enables her to spot the traps that other lesbians foolishly walk straight into. Moreover, only she has the wisdom, perception and authority to see and name the *truth* of other lesbians' experiences. The smugly patronizing tone of this short passage is indistinguishable from the voices of psychiatrists, priests and doctors derisively 'explaining' lesbian desire in order to bring it firmly under control. Even while she attacks the semantic strategies of the patriarchy as 'the Patriarchal Universe of Discourse (PUD)', Penelope is playing the same word games herself.

And this, perhaps, offers the thread which may help to disentangle the knots in this particular argument. With one group of politically radical, thoughtful women insisting that 'lesbian' *must* be sexual in the interests of the struggle against lesbian oppression and another group of equally radical, equally thoughtful women asserting that lesbian *must not* be sexual in the interests of the same struggle, which is the 'right' position?

A bit of what you fancy does the revolution good?

It is no doubt obvious that anyone who calls a book *Finger-Licking Good* is not going to advocate celibacy in the interests of the movement. So you are not expecting me to conclude this chapter by declaring that the word 'lesbian' has nothing to do with sex and that, come the revolution, I'll be first in line for my place in the daisy field. However, I *am* a feminist (albeit a queer one), and my reasons for rejecting the idea of desexed lesbianism are not purely selfish. It goes without saying that any woman who luxuriates in beds that 'delude' her to the extent that I do is going to resist being told that she is deluded. But I do not believe that my rejection of the non-sexual lesbian springs from a brain so driven by politically suspect lusts, so drugged by male-identified orgasms that I can no longer think straight. For, let us be clear, this is the thread which runs through anti-erotic lesbian-feminist discourse. Sexual pleasure is the enemy of the revolution because it seduces women into counter-revolutionary behaviour. It is time to revisit the anti-lesbian arguments of the anxious men.

Patriarchal discourse works hard to construct a 'lesbian' whose sexuality is: passive (because she is female, and female *means* sexually passive, as it is the 'opposite' of male which *means* sexually active); fake (because she has no penis, and all women *need* a penis for real sex); pathetic (because she can never get a penis and never be a man); infantile (because sex without penile penetration is just 'foreplay', and because clitoral orgasms are 'immature'); dysfunctional (because proper women want proper men, and something must have 'gone wrong' to explain why this is not the case for lesbians); and non-sexual (because lesbians want a mother to cuddle them, not a lover to fuck them). It is important to note at this point that all of this revolves around masculinity and depends on the primary symbol of male power, the phallus. In other words, patriarchal discourse defines lesbians *in relation to men*. This is unsurprising, since patriarchal discourse inevitably constructs meaning in relation to men.

Turning to anti-sex feminist discourse we are told variously that 'a lesbian is the rage of all women condensed to the point of explosion'[59] (rage against whom? against *men*); 'a lesbian is a woman-identified woman who does not fuck *men*',[60] (my italics) and that 'the emphasis on genital sexuality ... was the *male style*'.[61] As Kathryn Harriss puts it, 'lesbianism was set up as a kind of charmed space, outside of patriarchal values'.[62] In other words, 'lesbian' was/is defined within feminist discourse *in relation to men*. Again, this is unsurprising, since feminism is predicated upon resistance to male power. It is, however, powerfully ironic that the construction of 'lesbian' within this strand of feminist discourse was indistinguishable from the construction of 'lesbian' within traditional patriarchal discourse.

When male anxiety represents lesbian sexuality as passive, these feminists agree, because (in obedience to patriarchal dogma) they understand sexual agency and desire to be male. When male anxiety declares that lesbian sex is no more than foreplay, these feminists agree, because (in obedience to patriarchal dogma) they understand penetration to be something done to women by men. When male anxiety represents lesbian sexuality as not really 'sexual', these feminists agree, because (in obedience to patriarchal dogma) they understand female sexuality to be somehow 'above' striving for orgasm and sexual gratification. And when Roger Scruton depicts lesbian sex as an orgy of waiting, wishing and praying with 'troubled fervour', these feminists agree, because (in obedience to patriarchal dogma) doing anything else would be 'unwomanly'.

It is not, of course, possible somehow to abstract lesbian sexuality in its entirety from the world of heterosexuality and men's power over women. It is only necessary to compare average lesbian earnings with average gay men's earnings to understand something about the nature and extent of male social and economic privilege, and to appreciate the folly of believing that lesbians are exempt from women's material disadvantage. So there is little point in proposing the construction of a lesbian sexuality 'uncontaminated' by heterosexual or patriarchal assumptions. Nor is it appropriate to speak of a 'real' or 'authentic' female sexuality, currently warped or hidden by the detritus of centuries of patriarchal ideology and simply waiting to be discovered or set free by feminist struggle. As Harriss comments, anti-sex feminists 'constructed a model in which male sexuality was seen as innate, whereas women's sexuality was patriarchally *conditioned*',[63] and you really cannot have your theoretical cake and eat in it this way!

If we accept that sexuality is always already socially constructed, that there is no pure, natural female or lesbian sexuality waiting to be liberated, we have to accept that we do not and cannot know what desire and sexual behaviour would be like without patriarchy, heterosexism, homophobia, racism or capitalism. Indeed, when and if sexuality is no longer determined by these social and economic networks of power, it will be structured by whatever takes their place. So we cannot simply turn our backs on mainstream society and construct lesbian sexuality as we would wish it to be without reference to that mainstream – whether our ideal 'lesbian' is pure and untainted by lechery or shot through with desires and perverse pleasures.

None of this means that the notion of lesbian 'identity' can be removed from the political arena, any more than it can be removed from the sexual arena. Whichever way any one of us chooses to enact our lesbian identity and desires is inevitably and unavoidably political, simply because we live in a culture which persists in demonizing, criminalizing and hounding queer people. So the relationship between 'lesbian' and 'sex' cannot be a simple matter of personal preference, with fist-fucking leather dykes and hand-holding political lesbians ranged on some continuum according to choice. Rather, it is always a *strategic* relationship, inescapably making a contribution to the vast and fluid cultural 'conversation' of sexual meanings in our own fractured communities, the wider societies in which those communities are rooted, and in the entire global village.

To make a political choice between daisy-field radical-lesbian feminism and self-consciously transgressive bad-girl queer chic is neither appropriate nor necessary. What is necessary is simply to respect each other's choices, each other's 'lesbianism'. Of course, this is easier said than done. The atheist is able to tolerate the existence of true believers, because atheism does not demand the conversion of every soul on the planet; the true believer on the other hand cannot tolerate the existence of the atheist, because failure to believe challenges belief itself. Likewise, the sex-radical or sexual libertarian dyke is able to tolerate the anti-sex lesbian feminist, since sexual liberalism is happy to grant that individuals have widely different sexual desires, and the desire to avoid sex for political reasons is, from this perspective, no different in kind from the desire to cross-dress or be tied down. The anti-sex lesbian feminist, on the other hand, cannot tolerate the sex-radical or sexual libertarian lesbian, because her sexual behaviour sins against the doctrines of political lesbianism. The inevitable conclusion is that political lesbians become missionaries, attempting in the time-honoured (and dishonourable) tradition of missionaries everywhere to control the sexual behaviour of *all* lesbians.[64]

We have paid a high price for all this missionary zeal. Feminism has lost credibility among many lesbians and, in consequence, has lost the support of lesbian communities and the opportunity to develop a truly radical and transgressive politics of gender and sexuality. For many women, the fact that some feminists had chosen to fall back upon the traditionally patriarchal strategy of promoting their own position as the one true gospel, and of trying to control the intimate behaviour of other women, signalled the moment when feminism failed as a radical political movement. '[W]hen the radical becomes correct,' commented Muriel Dimen, 'it becomes conservative. The politically correct comes to resemble what it tries to change.'[65] A social/political movement struggling for liberation surely fails at the moment when it begins to collude with the very oppression it is fighting. Women's sexual desire, agency, activity and pleasure have been policed for centuries in the interests of maintaining their subordination to men. Within the terms of this gender power struggle, queer desires – both women's and men's – have been anathematized and punished. It is simply not possible to 'liberate' women by policing their sexuality.

It seems to me that a radical transformation of gender relations (the shared, although differently expressed, goal of both feminist and queer activists) depends upon asserting that most basic of human rights, the right to bodily autonomy. This incorporates a broad range of human freedoms, from the right to euthanasia by choice to the right to abortion on demand, the right to freedom from torture (including genital mutilation for religious or cultural reasons) and the right to fully informed consent during medical treatment. It also, centrally, incorporates the right to enjoy consensual sexual activities of choice – a right which is simply and literally unimaginable for the vast majority of the world's women and for a surprising number of the world's men.

Moreover, it does seem to me that feminists such as Sheila Jeffreys and Julia Penelope have simply got it wrong. The anxious male construct of 'woman' as innocent of desire, disinterested in the purely physical business of sex and more concerned with matters of emotion and spirit than with lust is historically and culturally specific. It is the product of an extraordinarily complex web of historical shifts: the development of modern capitalism, industrialization and urbanization; white colonialist exploitation; the birth of the nuclear family; the rise to power of the medical profession; the history of the sexually transmitted diseases (perhaps especially syphilis), political resistance to women's increased participation in public life, and other factors as yet unrecognised. It represents a cornerstone of Victorian paternalistic power, and has been a key element in the social control of women ever since.

In this context, it seems likely that the pursuit of sexual pleasure, far from being the dangerous delusion which Penelope suggests it is, or the 'heresy' which Jeffreys believes it to be, is an important element in the radicalization of lesbianism. The non-sexual lesbian may be 'politically correct' in terms of obedience to one vision of the feminist political agenda, but the desexualization of lesbianism is an uncannily accurate reflection of the strategies which have been so successful in maintaining women's subordination to men in the modern era. It is ironic that political lesbianism, seemingly among the most radical strategies of radical feminism, should replicate with such docility the doctrines of the patriarchs. I have a nagging suspicion that women who revel unapologetically in their lust for each other represent more of a threat to the straight boys than women who allow their sexual behaviour to be dictated by what men do. Perhaps, after all, it is sex rather than sisterhood which lies at the heart of lesbianism, and of lesbian feminism.

Notes

1. In Dorothy Allison *Skin: Talking about Sex, Class and Literature* (London: Pandora, 1995) p. 136.
2. Marilyn Frye (1988), 'Lesbian "Sex"' reprinted in Judith Barrington, *An Intimate Wilderness: Lesbian Writers on Sexuality* (Portland, Oreg.: Eighth Mountain Press, 1991), p. 1.
3. Berson wrote this in 1975; it is cited in Carol Anne Douglas, *Love and Politics: Radical Feminist and Lesbian Theories* (San Francisco: ism press inc., 1990), p. 148.
4. Judith P. Stelboum, 'Sliding into Home: Identifying Lesbian sex' in Mona Oikawa, Dianne Falconer and Ann Decter (eds.), *Resist! Essays against a Homophobic Culture* (Toronto: The Women's Press, 1994), p. 166.
5. Arlene Stein, 'The Year of the Lustful Lesbian' in Stein (ed.), *Sisters, Sexperts, Queers: Beyond the Lesbian Nation* (Harmondsworth: Penguin, 1993), p. 16.
6. I say 'so-called' because there is much more to this political position than a straightforward puritanism and erotophobia, as I hope this chapter will make clear. However, it is hard to avoid the impression that the more extreme revolutionary feminists are on some level hostile to sex itself.
7. Sheila Jeffreys, *The Lesbian Heresy: A Feminist Perspective on the Lesbian Sexual Revolution* (Melbourne: Spinifex Press, 1993).
8. Review of *The Lesbian Heresy* by Ruth Margerison, *Journal of Australian Lesbian Feminist Studies*, No. 4, June 1994, pp. 108–109.
9. Cited in Cherry Smyth, *Lesbians Talk Queer Notions* (London: Scarlet Press, 1992), p. 44.
10. Stein (ed.), *Sisters, Sexperts, Queers*, p. 16.
11. The definition of 'lesbian porn' in these circumstances is likely to be ill thought-out and broad. My own community bookshop in the (relatively large) city of Bristol refuses to stock Joan Nestle's books or the Sheba collection *Serious Pleasure*, although its shelves are full of those Naiad novels known with affection locally as 'the juicy wetness genre' or 'Mills and Boon for dykes'.
12. Radicalesbians (1970), 'The woman-identified woman' reprinted in Sarah Lucia Hoagland and Julia Penelope (eds.), *For Lesbians Only: A Separatist Anthology* (London: Onlywomen Press, 1988), p. 17.
13. The phallus is not the same as the penis, and a penis can never be or become a phallus. The phallus is the imaginary symbol which represents male power – economic, social, political and cultural as well as sexual – and as such may be 'owned' by anyone, regardless of biological sex. For more of this, see Chapter 6.
14. I use inverted commas here because this is 'butch' and 'femme' as the male experts see them, not as self-identified butches and femmes experience their lives and desires.
15. R. von Krafft-Ebing (1882) *Psychopathia Sexualis* reprinted in 1965, Trans. M. E. Wedneck (New York: Putnams), p. 28.
16. Diane Richardson, 'Constructing Lesbian Sexualities' in Ken Plummer (ed.), *Modern Homosexualities: Fragments of Lesbian and Gay Experience* (London: Routledge, 1992), p. 192.
17. David Reuben (1969), *Everything You Always Wanted to Know about Sex* cited in Vera Whisman, 'Identity Crises: Who is a Lesbian Anyway?' in Stein (ed.) *Sisters, Sexperts, Queers*, p. 49.
18. Germaine Greer , *The Female Eunuch* (London: Granada, 1970), p. 307. Greer, who at the time was

known in the underground press as 'Dr G the Groupie', had a reputation for sexual adventurousness. The limits to this adventurousness are entertainingly exposed by this revelation that the only thing she can imagine 'filling' a vagina is a penis!

19. Roger Scruton, *Sexual Desire: A Philosophical Investigation* (London: Weidenfeld & Nicolson, 1986).

20. Anthony Storr, *Sexual Deviation* (Harmondsworth: Penguin, 1964) p. 140. Storr cannot account for the large numbers of women who leave marriages and heterosexual relationships in order to become lesbian.

21. Richardson, 'Constructing Lesbian Sexualities', p. 190.

22. Cited in Richardson, *ibid.*, p. 194

23. Anna Marie Smith, 'Resisting the Erasure of Lesbian Sexuality: A Challenge for Queer Activism' in Plummer (ed.), *Modern Homosexualites*, p. 207.

24. *Ibid.*, p. 210.

25. Phyllis Lyon, Foreword to Pat Califia, *Sapphistry: The Book of Lesbian Sexuality* (Tallahassee, FL: Naiad, 1988), p. x

26. Anna Marie Smith, 'Resisting the Erasure of Lesbian Sexuality', p. 211.

27. Germaine Greer, 'The Politics of Female Sexuality', *Oz*, No. 29, July 1970, p. 32.

28. For accounts of this shift see for example Lynne Segal, *Straight Sex: The Politics of Pleasure*, (London: Virago, 1994), and Tamsin Wilton, 'Orthodoxy within disobedience: lesbians and feminists' in Wilton, *Lesbian Studies: Setting an Agenda* (London: Routledge, 1995).

29. For example, see Richardson, 'Constructing Lesbian Sexualities'.

30. Margaret Cruikshank, *The Gay and Lesbian Liberation Movement* (London: Routledge, 1992), p. 151.

31. Jeanne Cordova, 'Butches, Lies and Feminism' in Joan Nestle (ed.), *The Persistent Desire: A Femme-Butch Reader* (Boston: Alyson, 1992), p. 282.

32. Pat Califia, Introduction to *Sapphistry* (3rd edn., 1988), p. xi.

33. Dorothy Allison, 'Survival is the least of my desire' in Allison, *Skin*, pp. 214–15.

34. For a history of anti-lesbianism in feminism, see for example Sydney Abbott and Barbara Love, *Sappho Was a Right-On Woman: A Liberated View of Lesbianism* (New York: Stein & Day, 1972); Tamsin Wilton, 'Queer Subjects: Lesbians, Heterosexual Women and the Academy' in Mary Kennedy, Cathy Lubelska and Val Walsh (eds.), *Making Connections: Women's Studies, Women's Movements, Women's Lives* (London: Taylor & Francis, 1993).

35. Ginny Vida (ed.), *Our Right to Love: A Lesbian Resource Book* (Englewood Cliffs, NJ: Prentice-Hall, 1978).

36. Cited in Stein (ed.), *Sisters, Sexperts, Queers* p. 17.

37. Rita Laporte, 'A Document' in Barbara Grier and Coletta Reid (eds.), *The Lavender Herring: Essays from The Ladder* (Baltimore: Diana Press, 1976), p. 144.

38. Cited in Kathryn Harriss, *What Is this Big Fuss about Sadomasochism? Lesbian sexuality and the Women's Liberation Movement* (University of Kent at Canterbury, Women's Studies Occasional Papers., 1988), p. 7.

39. Elizabeth Wilson, 'I'll Climb the Stairway to Heaven: Lesbianism in the Seventies' in Sue Cartledge and Joanna Ryan (eds.), *Sex and Love: New Thoughts on Old Contradictions* (London: The Women's Press, 1983), pp. 180, 189.

40. *Ibid.*, p. 180.

41. Ti-Grace Atkinson (1974), cited in

Douglas, *Love and Politics* p. 141.

42. Harriss, *What Is this Big Fuss about Sadomasochism?*, p. 3.

43. Gillian Hanscombe, 'In Among the Market Forces?' in Barrington (ed.) *An Intimate Wilderness* p. 218.

44. Leeds Revolutionary Feminist Group (1981), 'Political Lesbianism: The Case Against Heterosexuality' reprinted in Onlywomen Press's pamphlet *Love Your Enemy? The Debate Between Heterosexual Feminism and Political Lesbianism* (London: Onlywomen Press), p. 5.

45. Pat Califia (1983), 'A Secret Side of Lesbian Sexuality', cited in Sharon P. Holland, 'To Touch the Mother's C(o)untry: Siting Audre Lorde's Erotics' in Karla Jay (ed.) *Lesbian Erotics* (New York: New York University Press, 1995), p. 212.

46. Carole Vance, 'Gender Systems, Ideology and Sex Research' in Ann Snitow, Christine Stansell and Sharon Thompson (eds.), *Desire: The Politics of Sexuality* (London: Virago, 1983), p. 385.

47. Joan Nestle, A Restricted Country: Essays and Short Stories (London: Pandora, 1987), p. 105.

48. *Ibid.*

49. Allison, *Skin*, p. 23.

50. *Ibid.*

51. Anna Marie Smith, 'The Regulation of Lesbian Sexuality Through Erasure: The Case of Jennifer Saunders' in Jay, *Lesbian Erotics*, pp. 175–6.

52. I have to say, I think this is unlikely! The claim that the sex-radical lesbian is a new improved version demonstrates an ignorance of lesbian history; lesbians have been saying and doing perverse and erotic things for centuries, as a quick flick through the relevant literature reveals (see, for example, Nestle, *The Persistent Desire*; Allison, *Skin*; and Emma Donoghue, *Passions Between Women: British Lesbian Culture 1668–1801* (London: Scarlet Press, 1993)).

53. Cited in Whisman, 'Identity Crises', p. 48.

54. Allison, *Skin*, pp. 140–1.

55. Kirsten Hearn, 'A Woman's Right to Cruise' in Christian McEwen and Sue O'Sullivan (eds.), *Out the Other Side: Contemporary Lesbian Writing* (London: Virago, 1988), p. 50.

56. Cheryl Clarke, cited in Wilton, *Lesbian Studies*, p. 126.

57. Karen/Miranda Augustine, 'Bizarre women, exotic bodies and outrageous sex: or, if Annie Sprinkle was a black ho she wouldn't be *all* that' in Mona Oikawa *et al.* (eds.) *Resist!*, p. 45.

58. Julia Penelope, *Call Me Lesbian: Lesbian Lives: Lesbian Theory* (Freedom, CA: The Crossing Press, 1992), pp. 98–100.

59. Radicalesbians, 'The Woman-Identified Woman', p. 17.

60. Leeds Revolutionary Feminist Group, 'Political Lesbianism', p. 5.

61. Robin Morgan, cited in Harriss, *What Is this Big Fuss about Sadomasochism?* p. 7.

62. *Ibid.*, p. 7.

63. *Ibid.*

64. Don't forget that the missionary position of heterosex is so-called because Christian missionaries restricted themselves to this position and *insisted that their pagan converts did likewise.*

65. Muriel Dimen (1984), cited in Nestle, *The Persistent Desire*, p. 36.

2

Do You Always Love the One You Hurt? Lesbian Sadomasochism

Before I launch into this chapter, I'd better confess! Perched on top of my wordprocessor, her knee-high, tight-laced, pervy, black plastic boots impaling little blobs of Blu tack, five-inch whip trailing from her black-gloved hands, is a model of Catwoman in full leathers. She's a child's toy, one of a series of spin-off 'collectables' from the *Batman* films, and I bought her in Woolworth's. The reasons why she lives on top of my wordprocessor give some pretty clear insights into my personal feelings about sexual s/m. She is not there as a constant reminder of the insidious penetration of patriarchal images of female sexuality throughout society (although the fact that such an erotically perverse little figurine is manufactured as a children's plaything is something I find peculiar, and worthy of further deconstruction when I've got a spare hour or two). She is there to remind me of how much I enjoyed the spectacle of Michelle Pfeiffer hamming it up in the film, and because I have adopted her to represent the muse which guides my writing. Living and working as I do in an academic environment, I need her to remind me that it is my perversion/transgression – of both the laws of correct sexual behaviour and the rules of gender – which motivates my work. So, although I do not identify as an s/m dyke,[1] you can guess that I'm not going to spend this chapter trying to prove that lesbian sexual sadomasochists are dupes of the patriarchy who ought to be thrown out of our communities.

This chapter has proved to be one of the most difficult I have ever had to write. To begin with, I had to pick my way through such enormous quantities of material: more words seem to have been devoted to lesbian s/m than to almost any other topic in the area of lesbian sexuality. Then there was the nature of the material. I'm not complaining at having to read sexually explicit writings from s/m dykes – it's dirty work, but someone's got to do it – nor at having to disentangle the dense theoretical language in which some of the debate has been couched.

What *is* unpleasant is confronting the nasty, bullying and frankly woman-hating rhetoric with which so much of the feminist literature *against* lesbian s/m is saturated. And I had to read lots of it. Out of the sixteen books and pamphlets which formed the bedrock of my research into lesbian s/m, three were directly supportive, three were various shades of neutral and ten were vehemently opposed.

Sexual s/m occupies a strangely intellectualized space in white Western culture. It has been the subject of theoretical analysis by the whole gamut of the intelligentsia, from heavyweights like Deleuze at the top (bottom?) through to PhD students. As a result a wide range of theoretical models for sexual s/m have developed, including the psychological, physiological, political, philosophical, sociological, feminist and even economic. Some of these are discussed below. It is important to recognize, however, that almost all mainstream discussion of s/m is concerned with the heterosexual variety, with its specific gendered power dynamics. Discussion of lesbian s/m is almost exclusively confined to feminist texts, the only exception to this being mainstream newspapers and magazines, which occasionally include a sentence or two on lesbian s/m tacked on to general articles about the subject.

This is an important point. It means that access to information about lesbian s/m sexuality is through the feminist machinery of representation and is, therefore, largely controlled by feminist gatekeepers. Since there is a long history of s/m dykes being refused a voice, and s/m speech being silenced and censored within feminist circles,[2] some dykes who identify as sadomasochists, or who are perceived as such, have been obliged to shift away from feminist communities and gain support from mixed queer milieus or from mixed (queer and het) s/m groups. This enforced shift then becomes integrated into the anti-s/m feminist attack. As Pat Califia, leading light of lesbian-feminist s/m group SAMOIS, notes, 'Those who accuse SAMOIS of being male-identified should remember that the group has always gone first to feminist institutions, and has been forced to find alternatives when those institutions won't accept our support.'[3] Far from accepting lesbian sadomasochists, there are feminists who deny that such creatures exist. Andrea Dworkin, for example, famously referred to female sadists as nothing more than a 'male pornographic conceit', having no existence outside this fictional discourse.[4]

What is going on here? How come feminists, whose politics are founded on respect for women, feel entitled to be so hostile, malicious and downright rude to these women *in the name of feminism*? What is lesbian s/m sex anyway, and whose rules does it break? Are lesbian sadomasochists an oppressed sexual minority, colluders with women's oppression or simply fashion victims? These are questions which have been rattling around in the back of my mind for some years now, and which I hope this chapter will go some way towards answering.

Infighting in the sisterhood – a recent history

My interest in lesbian s/m began in earnest in the summer of 1988. Before that, I had merely a vaguely detached curiosity about the subject. I had read *Justine* in early adolescence, and *The Story of O* at teacher-training college. Both had turned me on, but had not instilled in me any desire to participate in any of the activities described. Clearly they spoke powerfully to something in me on the level of fantasy, but equally clearly I was not 'like that' in reality. I was content to accept that I shared the planet with people whose sexual desires seemed simply incomprehensible; after all, people enjoyed football, mathematics, eating apricots and train-spotting, all of which I found equally unintelligible. And then I found myself on the fringes of a major storm in my own community.

In 1988 I travelled up to London for the Lesbian Strength march. I went with a group of friends, the day was sunny, we were having a great time. Then someone thrust a leaflet into my hands. The leaflet urged that s/m lesbians, or any lesbian wearing chains, bondage gear or leather, be ejected from the march. Still reading the leaflet, I wandered off to the nearest public convenience. When I emerged from my cubicle, I found the place had filled up with women wearing black leather, chains and studded belts. Many of them had dyed black hair and looked more punk than anything, but these were clearly the terrible women the leaflet was warning me against. I felt suddenly depressed and angry. Lesbian activism and lesbian feminism are both supposedly grounded in a politics of unapologetic self-definition. For lesbians to try and exclude another group of lesbians from our parade seemed to me to be both contradictory and politically disastrous.

As I read more about lesbian s/m it became clear that this was not an isolated incident. Rather, the attempt to exclude s/m dykes from community spaces was routine. In 1979 attempts were made to ban

SAMOIS from the Gay Freedom Day Parade in San Francisco,[5] and in the 1980s the group was refused permission to rent space in the San Francisco Women's Building – a particular irony, coming from a feminist organization which, as Gayle Rubin[6] points out, was perfectly happy to rent space to heterosexual weddings (unarguably a far more important instrument of women's oppression than sadomasochism could ever be). In 1980 the National Organization of Women – the most powerful feminist organization in the USA – passed a resolution condemning 'sadomasochism, pornography, public sex and pederasty',[7] in a motion supposedly in support of gay rights. In 1985, the London Lesbian and Gay Centre was the scene of heated conflict when a group of lesbian feminists tried to prevent s/m dykes being admitted to the centre; when they failed to prevent this, they attempted to have the centre's funding stopped by lobbying the Greater London Council. As Susan Ardill and Sue O'Sullivan comment, 'It's quite a turn-up when lesbian feminists, some of whom advocate withdrawal from men on an individual sexual basis as a political stance, run to a male-dominated bureaucracy to denounce other lesbians and gay men.'[8]

More recently, *Sisterwrite*, a London feminist bookshop (now closed), refused to stock either the British lesbian sex magazine *Quim* or Della Grace's book of lesbian photographs *Love Bites,* on the grounds that they included 'violent [material which] could cause offence to some of our customers'.[9] So taken for granted is it among certain feminists that s/m is the epitome of bad behaviour that Jenny and Celia Kitzinger feel able to write that 'The two issues of *Quim* which we have seen ... are heavily reliant on the traditional pornographic paraphanalia [*sic*] of sadomasochism', without bothering to explain *why* this should be a bad thing.[10]

It is not the case that feminist opponents of lesbian s/m are all simply narrow-minded bigots – although, sadly, plenty of them are! Many of the leading feminist thinkers, including Mary Daly, Julia Penelope, Ti-Grace Atkinson, Robin Morgan, Sarah Lucia-Hoagland, Claudia Card, Susan Griffin and Alice Walker, have publicly condemned S/M between women. I am especially saddened by the anti-s/m stance of Audre Lorde, a writer whose work has meant much to me, and somewhat surprised that Judith Butler (calling herself 'Judy' in this avatar) contributed a piece to the book *Against Sadomasochism: A Radical Feminist Analysis,*[11] although her piece is also critical of the feminist anti-s/m stance. Although many of these writers do seem to lose all rationality and coherence when they write about s/m (see below for a closer reading of some of these texts), many of them do not; for some of them their opposition to lesbian s/m is based on carefully thought through reasoning. It is reasoning which I believe to be profoundly flawed, as this chapter will, I hope, demonstrate. Before starting to examine these feminist texts in detail, it is important to establish a wider understanding of how s/m is located in late-modern/postmodern Western capitalist societies.

Mad, bad and distinctly dangerous – s/m in mainstream discourse

Tracing s/m back through history is fiendishly difficult, for the same reasons that tracing 'lesbianism' back through history is problematic: only after the practice was first given a name in the nineteenth century did it acquire an 'identity'. Foucault (incidentally one of the better-known s/m gays) is famous for his provocative statement that homosexuals were invented in the nineteenth century, although lesbian and gay historians have now fairly conclusively disproved this,[12] and it is probably as true to say that the sadomasochist was invented at the same time. The kind of historical work which has been carried out by lesbian and gay historians unearthing queer history remains to be done for sadomasochists, and it is to be hoped that s/m history will eventually burgeon as queer history has in recent years.

There are wall paintings from the ancient city of Pompeii which date from 90–80 BC and depict a female winged figure whipping a naked young woman in what appears to be an initiation ritual,[13] but with the spread of Christianity s/m images became the staple fare of martyrdoms and saintly suffering. The links between s/m and certain kinds of spirituality are present quite overtly throughout European culture – the lives of many saints, hermits and visionaries, for example, were entirely constructed around bodily degradation and pain - but individuals whose behaviour conforms to modern ideas of sexual s/m have left few traces on the historical record. It is only with the modern era, starting in the eighteenth century, that s/m as we know it began to take shape.

The twin poles of s/m derive – both as ideas and as names – from the European male aristocracy of the eighteenth and nineteenth centuries. From the Austrian novelist Leopold von Sacher-Masoch, author of

Venus im Peltz (*Venus in Furs*), comes the name and the notion of sexual masochism. From the better-known Marquis de Sade, author of *Justine* (among others), comes the name and the notion of sexual sadism. There is no doubt that de Sade was a cruel and violent man, whose assaults on female prostitutes put him in prison for many years. It was the Victorian sexologist Richard von Krafft-Ebing who coined the term 'masochism', intending it to mean the opposite of sadism. The two were regarded as separate phenomena at first, but by 1905 Freud regarded them as two sides of one coin:

> masochism is [often] nothing more than an extension of sadism turned round upon the subject's own self. ... A person who feels pleasure in producing pain in someone else in a sexual relationship is also capable of enjoying as pleasure any pain which he may himself derive from sexual relations. A sadist is always at the same time a masochist.[14]

From this point, sadism and masochism were generally thought of together, and referred to as sadomasochism. However, some recent writers, especially certain feminist commentators, have suggested that it remains necessary to think about them separately.

As with other sexual practices deviating from the reproductive heterosexual 'norm' – including male homosexuality and lesbianism – the first formal recognition of sadism and masochism was made within the emerging discourse of sexual psychopathology. Sadists and masochists, spoken of by 'experts' in this way, were constructed as sick. Indeed, it was not until 1995 that the *Diagnostic and Statistical Manual of the American Psychiatric Association* ceased to classify sadomasochists as mentally disturbed.[15] Because the idea of s/m first crystallized within psychology and psychoanalysis, and because many feminists have incorporated psychoanalysis into their work, it makes sense to start with a brief account of some psychological theories of s/m.[16]

Some non-specialist writers simply take it for granted that adult s/m is symptomatic of childhood physical or sexual abuse. Typical of this position is Julia Penelope who writes, without feeling the need to cite one shred of evidence in support of her claim, that 'Sado-masochism depends upon our memories of the power differential that exists between those who have power, adults, and those who don't, children, and our experience of the violent acts committed against us because they could'.[17] Penelope has a particularly irritating (and dangerous) habit of presenting conjecture as hard fact. She goes on to say:

> That sado-masochists have sexualized the differences in power and authority, like the relationship of parents to child, constructed by HP society [she means HeteroPatriarchal], is a fact. If the difference in power between adults and children did not exist, the situation would not be sexual for sado-masochists.[18]

Apart from the difficulty of imagining the (absurd) situation of equal power between adults and children, and the consequences of that for *every* society, culture and human activity, it is surely ironic that Penelope is here making use of a version of psychoanalytic theory, probably the most heterosexualizing model of human nature possible. Gay writer Edmund White, in an early essay on s/m, elegantly incorporates Freud's theory of 'repetition compulsion' into a more social model. Freud formulated the repetition compulsion theory to explain why survivors of trauma often re-enact the traumatic event in detail, sometimes repeatedly. He placed repetition compulsion 'beyond the pleasure principle', and suggested that it is an attempt to gain control of overpowering events by stage-managing them. White suggests: 'The repetition compulsion seems an elegant model for sadomasochism, in which both partners, functioning under the benign dispensation of make-believe, re-enact not their own private troubles but rather our society's nightmarish preoccupations with power, with might.' Within this psycho-social paradigm, the sadomasochist becomes almost the symbolic bearer of ethical clarity in a world gone mad:

> The same relief we experience in watching a Shakespeare play, the relief of participating in action devoid of irony and freighted with clear values, is the release offered to the sadist and the masochist. The couple perform the mysteries of domination, of might, that obsess our cultures.[19]

Although firmly grounded in Freud, White's social catharsis model of s/m is as far removed from empirical evidence as Penelope's child-abuse model. Since he is not attempting to discredit, exclude or control sadomasochists, this is less of a problem than it is with Penelope's overt propagandist approach, but it remains, nevertheless, a personal vision.

Mandy Merck[20] identifies three feminist psychoanalytically informed models for s/m. The first is developed by Parveen Adams, who 'discovers in lesbian s/m a unique separation of sexuality from gender' and hence proposes a politically radical status for this most reviled of lesbian behaviours. Based on a reading of Freud's Oedipus complex, Adams develops an account of lesbian S/M as a fetishism which, unique among fetishisms, 'recognises that no one has the phallus'[21] and therefore constitutes a 'new sexuality'.

The second model cited by Merck is provided by Julia Creet, who examines within a psychoanalytic framework the dynamic between 'feminism' as a powerful mother figure and lesbian sadomasochists as rebellious daughters. This mother/daughter symbolism is a fairly common thread running through debates on lesbian feminism and s/m. For example, SAMOIS member Katherine Davis describes the anthology *Coming to Power*[22] as calling for 'a re-evaluation of existing lesbian-feminist ethics', saying 'You must own your "illegitimate" children.' Creet firmly establishes feminism as the disciplinary mother in a kind of macro-level sadomasochistic fantasy, into which she introduces an Oedipal/generational dynamic. According to Merck:

> Creet pursues the disciplinary implications of a community ethic which regulates sexual conduct in the name of politics. She further observes how this regulatory power is displaced on to the previous generation to equate morality with maternity, and both with feminism. ... Beneath their objections to its censoriousness, Creet discerns regret that the Symbolic Mother is *not powerful enough*.[23]

What is important about Creet's model is that, rather than attempting to explain s/m in isolation as the product of an individual's psychological development, she takes a *social* focus and assesses lesbian s/m in relation to the specific socio-political context in which it is embedded. She also firmly avoids pathologizing the actors in this conflict. Indeed, the implication of her theory is that the power dynamics inherent in feminism, transforming with the passage of time, make the symbolic confrontation over s/m inevitable, if not necessary.

Merck goes on to discuss the related account given by Tania Modleski, the third feminist psychoanalytical model for lesbian s/m. Modleski sees the 'top' in the lesbian s/m dyad, rather than authoritarian feminists, as representing the Symbolic Mother. As such, she too accords lesbian s/m a radical status, for this maternal power transgresses, and offers an alternative to, patriarchal power. She describes the 'top' as 'initiating the woman into the symbolic order, but transferring and transforming a patriarchal system of gender inequities into a realm of difference presided over by women'.[24]

All three theories, then, understand lesbian s/m in terms of the gendered relations of power which are hegemonic in the cultural settings in which it is acted out. Moreover, all propose that lesbian s/m represents a radical departure from, or transgression of, the heterosexual power relations whereby symbolic (and material) power is differentially invested in maternal and paternal authority. This incorporation of the psychoanalytic perspective into a social and political paradigm is characteristic of the uses which feminists have made of psychoanalysis, and it offers a useful tool for investigating not only the dynamics of lesbian s/m but also the dynamics of the struggles over s/m in general.

There are mainstream theories located in disciplines other than psychology which attempt to account for s/m, although lesbian s/m is characterized by its absence from these accounts, which generally focus on heterosexual (or sometimes gay male) s/m. There have, for example, been attempts to interpret the desire to engage in sadomasochistic sex in terms of physiology: as an addiction to the endorphins produced in the body in response to pain and stress.[25]

Once again, it is important to remember at this point that the attacks on s/m are not confined to community conflicts within feminism or within queer communities. The establishment legislates against, polices and punishes s/m sexuality with a degree of power and effectiveness which marginalized groups simply lack. The case of Operation Spanner the UK, where s/m gay men were charged and imprisoned for consensual s/m acts[26] (which the law deemed to be assault), has recently come before the European Court of Human Rights in Strasbourg. As I write this, a test case has been ruled admissible and it remains to be seen whether the right to engage in consensual s/m will be upheld by the Court.

Discipline and control? The anti-s/m feminists

It is within feminist discourse that the practice of lesbian s/m has been subjected to the most vitriolic attack. Lesbian sadomasochists have been accused of every harm imaginable, from colluding with the destruction of the earth to aiding and abetting violence against women. So much anger and hostility is vented on lesbian s/m that it is tempting to suggest that if s/m dykes didn't exist, feminism would have to invent them. Audre Lorde's position is fairly typical of the tendency within this discourse to position lesbian s/m sexuality firmly in the 'enemy' camp, and to see it as implicated in some quasi-religious vision of evil forces (seen as male) threatening to engulf life on earth (seen as female). She writes:

> SM is not the sharing of power, it is merely a depressing replay of the old and destructive dominant/subordinate mode of human relating and one-sided power, which is even now grinding our earth and our human consciousness into dust.[27]

Anti-s/m feminist discourse has several problematic tendencies. Firstly, it falls back on the kind of simplistic universal dualism between good and evil exemplified by Lorde's statement. Within this dualism, the definition of s/m becomes exceedingly loose. At its extreme, this position states not that s/m is among the evils of patriarchy, but that evil or destructive practices *constitute* s/m. By means of this (cynical?) sleight of hand it becomes impossible to support s/m, because *all* destructive behaviours are labelled s/m and support for the practice becomes perverted into support for all the evil and cruelty in the world.

Radical feminist theologian Mary Daly, who plays with language so that it means what she wants it to mean, writes about '*sado*feminism', which she defines as 'a species of plastic feminism marked by malignant hatred of and/or indifference to women and characterized by scapegoating, sadomasochism (both physical and psychic) and attempts to destroy female creativity and bonding'.[28] She constructs new words for 'degraded caricatures of Lesbian reality', which she terms '*pseudo-Lesbian* or *sadolesbian*', and characterizes Western society *in toto* as 'sadosociety: [a] society spawned by phallic lust; the sum of places/times when the beliefs and practices of sadomasochism are The Rule'.[29] Daly has simply chosen to use 'sadomasochism' opportunistically to refer to any and every practice and institution which she disapproves of. In so doing, she simultaneously constructs a relentless, almost hypnotic, association between the word 'sadomasochism' and the direst evil. Moreover, she encourages her readers to join her in this dubious enterprise: 'Clearly many other *sado*-words could be listed and defined. Any Crone is free to compose such words when she deems this necessary or appropriate'.[30] I doubt whether any clearer appeal to unthinking prejudice could be found in print.

Vivienne Walker-Crawford's critique of lesbian s/m is one of many which become hopelessly tangled up in the twisted logic of this approach; so much so that she ends up comparing s/m with an overindulgent consumption of alcohol or coffee:

> I define sadomasochism as any mode of behaviour that demonstrates hate and blocks the achievement of personal and political ambitions. ... It's the one drink too many that makes us too drowsy to rise and jog the next morning. ... Jolting the nerves of the body with pin pricks for sexual sensation is no better or worse than jolting the nerves of the body with caffeine for an alerting [sic] sensation.[31]

This is semantic game-playing at its most foolish! If you choose to define s/m as anything which 'demonstrates hate and blocks the achievement of personal and political ambitions', then 'sadomasochism' becomes a meaningless word, a way of stamping your foot at the world when you are thwarted. Equally suspect is Lorena Leigh Saxe's analogy whereby lesbian sadism is equated with the tobacco industry:

> Some ways of interacting with another Lesbian are not acceptable ... sexual sadism is one of those unacceptable ways of treating a lesbian. ... Tobacco companies profit from behaviour that shows disrespect, even contempt, for the lives and health of women. To show a basic disrespect for a woman is unacceptable, to profit from such contempt unjust, *even if she is not harmed or even if she enjoys it.*[32] (my italics)

This opportunistic analogy reveals what seems to be a degree of basic misunderstanding of lesbian s/m common among anti-s/m feminists. The idea that the lesbian sadist is disrespectful or contemptuous of the lesbian masochist is in itself disrespectful and contemptuous of s/m lesbians, who stress the mutual respect and care involved in s/m sex. Claudia Card, in an essay unusual for its open-mindedness, describes lesbian s/m, 'not as an example of horizontal hostility but as a puzzling set of practices whose participants generally wish each other well and respect each other's choices'.[33]

The second general problem with the anti-s/m lesbian-feminist position is its patronizing assumption that anti-s/m lesbians know what lesbian s/m is really all about *better than the s/m dykes themselves*. In this, it not only projects the mummy-knows-best smugness which seems to fit it so well into the Symbolic Mother role assigned to it in variations on the psychoanalytic theme, it also echoes in a disturbing way the disempowering and oppressive practices of the therapeutic professions as criticized by Jeffrey Masson[34] and others. One particularly distressing example of this approach can be found in Sarah Lucia Hoagland's essay 'proving' that lesbian sadism and masochism are inconsistent with lesbian feminism:

> It is so obvious to me that they are inconsistent with Lesbian-feminism that I have found myself ... essentially speechless. If you have on a pair of socks and cannot see that they do not match what can I say? I can test your eyes for colour blindness and I can check to see you understand what the word 'match' means. But if your vision is fine and your understanding of English good, then beyond pointing out the mismatch to you, is meaningful dialogue possible?[35]

This passage simply erases any difference there may be between Hoagland's personal belief (that lesbian s/m is inconsistent with lesbian feminism) and universally accepted 'truth' (that unmatched socks are recognizable by able-bodied and able-minded people), and in doing so constructs those who disagree with her as deluded. Similarly, the authors of a health guide for lesbians feel quite free to promulgate an anti-s/m *political* position as health-promoting: 'Just as Lesbian communities support recovering alcoholics with substance-free events, we can support recovering sadomasochists by helping them channel their erotic impulses positively. They can be helped so that they see all the choices available to them sexually.'[36] As though lesbians fell back on s/m sex through ignorance of other sexual possibilities! This addiction model of s/m (which is discussed later in this chapter) is taken for granted without any recognition of its problematic status. Indeed, the notion that this urge to 'help' s/m dykes 'recover' from their sickness springs perhaps from a misreading of lesbian s/m is allowed to stand, since there is an explicit refusal to try and understand: 'We do not need to explore and explain sadomasochism,' they continue, 'We need to name the violence.'

It is difficult to understand why this stance is acceptable. In what other context could a group of people be dismissed as sick by critics who expressly refuse to deny or remedy their own ignorance? This account covertly excludes s/m lesbians from its addressed readership (perhaps doing s/m makes you so healthy you don't need a lesbian health guide?) by the presumptuous use of 'us' to refer to non-s/m lesbians: 'Sadomasochists tell *us* that they are stigmatized because of their desires ... and all the rest of *us* "Vanilla Dykes" must simply fear the truth of the power relationships they portray.'[37] (my italics) Such unexamined textual practices work powerfully to construct 'insider' and 'outsider' groups. The message is clear: if you are into s/m, this book is not for you.

Accepting these flaws in the anti-s/m feminist position, what are its goals? What precisely does it mean to claim that s/m is not a 'valid sexual practice'[38] (and what would a 'valid' sexual practice look like?), or that one is 'against sadomasochism'? Clearly, it is more than a simple statement of sexual taste; it is not necessary to write full-length books or to call upon feminist political theory in order to refuse personal participation in s/m sex. Nor, apparently, does it imply a desire to stop s/m sex from taking place. Many anti-s/m feminists explicitly state that they do not want this to happen. Robin Linden, Bat-Ami Bar On, Jeanette Nichols, Darlene Pagano, Margaret Rossoff and Susan Griffin are among those who write that they are not seeking to deny lesbian sadomasochists the right to their chosen sexual behaviours – although there is a covert understanding that this should take place in private.

The ultimate aim of anti-s/m feminists is to exclude s/m dykes from feminism in some way, because lesbian s/m is perceived as *intrinsically antagonistic to the goals of feminism*. Mary Daly insists that the conflict over lesbian s/m is not a conflict within feminism at all, because supporting s/m (or pornography) is so hostile to feminism that to do so puts women *outside* feminism altogether:

> When women ... whose consciousness has been ... destroyed pro-claim themselves pro-sadomasochism ... they are speaking neither *as* feminists nor *for* feminists. Since the inherent logic of their position is simply anti-feminist, they do not represent a 'split' or a 'struggle' *within* the feminist movement. Rather, they have become tools of the sadosociety in its continuing effort to destroy female consciousness.[39]

The attempt to cast s/m lesbians out of the feminist body politic on the grounds that s/m is always already anti-feminism is presented over and over again, as the following excerpts demonstrate:

SAMOIS is entitled to exist as a group devoted to S/M, but why should we let them get away with calling themselves lesbian-feminist?[40]

sadomasochism is used to delegitimize lesbian-feminism, lesbianism and feminism.[41]

sadomasochism is anti-feminist and anti-liberatory for many reasons ... Two world views – one nourished by and nourishing sadomasochism, the other, Lesbian feminism – are irreconcilably at odds.[42]

So now here comes this whole sadomasochism issue. ... And it's being represented as a feminist issue, a lesbian-feminist issue. It's bullshit! ... The part of it that concerns me is when it is presented as a feminist issue or when it's held out as being part of the feminist movement, lesbian-feminist movement, that's when I draw the line.[43]

In my opinion sadomasochism is a manifestation of sickness. ... It is destructive to the women's movement as well as to the individual women involved. We need to be aware of how the promotion of sadomasochism can be subterfuge [sic] to the women's movement.[44]

sadomasochism is not a feminist activity. It should not be falsely justified with the language of liberation movements.[45]

The 'debate'... started when sado-masochists claimed that sado-masochism was the *avant garde* of the 'sexual revolution' and defined their ideology as 'Feminist', thereby equating the politics of Feminism with the *Playboy/Penthouse/Hustler/Screw* 'sexual revolution'. Feminists, however, said that sado-masochism is a sexuality constructed by the heteropatriarchal (HP) values and assumptions that Feminism seeks to eradicate.[46]

This last extract, from Julia Penelope, is a clear example of a common semantic strategy used by some feminists to exclude s/m lesbians from feminism in a covert way. Note that Penelope is here setting 'sado-masochists' and 'feminists' up as *opposing groups* ('sado-masochists claimed' and 'feminists said'). Yet the lesbian sadomasochists she is referring to publicly identify as lesbian feminists. SAMOIS is a lesbian-feminist organization and has publicly stated as much. Penelope is herself critical of what she alleges to be the 'rhetorical ploy' of feminists who call themselves pro-sex:

> the 'pro-sex' label has been used as a rhetorical ploy to discredit dissenters in advance, with about the same substance as the 'pro-life' line. This facile word-trick attempts to stifle disagreement by forcing dissenters to start out in a negative and, therefore, hostile position.[47]

The spectacle of women playing manipulative rhetorical games, while furiously accusing those who disagree with them of the same tactics is not a pretty one. Both s/m dykes and anti-s/m feminists, together with certain feminists who come close to neutrality on this issue, have drawn attention to the disturbing implications of anti-s/m hostility. Lesbian sadomasochist Pat Califia writes, 'I continue to be amazed at the humiliation and degradation which vanilla lesbian feminists force on S/M lesbians against our will',[48] while lesbian feminist philosopher Claudia Card suggests that 'A better candidate for horizontal hostility than consensual sadomasochism may be the sparring ... between lesbian sadomasochist liberationists and lesbian feminists who oppose sadomasochism'.[49] But it is anti-s/m lesbian feminist Sarah Lucia Hoagland who makes the clearest case for rejecting such tactics. It is worth citing her at some length:

> While we may find we lose respect for a lesbian at a given time as a result of something she's done, we don't have to act to destroy her. Such desires involve a scenario of one lesbian saying 'fie on thee foul dyke' and the other saying 'hit me again', while the community sits in silent approval. The scenario we would enact is sadomasochism pure and simple ... by engaging in [such strategies] we make plausible the idea that a lesbian should give up her judgement to the mothers; we make plausible the idea that undermining a lesbian's moral agency is legitimate (has a social function); we make plausible the idea that within [a] community it is appropriate for us to de-moralize a lesbian.[50]

The sharp-eyed reader will have noticed that Hoagland is herself colluding with the scenario she abjures by her presumptuous use of 'sadomasochism' as a descriptor of a destructive set of behaviours! Nevertheless, this remains a powerful indictment of the more shameful excesses of anti-s/m discourse. Name-calling and dismissal have not, of course, been confined to the anti-s/m camp, although they are markedly more widespread among anti-s/m feminists than among pro-s/m writers and activists. I have not, for example, come across anything written by a lesbian sadomasochist which parallels the dismissive rudeness of Gillian Hanscombe's description of 'enthusiasts for sadomasochism (empty-headed, wrong-headed, disreputable, disrespectful, decadent)',[51] although there is certainly much anger and bitterness in lesbian s/m writing.

It is abundantly clear that large numbers of feminist writers believe that lesbian s/m is at the very least non-feminist, if not actively anti-feminist. This is a problematic assertion, given the basic feminist principle of validating women's personal experience, and given s/m lesbian feminists' opposing assertion that 'Anti-S/M attitudes are embedded in many areas of lesbian feminist ideology. As S/M lesbians, we say that our experience contradicts many of those closely held theories, and that this examination of our experience is a feminist inquiry'.[52] Both sides in this debate lay claim to the label 'feminist'; the crucial distinction seems to lie in the fact that, whereas s/m dykes and their supporters do not claim that theirs is the *exclusive* feminist position and that those who disagree with them forfeit the right to the title 'feminist', many anti-s/m feminists do make these claims.

If the practice of s/m *is* contrary to feminist political ideology, it is unclear what the implications might be. Feminism is not a membership organization from which women may be ejected for improper behaviour – although feminists such as Julia Penelope clearly believe this to be the case. However, the hostility which s/m lesbians have faced from anti-s/m feminists is damaging both to feminism – which is already widely dismissed by queers and sex-radicals as erotophobic – and to s/m lesbians. The cost to s/m dykes has been high. All too often they have been denied access to feminist community resources and communications networks. As a profoundly stigmatized, criminalized and despised group, such resources would have provided much-needed support at a time when s/m dykes were beginning to organize in resistance. If the reasons for their exclusion were not ethically and politically rock-solid, this stands as one of the most shameful failures in the history of feminism. The personal cost has also been high for many s/m dykes, who initially turned to the women's movement confident of support. Pat Califia writes:

The things that seem beautiful, inspiring, and life-affirming to me seem ugly, hateful and ludicrous to most other people. This may be the most painful part of being a sadomasochist. ... We know we are ugly before we have even seen ourselves, and the injustice of this, the falsehood, chokes me. ... Do these people hate me, do they want sadomasochists to cease to exist, because of a different notion about what constitutes the good and the beautiful?[53]

If it is no more than this, if the feminist critique of s/m is premised on 'a different notion about what constitutes the good and the beautiful', then anti-s/m feminists have been simply colluding with the oppression of a socially marginalized group of women. It is important, therefore, to ask *why* anti-s/m lesbian feminists believe lesbian s/m sex to be in opposition to feminism.

What's wrong with s/m? The feminist argument dissected

Anti-s/m lesbian feminists make many specific accusations against the practice of lesbian s/m sexuality. They have said that it is intrinsically heterosexual, that it supports capitalism, is racist and anti-Semitic, male-identified and pro-establishment, that it is offensive to battered women, is never consensual, reinforces male power and is addictive. I don't have the space to engage with all these points – to do so would require another book – but some of the key anti-s/m arguments are too important to ignore here. Not all rejections of lesbian s/m come from a primarily political agenda, some women place great faith in what can only be called a 'gut reaction'. Thus Susan Leigh Starr writes that 'Sadomasochism troubles my street sense. If I were a cat, I would say that I arch my back in its presence',[54] while Cheri Lesh claims that accounts of s/m scenarios remind her of being tortured in previous incarnations: 'I told her I did not want to listen to this [s/m] scenario, it pushed my buttons, my old memories of being tortured in past lives flickering through me like the Inquisitor's fires.'[55] Although I do not wish to dismiss anyone's belief in reincarnation, it seems doubtful whether the avoidance of behaviours which may 'push buttons' from past historical eras is either realistic or helpful as a lesbian feminist strategy. It is not, however, possible to engage with this debate on the level of 'street sense' or previous lives. If feminists claim that the argument is a political one – and feminists on both sides do – then it is the political objections to s/m that must be examined.

Is lesbian s/m intrinsically heterosexual?

Many anti-s/m lesbian feminists reject lesbian s/m on the grounds that it is heterosexual. It is important to recognize that, in the terms of this discourse, 'heterosexual' is politically determined, as relations between men and women are understood to reinforce women's submission to male power:

> If you engage in any form of sexual activity with a man you are reinforcing his class power. ... Only in the system of oppression that is male supremacy does the oppressor actually invade and colonise the interior of the body of the oppressed.[56]

To be labelled 'heterosexual' in this paradigm is to be labelled a collaborator in the oppression of women and a supporter of male power. It is especially offensive to many queer people, given the complex and oppressive history of our struggles against heterosexual supremacy. To label lesbian s/m sexuality 'heterosexual' is strongly derogatory, and quite common in anti-s/m feminist writing:

> The s/m scenario ... based upon fetishised masculinity and femininity, should make clear, supposing any doubt remains, that the traditional heterosexual system is an s/m romance. Through the exaggeration of the characteristics of gender roles, the naked, eroticised power dynamic which fuels heterosexuality is laid bare.[57]

> Without the idea of 'power over' another person assumed to be one's inferior, taken unapologetically from heteropatriarchal structures, sado-masochism would not exist.[58]

> the occurrence of sado-masochistic fantasies and/or behaviours among lesbians, and the far more prevalent occurrence of both among faggots, are, to me, a function of the enforced identification of the homosexual with heterosexual roles in a patriarchal culture.[59]

> Sadomasochism is not a 'kinky' deviation from normal heterosexual behaviour. Rather, it is the defining quality of the power relationship between men and women. Sadism is the logical extension of behaviour that arises out of male power.[60]

The norm of femininity as it manifests itself in normal women is masochism. Force actualises femininity. Violence is sex. Pain is pleasure for the woman.[61]

It is difficult to engage with the assertion that lesbian s/m is intrinsically heterosexual, because it is premised on two strategic word-games. Firstly, there is a general tendency within anti-s/m radical-lesbian feminist discourse to use 'heterosexual' not to mean sexual acts or relationships between men and women, but rather acts which express hatred of women or which attempt to exert control over women, or (in Sheila Jeffreys's use of the word) *relationships constructed around or including any power differential.*[62] This by now familiar tactic of broadening the definition of a word to the extent that it becomes virtually meaningless implies that any feminist can use 'heterosexual' to mean what she chooses, so that any challenge to the links drawn between s/m and heterosexuality is forced into a preacarious position.

The second semantic strategy is to base the claim that s/m is heterosexual on the prior assertion, considered as proven, that heterosexuality is sadomasochistic *because* it is always already implicated in men's control and abuse of women. This doubly tautological argument cannot be challenged because, fundamentally, it is meaningless.

Stripped of the word-games, the argument appears to be as follows. Women are subordinated by men, and both heterosex (as a sexual practice) and heterosexuality (as a social institution) are important elements in that subordination. Women are commonly beaten, humiliated, raped and terrorized by men without their consent, and this abuse – which helps to maintain male power and to control women – is routinely eroticized and/or set in a sexual framework by both women and men. *Therefore* when one woman engages with another woman in consensual sexual behaviours which appear to resemble these abusive acts, they are behaving in a heterosexual way and hence reinforcing men's power over women. This argument contains – although its proponents generally choose to ignore the fact – several unanswered questions. What is the social, psychic or cultural mechanism whereby sexual activity between two women translates into increased power for men? What should we make of s/m dykes' insistence that their actions, far from being abusive or cruel, are mutually pleasurable (it is not enough simply to assert some kind of superior insight and claim that they are wrong about their own experiences)? If 'heterosexual' may be freely applied to sexual behaviours between women, between men or between men and women, does this mean that there is *no difference in kind* between 'lesbian heterosexuality' and 'heterosexual heterosexuality'? If this is the case, what implications does it have for the revolutionary feminist position that it is better for a feminist to be a lesbian than to be heterosexual – does it not imply that politically radical 'lesbian' sex is as possible between a man and a woman as politically reactionary 'heterosexual' sex supposedly is between two women?

I do not believe that, as it stands, the argument that lesbian s/m is heterosexual, or even that it is a simulacrum of heterosex, represents anything other than a propagandist semantic ploy. Perhaps there are important questions to be asked concerning the relationship between the practice of lesbian s/m and heterosexuality (such as the link between practising s/m and the perceived *rejection* of prescribed feminine powerlessness), but these questions can only be answered by lesbians who practise or who have practised s/m.

Does lesbian s/m support the capitalist system?

Accusations that s/m is an expression of commercialized sexuality and that it profits (male-controlled) capitalism are comparatively rare. This is perhaps unsurprising, since the feminist arguments against s/m have taken place almost exclusively on the level of the symbolic rather than the material, as Gayle Rubin points out:

> this [lesbian-feminist] analysis is not based on the realities of sexual behaviour. It is predicated on a limited notion of the symbolic valences of both lesbianism and S/M. Torn from real social context, sexual differences can symbolize all kinds of other differences, including political ones.[63]

The materialist arguments against s/m are largely confined to the claim that it is an expensive practice, requiring the purchase of equipment – whips, bondage gear, leather harnesses and clothing, pornography, etc. – which must be provided by male entrepreneurs, and that s/m imagery is used in advertising:

who profits from sadomasochism? According to an article in *Mother Jones* there is an enormous profit being made from the manufacture and sale of adult sex 'toys'. ... Major department stores have discovered that sadomasochistic themes or situations in their display windows lure customers. Sadomasochism, besides being marketed itself, is also used to sell a wide variety of products.[64]

It is certainly the case that sadomasochists, like lesbians and gay men before them, have historically been exploited by cynical manufacturers. But it is also the case (again paralleling the experience of lesbians and gay men) that the s/m community incorporates a small specialist market in which practitioners design, manufacture and supply equipment. Of particular note in this context is the growth – in the UK and elsewhere in Europe, in North America, Australia and New Zealand – of lesbian-run and lesbian-owned sex-toy cottage industries. Which is not to claim that lesbian s/m occupies some sort of magical uncontaminated space outside the capitalist economy. Nor, of course, does feminism. The argument that lesbian sadomasochists are propping up capitalism would only be significant if vanilla lesbians had found some way of avoiding doing so. Clearly, given the exploitation of both feminism and lesbianism by the commercial mainstream (perhaps especially in the mainstream adoption of lesbian and feminist codes in advertising), this is not the case.

Is sadomasochism racist or anti-Semitic?

The charge of racism or anti-Semitism is probably the most troubling of the many charges levelled against lesbian s/m. It is also probably the most frequent. As Susan Ardill and Sue O'Sullivan note in the context of the attempt to deny sadomasochists access to the London Lesbian and Gay Centre, 'SM Dykes became the walking repositories of racism, fascism and male violence'.[65] Lesbian sadomasochists may be accused of racism, anti-Semitism or fascism because some s/m scenarios reputedly incorporate elements of slavery or Nazism into their fantasy, or because the wearing of swastikas, Nazi uniforms, black peaked caps or black leather has fascist connotations, or simply because the foundational s/m fantasy of dominance and submission is in itself seen as fascistic. (There is a very important distinction to be drawn between the use of semiotic codes which reference Nazism directly and consciously – such as swastikas – and the use of multivalent codes which may or may not reference Nazism – such as black leather. The use of swastikas in s/m is discussed in detail below.)

Anti-s/m lesbian feminists frequently exploit the history of the Holocaust in order to demonize lesbian s/m. This is generally done in a quite thoughtless and manipulative way, as these extracts show:

> I am appalled by Samois' advocacy of 'dominance' and 'submission' between lesbian-feminist lovers, and by Samois' advocacy of the cultivation of pain. ... I associate the cultivation of pain with the horrors of the Nazi Third Reich and the medieval Inquisition. Historically, cultural desensitization to pain has led to incredible butchery.[66]

> Marie Robinson['s] book *The Power of Sexual Surrender* is to women what a tome called *Why You Know You Love It on the Plantation* would be to blacks or one titled *How to Be Happy in Line to the Showers* would be to Jews.[67]

Or, in this argument attempting to justify the refusal of lesbian-feminist publications to carry s/m material:

> Lesbian-feminist publications do not exist to print anything and everything anyone might wish to publish. Our publications do not print speeches and papers by nazis. We do not print essays advocating a return to slavery ... racism and anti-Semitism are not consistent with Lesbian-feminism. ... Nor is sadomasochism. I work to create a world in which not only are lynching, pogroms, rape and sissy-beating not practiced [*sic*], they are inconceivable; I work for a world in which dominance and submission are inconceivable.[68]

> The ... 'passion' frequently described in sado-masochistic literature reflects the sexualization of conceptual oppositions and hierarchies of domination such as racism, classism, anti-Semitism. ... What, then, is the 'real' content of sado-masochism? Primary HP [heteropatriarchal] dichotomies ... are labelled sadist/masochist ... and acted out in sado-masochistic 'scenes' as master (mistress)/slave, top/bottom ... Nazi/Jew ...[69]

Many have argued that sadomasochism is consistent with, and even strengthens, such oppressions as anti-Semitism, racism and sexism by both sexualising and publicly displaying the symbolisms of Nazism, slavery, prostitution and incest ... sadomasochists are not playing with power and control in the abstract. For the purposes of fun the drama in their scenes uses (publicly, thus endorsing) the real-life horrors of oppression that real women and Lesbians have endured.[70]

In emulating Nazi/Jew or master/slave scenes, for example, sadomasochists contribute to the context which allows such institutions to flourish, thereby validating them ... such practices lull us into acceptance and resignation.[71]

Warning. Do not go to the London Lesbian and Gay Centre unless you are prepared to be in an environment that is rife with fascists, racists, misogynists and sadomasochists.[72]

What an irony that a word like 'liberation' should be applied to sadomasochism! ... The sadomasochistic act [sic] requires the renunciation of freedom and choice. It requires a master and a slave. ... Oh yes. We have seen these two before. The guard to the prisoner. The Nazi to the Jew. The white master to the black slave.[73]

O's abandonment of her own freedom reminds one of the German masses' allegiance to Hitler.[74]

While they [s/m lesbians] talked of liberation and uninhibited pleasure their pain and fear and rage filled the room like invisible poison gas, squeezing my lungs narrow. 'What are you afraid of, we're only on our way to the showers' they say, and all the while their eyes and nervous hands speak what they know. We are in the death camps.[75]

This elision of lesbian sadomasochistic sex play with the horrors of slavery and the Holocaust constitutes opportunistic and irresponsible game-playing. Firstly, it presents 'slavery' and 'Nazism' as though they were examples of a single phenomenon, 'dominance and submission'. This is deeply problematic, and ignores the real history of both. Although the Third Reich involved slave labour, Nazism and slavery are simply not the same thing. They must be discussed separately.

In anti-s/m feminist discourse, partly because most of the writers are from the USA, 'slavery' refers to one episode of enslavement in history, the trade in African women and men shipped to the plantations in the Americas and the Caribbean Islands (the original inhabitants of those islands, the Arawak, Carib and others, having been virtually wiped out by white colonialists). The history of slavery in human civilization is of course much longer and more complex than this, but the defining features of this particular episode are its racialized nature – those who profited by the slave trade were mostly (although not exclusively) white; those subjected to its brutalities were black – and the fact that slaves worked the plantations in a country which *defined itself* around an ideology of individual freedom. From this complex history, anti-s/m feminists have extracted the racialized relation between black African slave and white American trader/owner/overseer as significant. Master/slave fantasies, they argue, exploit for pleasure an evil historical moment of racist abuse and are therefore *intrinsically* racist.

Similarly, direct comparisons are drawn between Nazism and lesbian s/m. These tend to concentrate on one aspect of the complex phenomenon of Nazism – the torture and murder of Jews in the concentration camps – or (less commonly) to suggest that s/m was an intrinsic part of the decadent society which allowed the Nazis to rise to power. The London group, Lesbians Against Sado-Masochism (LASM) claimed that 'SM was a significant part of the "decadent" social scene in 1930s Berlin – part of the political climate of the day. *People acclimatized to SM brutality would have failed to notice the threat of the "real Nazis"* approaching'[76] (my italics).

This (ludicrous) vision of a world in which s/m was such an accepted mode of sexual expression that people became too dull-witted to tell the difference between sex games and political policies both trivializes 'real' Nazism and distorts historical fact. In particular, it erases the suffering of lesbians and (especially) gay men at the hands of the Nazis, a history which lesbians surely have a responsibility to make visible, not to deny. As Edmund White comments, 'Actual gay sado-masochism, as practiced by some of Ernst Roehm's followers, was exterminated by the Nazis'.[77]

Because the Holocaust stands as the most potent symbol of brutality, injustice and inhumanity in the twentieth century, some choose to use it as a free-floating signifier, an incantation which damns lesbian sadomasochists simply by being spoken in the same breath. In an account of the 1986 *Feminism, Sexuality and Power* conference at Mount Holyoake College, Margaret Hunt describes an anti-s/m presentation by Janice Raymond: 'At one point she compared people with tolerant attitudes towards pornography and S/M to those who deny the Holocaust ever happened.' This strategy, by asserting that tolerance towards porn and s/m is *the equivalent* of denying the Holocaust, not only casts sexual tolerance as equal to the most offensive anti-Semitism but also constructs pornography and s/m as *of the same order as* the atrocities committed at that time. Hunt observes, 'This was very distressing not only to some of the people in the audience who did S/M (including several who were Jewish), but to a prominent feminist historian of the Holocaust who was attending the conference'.[78]

Those who claim that Nazism and lesbian s/m are *the same thing* tend themselves to sexualize Nazism, as this account by Sarah Lucia Hoagland shows:

> Have we forgotten or failed to inform ourselves that some nazi men found the torture of Jews highly erotic? Have we forgotten or failed to inform ourselves that some nazi men experienced orgasm while watching Jews being beaten, tortured, mutilated, gassed, destroyed?[79]

This passage makes subtle use of guilt to manipulate the reader. If you happened *not* to know these unpleasant details, you have '*failed* to inform' yourself. It is perhaps the cynical social scientist in me who demands that, if Hoagland is so determined that her readers should know these things, she should at the very least give us references to her sources so that we may better inform ourselves. This she does not do. I am not suggesting that these things did not happen, only that it is important that Hoagland should not be the filter through which we gain our knowledge when there are more direct avenues available to us. By keeping the doors to such knowledge firmly shut, rather than giving her readers the key, Hoagland is asserting her right to retain control of this knowledge and demanding that we accept *her* as the expert. She concludes, 'It is just not true that all areas of eroticism should be explored by Lesbian-feminists or anyone else'.

But it is the content of her words, not simply the semantic strategy, which is significant. By stating that some Nazis found torture sexually pleasurable (and does this surprise anyone?), she is trying to prove that the practice of s/m can damage women's sexual responses: 'while repression, sexual and otherwise, can shape our erotic response, so can dominance or submission'. She is claiming here that sexual games involving dominance and submission *are the same as* the mutilation and murder of Jews by Nazis. How can this not be offensive to Jews, to Holocaust survivors and to lesbian sadomasochists? This elision of sexual sadism and the horrors of genocide is a common tactic in feminist anti-s/m writing, and it sets up a confusion between the two which is both offensive and unhelpful as Edmund White makes clear:

> The concentration camps were not sexual playgrounds but scenes of real, not make-believe, genocide. ... The confusion arises from our double use of the word sadism to mean both criminal, brutal acts of non-sexual violence and harmless erotic games. They are not the same thing. The obscenities of war are not equivalent to the eccentricities of the bedroom.[80]

To reject the critique of s/m as intrinsically replicating Nazism is not to endorse the conscious public use of Nazi symbols by s/m lesbians. In particular, I do not think that swastikas can be extracted from their context – not only the historical co-option of the swastika[81] by the Nazis but its current use by resurgent fascist groups in Europe and the USA. The public wearing of the swastika is undoubtedly directly disrespectful to Jews:

> I am a Jew. Therefore swastikas and those symbols that are closely associated with them *bother me* ... in the case of swastikas, the connection with a *direct* threat to my physical well-being is recent in history. This threat is still alive, as demonstrated by recent acts of violence against Jews.[82]

Because of its semiotic status – as a sign signifying allegiance to fascist ideology – the wearing of the swastika constitutes an anti-Semitic act. It also indicates (at the very least) disrespect for other groups victimized by Nazism during the Third Reich or currently. I am not, however, convinced that the wearing of swastikas is a common practice among sadomasochists, and I am unsure to what extent other symbols may be regarded as signifying fascism or Nazism. The iron cross and the double-headed German eagle carry the same connotations as the swastika, but I do not believe that peaked caps, boots or black leather – all frequently described as 'fascist gear' in anti-s/m discourse – are so

densely laden with fascist meaning. That they may have (potentially troubling) associations with militarism is true, but so too do the shaved heads sported by many right-on lesbian feminists.

All too often the 'accoutrements of fascism' argument is wielded lazily and inaccurately. Ardill and O'Sullivan recount that anti-s/m feminists active in the fight to exclude s/m practitioners from the London Lesbian and Gay Centre often accused their opponents of coming to meetings 'dressed in fascist gear'. From their own experience: 'As far as dress goes, some strange outfits were worn, some leather and a few studded collars and leather caps. We saw no fascist gear'.[83] I have never seen a lesbian or gay man wearing fascist symbols, and have been unable to find a single swastika, iron cross or German eagle in my copies of lesbian sex magazines, in any SAMOIS literature, or in any lesbian erotic photography. This is not to deny that there may be lesbian sadomasochists who wear these things – for all I know lesbians in full Nazi gear may be two a penny on the streets of San Francisco – but it seems to be at most a hidden and rare practice. It is unreasonable and illogical to trash lesbian s/m *per se* for the offensive or ignorant actions of a few, just as it is unreasonable to criticize s/m by foregrounding the extreme practices of a highly specialized minority (such as scrotum-piercing among gay men[84]) or claiming that Gayle Rubin's support of 'intergenerational' sex is definitive of sadomasochistic principles.[85]

The accusation of racism is altogether more troubling. There is ample evidence that lesbian, gay, queer, feminist and s/m communities are as saturated with racism as any other part of white post-colonialist society. It would be surprising if racism were not sexualized, since the sexualization of racial difference was intrinsic to the ideology of racialization which evolved to justify the slave trade, and we all inherit this unpleasant legacy. From this position, it is as important to fight racism within s/m practices and communities as in any other context. This is, however, very different from fighting s/m because it is *intrinsically* racist. There is heated disagreement among black lesbians about the degree to which lesbian s/m may be called racist. Some black lesbians believe that s/m is a white women's problem: 'I do think it's a white woman's issue, I really do. It comes out of a luxury that I don't have'.[86] Yet there are black lesbian sadomasochists. The struggle over black lesbian s/m is a complex one. Heterosexual black feminist writer Alice Walker describes her horrified reaction to a TV documentary on s/m:

> the only interracial couple in it, lesbians, presented themselves as mistress and slave. The white woman, who did all the talking, was mistress. ... and the black woman, who stood smiling and silent was – the white woman said – her slave. ... All I had been teaching was subverted by that one image and I was incensed to think of ... the actual enslaved *condition* of literally millions of our mothers trivialized – because two ignorant women insisted on their right to act out publicly a 'fantasy' that still strikes terror into black women's hearts.[87]

Pat Califia's response to this is to point out that 'In an attempt to prove that s/m is racist, Walker describes these women as a white woman top and a black woman bottom. In fact, the top in this couple is a Latina lesbian'.[88] While this effectively draws attention to the misperception and misrepresentation which saturates feminist anti-s/m criticism, it does not answer Walker's charge that public exhibitions of mistress/slave scenarios trivialize the sufferings of black women slaves. There are no easy answers to this dilemma, although of course 'freedom' must include the freedom to choose 'slavery' if it is to be a meaningful concept. Cherríe Moraga, a thoughtful commentator who resists being drawn into either a pro- or anti-s/m position, sets an agenda for future debate:

Lesbian s/m has never been critically examined in any sensitive and realistic way, which could be useful to its feminist practitioners and to other feminists who simply want a right to their sexual desire, and at the same time, understand what that desire means in a racist/sexist and violent culture. ... So how does one build a sexual politic that incorporates this complexity? For example, what does it mean that some images and acts of s/m mirror actual acts of violence visited upon people of colour, Jews, and women as a group – and that some Jewish women and women of colour are sexually stimulated by these?[89]

I hope that it may now be possible to debate these questions without the constraints of the polarized framework imposed by anti-s/m feminist activism.

Consent and addiction

Two other feminist critiques of lesbian s/m warrant brief discussion. The first, in an attempt to challenge the notion of consensual exchange which is the bedrock of s/m's claim to be a morally and ethically defensible practice, states that no s/m act can *ever* be consensual, because consent in this context is meaningless. The second, in response to some sadomasochists' belief that s/m can be a cathartic experience which has the potential to help emotional release and healing, states that s/m is *addictive* rather than cathartic.

The addiction model of s/m is based on fairly shaky evidence, and perhaps owes much to the popularity in American lesbian (and gay) communities of the addiction model and the twelve-step programmes which accompany it. The assertion that s/m behaviour is addictive is generally made with no supporting evidence whatsoever:

I protest the claim that enactments of humiliation and pain bring catharsis, because I know that repetition of a behaviour, especially eroticized repetition, will more likely cause habituation or addiction.[90]

it has been noted that sadomasochism has an engulfing and addictive quality to it – partly in virtue of being (at least superficially) an outlaw culture ...[91]

Where evidence is provided, it is almost always in the form of appeals to the supposed findings of the (in)famous Stanford Prison experiment which took place in the USA in 1971. In this experiment, student volunteers were cast in the roles of 'prisoner' or 'guard' and placed in a 'prison' setting which was as realistic as possible. So overwhelming was the experience, with the 'guards' becoming authoritarian and cruel and the 'prisoners' becoming distressed and anxious, that it was discontinued. It remains contentious, and few psychologists would claim that it 'proved' anything at all (beyond the need for rigorous ethical standards in human experiments!). It is in any case inappropriate to generalize from this very specific experimental setting to consensual sex play. Nevertheless, the Stanford Prison experiment is the *only* empirical 'evidence' of the addictive nature of s/m which I have been able to locate in feminist texts:

> By generalising from the [Stanford] prison experiment to sadomasochism, we can infer that enacting dominant and submissive roles would be habituating rather than cathartic, thus creating a desire for increasingly intense sadomasochistic experiences instead of exhausting it.[92]

> Associating beatings, humiliation, domination and submission with orgasms is habituating rather than cathartic for the participants. Go back to the results of the Stanford Prison Experiment; guards with power became more and more abusive and violent ...[93]

It must be said that there is no empirical evidence to support the catharsis hypothesis either. However, many lesbians who do s/m have reported that the experience is cathartic for them. '*I* was a battered womyn [*sic*] for years,' writes one, '& claim the right to release & transform the pain & fear of those experiences in any way I damn well please.'[94] Personal accounts such as these are generally accorded the status of evidence within formal social scientific inquiry, and are usually privileged within feminism as authentic expressions of women's experiences. This being so, we must conclude that there is at present better evidence for the claim that s/m is cathartic than there is for the opposing claim that it is addictive. The final word goes to Claudia Card who points out that 'Both catharsis and addiction suggest a medical model, which has not been generally characteristic of lesbian feminist approaches to sexuality.'[95] I suggest that this uncharacteristic reliance on the traditional patriarchal medical model (otherwise stringently critiqued by feminists) indicates our lack of knowledge about the psychosociology of s/m and demonstrates the pointlessness of trying to debate the politics and/or ethics of an issue about which we know so little.

The question of consent is of a different order, since it is purely theoretical. It is not possible to establish the existence of 'consent' empirically. Sadomasochists insist that what distinguishes their sexual practices from cruelty and abuse is that both parties are fully consenting. The anti-s/m feminist response is to deny that consent to s/m is possible, generally on the grounds that women's subordinate status and our socialization into subordination render 'consent' a meaningless notion in a sexual context:

> The feminist defense of sadomasochism pivots on the apparent consensuality of sadomasochistic sexual encounters. ... However, I take the view, along with other feminists who oppose the practice of sadomasochism, that the psychological reality of 'consensual' sadomasochism is so abstracted from the actual social and historical conditions that shape human relationships and erotic desires as to be virtually meaningless.[96]

> I think the issue of 'mutual consent' is entirely beside the point. ... Since our sexuality has for the most part been constructed through social structures over which we have no control, we *all* 'consent' to sexual desires and activities which are alienating to at least some degree.[97]

> Sadomasochists argue that their sex is based on consent. ... One problem with this argument is that it fails to account for the fact that consent is created in the existing social context ... consent is meaningless in the context of sadomasochism.[98]

These arguments are logically inconsistent since, if individual actors are so constrained by the social construction of hegemonic gender roles that it is impossible to consent to s/m sex, it is by definition impossible for them to 'consent' to politically correct sex, or to anything at all. Though, as Margaret Hunt notes, 'The argument that there is no free choice in the world is never all-inclusive. It always admits the existence of a small group which is morally superior to the corrupt mass.'[99] More sophisticated feminist critics of s/m reject the 'consent impossible' position. As Bat-Ami Bar On admits, 'The consent-based appeal challenges the conceptualization of the practice of sado-masochism typical to the feminist opposition. The challenge cuts quite deeply. At present, feminist theory does not provide any basis for a response to the challenge.'[100]

The 'consent impossible' argument is yet another version of 'superior knowledge' – anti-s/m feminists *can* consent to sex (because the sex they have is 'good' sex), but clearly s/m feminists *cannot* consent to sex (because the sex they have is 'bad' sex). The peculiar illogic of this argument suggests that anti-s/m feminists oppose lesbian sadomasochism because it contradicts the vision of female *goodness* around which a particular utopian feminism (sometimes known as cultural feminism) is constructed.

Conclusion?

The historical relationship between s/m lesbians and anti-s/m feminists has been damaging to both parties, and the debate between the two parties has not reached any logical conclusion. Viewed from one perspective, the whole sad conflict seems to have been a farcical waste of time and energy. As Pat Califia so forcefully insists:

> The real danger is not that S/M lesbians will be made uncomfortable in the women's movement. The real danger is that the right, the religious fanatics, and the right-controlled state will eat us all alive. It is sad to be having to fight to maintain one's membership in the women's movement when it is so imperative to create broad-based coalitions against fascism. The level of internal strife around S/M should be reserved for more genuine threats to feminist goals.[101]

The questions which need answering do not centre on whether a 'good' feminist or a 'good' lesbian (or for that matter a 'good' queer) should be against s/m or for it. Sadomasochism is not a political party, and there are limits to what can or should be *done* from either a 'for' or an 'against' position. The important questions are about the conflict itself. Why did lesbian s/m become such an overdetermined sign at that particular historical moment and in that particular lesbian-feminist community? It is not substantial enough to carry the weight of either side's symbolism. Lesbian s/m sex play is neither going to overthrow the patriarchy nor ensure that it survives and prospers. What makes otherwise rational and thoughtful lesbian feminists set themselves up to condemn the practices of other lesbian feminists from a position of smug, self-righteous ignorance, making use of guilt, manipulation and verbal trickery to do so? As Judith Butler suggests, both s/m lesbian feminists and their opponents 'can ... be seen as attempt[ing] to find a legitimate way of relating lesbian feminist theory and practice'.[102] The preconditions for this attempt require, at the very least, mutual respect.

It is the disrespectful treatment of lesbian sadomasochists and their supporters by anti-s/m feminists which is the most troubling feature of this 'debate'. Rather than following the feminist principles of listening to and believing what women say, anti-s/m feminists have rejected empirical evidence and chosen instead to use deceit, misrepresentation, semantic manipulation and infantile name-calling in order to attack lesbian sadomasochists. This simply turns 'lesbian feminism' into a parodic s/m relationship, with 'feminism' acting as the dominatrix and 'topping' 'lesbian'. Only, contrary to the ethical codes of s/m, feminism is attempting to control, restrain and inflict pain on s/m lesbians *without their consent*, and without paying any attention to their anger or pain. I believe this to be one of the most shameful moments in feminist history.

I will leave the last word to Pat Califia:

> I do not believe that sex has an inherent power to transform the world. I do not believe that pleasure is always an anarchic force for good. I do not believe that we can fuck our way to freedom ... [But] if you live in a society that wishes you didn't exist, anything you do to make yourself happy disrupts its attempts to wipe you out, or at the very least, make you invisible.[103]

Notes

1. I do not mean by this that my fantasies or my sexual behaviours exclude anything which could be called s/m. On the contrary. However, s/m does not form part of my social, political or sexual 'identity', I don't belong to any s/m communities or groups, and there are major aspects of s/m (such as the fairly central question of pain or humiliation as erotic) which I just don't relate to. I want this to be understood in terms of my own sexual preference, not in terms of a political rejection of s/m.

2. For accounts of the degree to which s/m dykes have been silenced within feminist communities, see (from an American perspective) Pat Califia 'A Personal View of the History of the Lesbian S/M Community and

Movement in San Francisco' and Gayle Rubin, 'The Leather Menace: Comments on Politics and S/M', both in SAMOIS (ed.), *Coming to Power: Writings and Graphics on Lesbian S/M*, (3rd edn.) (Boston: Alyson Publications, 1987); or Kathryn Harriss, *What Is this Big Fuss About Sadomasochism? Lesbian sexuality and the Women's Liberation Movement*, (University of Kent at Canterbury, Women's Studies Occasional Papers), for an account of the British experience.

3. Califia, 'A personal view', p. 280.

4. Andrea Dworkin, *Pornography: Men Possessing Women* (London: The Women's Press, 1981), pp. 134–6.

5. Califia, 'A personal view', p. 261.

6. Rubin, 'The leather menace', p. 212.

7. Mandy Merck, *Perversions: Deviant Readings* (London: Virago, 1993), p. 247.

8. Susan Ardill and Sue O'Sullivan, 'Upsetting an Applecart: Difference, Desire and Lesbian Sadomasochism' in Christian McEwen and Sue O'Sullivan (eds.), *Out the Other Side: Contemporary Lesbian Writing* (London: Virago, 1988), p. 139.

9. Cited in Jenny Kitzinger and Celia Kitzinger, '"Doing it": Representations of Lesbian Sex' in Gabrielle Griffin (ed.), *Outwrite: Lesbianism and Popular Culture* (London: Pluto Press, 1993), p. 21.

10. *Ibid.* Apart from the unthinkingness of this position, their statement is simply untrue. See Chapter 6 for a fuller refutation of their assertion.

11. Robin Linden, Darlene Pagano, Diana Russell and Susan Leigh Starr (eds.), *Against Sadomasochism: A Radical Feminist Analysis* (San Francisco: Frog in the Well Press, 1982).

12. See, for example, Emma Donoghue, *Passions Between Women: British Lesbian Culture 1668–1801*

(London: Scarlet Press, 1993); and essays in Martin Duberman, Martha Vicinus and George Chauncey (eds.), *Hidden from History: Reclaiming the Gay and Lesbian Past* (Harmondsworth: Penguin, 1989).

13. Michael Grant, *Erotic Art in Pompeii* (London: Octopus, 1975).

14. Sigmund Freud, 'Three Essays on the Theory of Sexuality' in Freud, *On Sexuality* (Harmondsworth: Penguin, 1905).

15. 'International News' in *Wicked Women: A Magazine of Lesbian Sex and Sexuality* (Strawberry Hills, Australia) No. 25, 1995 p. 7. The DSM took this decision in response to campaigning from the s/m community – much as it agreed to remove 'homosexuality' in response to pressure from lesbian and gay activists - and now classes s/m as evidence of disturbance only in cases of 'clinically significant distress or impairment in social, occupational or other important areas of functioning'.

16. Readers who want to find out more about psychological/psychiatric theories of s/m are referred to Bill Thompson (1994) *Sadomasochism: Painful Perversion or Pleasurable Play?* (London: Cassell, 1994).

17. Julia Penelope, *Call Me Lesbian: Lesbian Lives, Lesbian Theory* (Freedom, CA: The Crossing Press, 1992). Penelope may, of course, be right in this suggestion. What is unacceptable, however, is the presentation of personal belief *as if it were scientific 'fact'* and, moreover, as if it were so well known as a 'fact' that she has no need to offer empirical evidence.

18. *Ibid.*, p. 121.

19. Edmund White (1979), 'Sadomachismo' in White, *The Burning Library: Writings on Art, Politics and Sexuality 1969–1993* (London: Picador, 1994), pp. 62–3.

20. Mandy Merck, 'The Feminist Ethics of Lesbian S/M' in *Perversions*.
21. *Ibid.*, p. 243.
22. SAMOIS (ed.), *Coming to Power*, p. 13.
23. Merck, 'Feminist Ethics of Lesbian S/M, pp. 252–3.
24. *Ibid.*, p. 254.
25. See Claudia Card, *Lesbian Choices* (New York Columbia University Press, 1995).
26. For more detail, see Thompson, *Sadomasochism*.
27. In Audre Lorde and Susan Leigh Star, 'Interview with Audre Lorde' in Robin Linden *et al.* (eds.), *Against Sadomasochism*, p. 66.
28. Mary Daly and Jane Caputi, *Webster's First New Intergalactic Wickedary of the English Language* (London: The Women's Press, 1987), p. 224.
29. *Ibid.*, p. 94.
30. *Ibid.*, p. 224. 'Crone' here is used positively in Daly's own brand of reverse discourse to mean a strong woman who survives in the face of great obstacles, and has 'Dis-covered depths of Courage, Strength, and Wisdom in her Self' (p. 115).
31. In Linden *et al.* (eds.), *Against Sadomasochism*, p. 149.
32. In Claudia Card (ed.), *Adventures in Lesbian Philosophy* (Bloomington and Indianapolis: Indiana University Press, 1994).
33. In Card, *Lesbian Choices*, p. 221.
34. Jeffrey Masson, *Against Therapy* (London: Fortuna, 1990).
35. In Linden *et al.* (eds.), *Against Sadomasochism*, p. 153.
36. Cuca Hepburn and Bonnie Gutierrez (eds.), *Alive and Well: A Lesbian Health Guide* (Freedom, CA: The Crossing Press, 1988), pp. 147–48.
37. *Ibid.*, p. 141.
38. Jesse Meredith in Linden *et al.* (eds.), *Against Sadomasochism*, p. 96.
39. Mary Daly, *Pure Lust: Elemental Feminist Philosophy* (London: The Women's Press, 1984), p. 66.
40. tacie dejanikus in SAMOIS (eds.), *Coming to Power*, p. 211.
41. Audre Lorde in Linden *et al.* (eds.), *Against Sadomasochism*, p. 67.
42. Lorena Leigh Saxe in Card (ed.), *Lesbian Philosophy*, pp. 66–67.
43. Rose Mason in Linden *et al.* (eds.), *Against Sadomasochism*, p. 100.
44. Maryel Norris in Linden *et al.* (eds.), *ibid.*, p. 106.
45. Jeanette Nichols *et al.* in Linden *et al.* (eds.), *ibid.*, p. 145.
46. Penelope, *Call Me Lesbian*, p. 114.
47. *Ibid.*
48. In SAMOIS (ed.), *Coming to Power*, p. 277. Califia is here lumping all 'vanilla [i.e. non-s/m] lesbian feminists' together as if all non-S/M lesbian feminists automatically exhibit hostility to s/m dykes. Speaking as a vanilla dyke (though, perhaps one who recognizes that nothing spices up vanilla like a little topping!), I feel that although this is perhaps unsurprising, given the degree of hostility to which Califia in particular has been subject, it is neither accurate nor helpful!
49. Card, *Lesbian Choices*, p. 221.
50. Sarah Lucia Hoagland, *Lesbian Ethics: Towards New Values* (Palo Alto, CA: Institute of Lesbian Studies, 1988), p. 270.
51. In Judith Barrington (ed.), *An Intimate Wilderness: Lesbian Writers on Sexuality* (Portland Oreg.: Eighth Mountain Press, 1991), p. 218.
52. Katherine Davis in SAMOIS (eds.), *Coming to Power*, p. 8.
53. Pat Califia, *Macho Sluts* (Boston: Alyson, 1988), pp. 9, 25.
54. In Linden *et al.* (eds.), *Against Sadomasochism*, p. 131.
55. Cheri Lesh in Linden *et al.* (eds.), *Against Sadomasochism*, p. 204.
56. Leeds Revolutionary Feminist Group (1981) 'Political Lesbianism: the Case

Against Heterosexuality', reprinted in Onlywomen Press (ed.), *Love Your Enemy? The Debate Between Heterosexual Feminism and Political Lesbianism* (London: Onlywomen Press, 1981), pp. 5–7. This statement ignores the ways in which 'invading the body of the oppressed' has been used to maintain the power of the oppressor in, [for example], racism/slavery, anti-Semitism, homophobia, the 'treatment' of those deemed mentally ill or intellectually handicapped, etc.

57. Shelia Jeffreys, *Anticlimax: A Feminist Perspective on the Sexual Revolution* (London: The Women's Press, 1990), p. 216.

58. Penelope, *Call Me Lesbian*, p. 117.

59. In Linden *et al.* (eds.), *Against Sadomasochism*, p. 116.

60. In Linden *et al.* (eds), *ibid.*, p. 28. This assumption cannot, of course, explain why heterosexual s/m dyads generally involve a male *masochist* and a female sadist.

61. Andrea Dworkin cited in Harriss, *What Is this Big Fuss about Sadomasochism?* p. 6.

62. For a detailed critique of Sheila Jeffreys's use of 'heterosexual' and 'homosexual', see my chapter 'Which One's the Man? The Heterosexualization of Lesbian Sex' in Diane Richardson (ed.), *Telling it Straight: Theorizing Heterosexuality* (London: Macmillan, 1996).

63. In SAMOIS (eds.) *Coming to Power*, p. 215.

64. Jeanette Nichols *et al.* in Linden *et al.* (eds.), *Against Sadomasochism*, p. 144.

65. Ardill and O'Sullivan, 'Upsetting an Applecart', p. 133.

66. Jesse Meredith in Linden *et al.* (eds.), *Against Sadomasochism*, p. 96.

67. Robin Morgan in Linden *et al.* (eds.), *Against Sadomasochism*, p. 109. I must confess to finding this 'joke' extremly offensive.

68. Sarah Lucia Hoagland in Linden *et al.* (eds.), *Against Sadomasochism*, pp. 154–5.

69. Robin Morgan in Linden *et al.* (eds.), *Against Sadomasochism*, p. 116.

70. Lorena Leigh Saxe in Card (ed.), *Lesbian Philosophy*, p. 67.

71. Hoagland, *Lesbian Ethics*, p. 59.

72. Lesbians Against Sado-Masochism (LASM) leaflet distributed in London before the 1986 Lesbian Strength March, after LASM had failed to get s/m practitioners banned from the centre. Cited in Ardill and O'Sullivan, 'Upsetting an Applecart', p. 139.

73. Susan Griffin in Linden *et al.* (eds.), *Against Sadomasochism*, p. 185.

74. *Ibid.* p. 193.

75. Cheri Lesh in Linden *et al.* (eds.), *Against Sadomasochism*, p. 204. This is a particularly transparent example of the claim to superior insight: *you* think you are having fun, *I know* you are in hell. It could be asked (at the risk of playing the superior knowledge game!) whether the author is not projecting her own 'pain, fear and rage' onto the s/m lesbians, and whether this might offer one (among many) means to make sense of the degree of irrational hostility shown by some lesbians towards lesbian s/m. I am a sociologist and tend to distrust psychological explanations, but in this instance it seems fairly obvious that the 'pain, fear and rage' belong to the writer herself.

76. In Ardill and O'Sullivan, 'Upsetting an Applecart', p. 138.

77. White, *The Burning Library*, p. 66.

78. In SAMOIS (ed.), *Coming to Power*, p. 86.

79. In Linden *et al.* (eds.), *Against Sadomasochism*, p. 155.

80. White, *The Burning Library*, p.66

81. The swastika was originally a

Sanskrit religious symbol for the life force. The Nazis reversed the direction of the arms and adopted it. The quasi-religious mythography of the Third Reich was a rag-bag of symbology, scavenged from Christianity, old Norse mythology, imperial Rome and (in the case of the swastika) Hinduism.

82. Susan Leigh Starr in Linden *et al.* (eds.), *Against Sadomasochism*, p. 132.
83. Ardill and O'Sullivan, 'Upsetting an Applecart', p. 135.
84. Sheila Jeffreys uses this tactic in her trashing of gay men's s/m in *Anticlimax*.
85. Julia Penelope does this in *Call Me Lesbian*. However problematic Rubin's support for 'intergenerational sex' may be – and this is not a debate about which I am well informed, so I am loathe to take sides – it is blatantly misused by Penelope to discredit Rubin as a defender of s/m, and to discredit s/m *per se*.
86. Karen Sims in Linden *et al.* (eds.), *Against Sadomasochism*, p. 99.
87. In Linden *et al.*(eds.), *ibid.*, p. 207.
88. In SAMOIS (ed.) *Coming to Power*, p. 270.
89. In Carla Freccero, 'Notes of a Post-Sex Wars Theorizer' in Marianne Hirsch and Evelyn Fox Keller (eds.), *Conflicts in Feminism* (London: Routledge, 1990), p. 312.
90. Jesse Meredith in Linden *et al.* (eds.), *Against Sadomasochism*, p. 97.
91. Lorena Leigh Saxe in Card (ed.), *Lesbian Philosophy*, p. 65.
92. Robin Linden in Linden *et al.* (eds.), *Against Sadomasochism*, p. 10.
93. Hepburn and Gutierrez, *Alive and Well*, p. 145.
94. Juicy Lucy in SAMOIS (eds.), *Coming to Power*, p. 30.
95. Card, *Lesbian Choices*, p. 231.
96. Linden in Linden *et al.* (eds.), *Against Sadomasochism*, p. 7.
97. Rian in Linden *et al.* (eds.), *ibid.*, p. 49.
98. Hepburn and Gutierrez, *Alive and Well*, pp. 145–6.
99. In SAMOIS (eds.), *Coming to Power*, p. 89.
100. In Linden *et al.* (eds.), *Against Sadomasochism*, p.78.
101. In SAMOIS (eds.), *Coming to Power*, p. 227.
102. In Linden *et al.* (eds.), *Against Sadomasochism*, p. 171.
103. Califia, *Macho Sluts*, p. 15.

3

Out of Sight, Out of Body?
The Visible Lesbian

Lesbians have never been particularly visible in 'first world' societies. In fact, we have been *invisible*, hidden, secret. Of course, this invisibility has been, until very recently, a necessary survival strategy, and continues to be so for many lesbians today. Indeed, it is probably true to say that the majority of lesbians continue to rely on the protection offered by invisibility at various times and places. It is one thing to be openly and visibly lesbian at a club, demonstration or other community event, it is quite another to display the same openness on a crowded train or in many workplaces. But this individual survival strategy does not in itself explain the degree to which lesbians are simply absent from mainstream discourse and culture. After all, gay men also slip in and out of the closet as their safety dictates, yet they have an acknowledged presence in many mainstream locations which lesbians have never had. There is no space in mainstream culture for a lesbian version of the drag queen,[1] no parallel to the widely recognized character of the limp-wristed pansy exploited by performers from Kenneth Williams to Frankie Howerd, no lesbian 'camp'. This is not to say that such things do not happen in lesbian culture, simply that they have not been the staple fare of mass culture in the way that some aspects of gay male culture have been.

Of course, sex itself – whether homosex or heterosex – has a peculiar cultural presence. Many aspects of the erotic are silenced, hidden, or represented obliquely or in restricted contexts (such as after an evening 'watershed' time on TV). This is not simply a matter of privacy or modesty, nor is it to do with the repression of sexuality in any straightforward sense, nor with the heritage of Victorian prudery. Indeed, as Michel Foucault[2] famously argued, the repressive prudery of the Victorian era (the era which so powerfully shaped our own modern 'first world' cultures) is an illusion. Foucault pointed out that, contrary to popular belief, sex has been more volubly spoken and argued about in modern Western societies than any other aspect of human behaviour, albeit often under the guise of control and repression. Indeed, we are now accustomed to an extraordinary proliferation of sexual and/or erotic images, most notably in the commercial arena, where it is generally recognized that sex is used to sell everything from toothpaste to cars. Indeed, radical political movements from the traditional left to feminism, from anti-racism to disability rights activism, have all critiqued the sexualization of contemporary culture.

Yet, in all this babble and contestation, there has been until recently an almost absolute silence about lesbians, and in particular about lesbian *sex*. Feminists, most importantly the American lesbian poet and writer Adrienne Rich, pointed out in the 1970s and 1980s that 'lesbian invisibility' is no accident. Rather, they suggest, it is both an indication of the threat which lesbians pose to male supremacy simply by existing, and a strategy on the part of men to restrict the flow of information about lesbianism in order to stop this dangerous perversion spreading. There is ample evidence to support this suggestion. For example, a trawl through British legislation on 'homosexuality' strongly suggests that the law maintains a conscious silence on *female* 'homosexuality' for reasons of its own:

> Lesbian practices were not referred to in the 1533 Act of Henry VIII on sodomy, the 1861 and 1885 laws on sodomy and gross indecency, the 1898 Vagrancy Act, the 1967 Sexual Offences Act, or Clause 25 of the 1991 Criminal Justice Bill. When attempts were made in 1921 to include lesbian practices in the category of gross indecency, Lord Desart argued that this inclusion would be inappropriate in that it would only bring lesbian sex 'to the notice of women who never heard of it, never thought of it, never dreamed of it'.[3]

This certainly seems to bear out the lesbian-feminist suggestion that allowing mainstream culture to reflect lesbian existence is too dangerous. Moreover, radical feminists (not all of whom are lesbians) have pointed out that the entire superstructure of patriarchy depends on women's heterosexuality. As Adrienne Rich concludes:

> the issue feminists have to address is not simple 'gender inequality' nor the domination of culture by males nor mere 'taboos against homosexuality', but the enforcement of heterosexuality for women

as a means of assuring male right of physical, economic and emotional access. One of the many means of enforcement is, of course, the rendering invisible of the lesbian possibility.[4]

As Rich points out, this invisibility is true of nearly *every* field of human activity, including the one arena which might be expected to pay adequate attention to lesbian existence – feminism. She writes of 'the virtual or total neglect of lesbian existence in a wide range of writings, including feminist scholarship'.[5] Indeed, her stated aim in writing *Compulsory Heterosexuality and Lesbian Existence* was for 'feminists to find it less possible to read, write, or teach from a perspective of unexamined heterocentricity'.[6] This simply hasn't happened. Although Rich's essay became a classic feminist text, feminism and women's studies carried on ignoring lesbians and refusing to integrate lesbianism into theories of gender and sexuality.[7] Of course, *lesbians* continue to talk, read, write and teach about lesbianism, both within and outside feminism/women's studies, but there is – infuriatingly – ample evidence that non-lesbian feminists cannot really be bothered. This tendency of non-lesbian feminists to ignore lesbianism entirely, combined with attempts on the part of some revolutionary or pro-censorship lesbian feminists to repress or restrict the expression and representation of lesbian sex, results in a feminism which is as firmly hostile to lesbian sexuality as the mainstream.[8]

This continuation of lesbian silence and invisibility within feminism is somewhat ironic, given the extraordinarily high profile which (some) lesbians and (some) lesbian issues have been given of late in mainstream culture. Now that they are finally out of their closets, the media are just as keen to discuss Martina's and kd's sexuality as their game play or music, and you'd be hard-pressed to find any British newspaper or magazine which considers itself 'serious' and which *hasn't* carried an article about lesbians in the past year or two. So is lesbian invisibility a thing of the past? Is the beginning of the twenty-first century to be characterized by the end of lesbian oppression, by our acceptance into the bosom of society and by the collapse of the powerful forces which have historically tried to eradicate lesbian love, desire, identity and sex?

The social position of lesbians in contemporary 'first world' cultures seems to contain some extraordinary contradictions. Increased cultural visibility is paralleled by increased political hostility. On the one hand, the resurgent right wing in the USA and the UK voted in governments which passed some of the most directly anti-gay and anti-lesbian legislation of the twentieth century. The USA, in particular, has seen the rise of a powerful alliance of biblical religious fundamentalism and far-right politics that has adopted sex as their chosen battleground on which a vicious political and ideological struggle over the very notion of 'America' is fought out. Homosexuality, reproductive rights, sex education and HIV/AIDS have been systematically targeted by this alliance, and the amount of money and energy expended in trying to prevent abortion, contraception, sex education, safer sex education and services for people living with HIV/AIDS is astronomical. For example, the Colorado-based group Focus on the Family devotes an annual income of $150 million to fighting gay rights and abortion; Virginia's Christian Coalition spends $25 million annually fighting gay rights, women's rights and abortion, while Concerned Women for America, based in Washington, spends $14 million each year fighting gay rights, abortion and sex education.[9]

Although this phenomenon is peculiarly American, there are similar alliances at work in Australia, New Zealand and many European countries including the UK. The long-lived British Conservative administration has introduced and/or passed (they have not always been successful) a number of laws which actively discriminate against lesbian and gay citizens. Such legislation encourages a general social climate where discrimination against and hostility towards queer people is the sanctioned norm. It would seem that efforts to repress, discipline and punish homosex have intensified across a wide geographical and political area, and that lesbians are more subjugated and more under siege with each passing year.

On the other hand, however, the cultural visibility of lesbians has never been so striking. Lesbian chic has become a widely debated topic, and a dash of dyke suggestiveness has been used to spice up the mainstream, from Michelle Pfeiffer's leather-clad Catwoman (resisting that once-in-a-lifetime proposal from Batman) to Telstra's Australian ads selling phones to dykes on bikes. Sandra Bernhardt has stalked through several episodes of the mainstream American comedy show *Roseanne* as a lesbian/bisexual good-time girl, Channel 4 in the UK offered fans of the soap opera *Brookside* the enormously sympathetic lesbian character Beth Jordache,[10] while Madonna's sexploitation bestseller *Sex* was heavily laced with lesbian, sub-lesbian and bisexual images of the material girl herself entangled with dykes, queers and queer wannabees. Mainstream culture appears to be so saturated with images of lesbianism that it drips.

There is a strange sense of dislocation between the cultural sphere and the socio-political sphere: while mainstream culture seems to be promoting lesbianism as chic and trendy, the lawmakers are engaged in stepping up the attempt to eradicate homosex altogether. Such dislocation is unlikely to be as dramatic as it appears – the relationship between the social and the cultural is more complex and mutable than that. So it is important to look closely at this new love affair between lesbians and the mainstream. Were they made for each other, or will there be tears before bedtime?

Who is that mysterious woman? The mainstream peeks in

To what extent does the cultural explosion of lesbian images challenge or contradict social and political hostility? Is it simply the case that politicians tend to be right-wing traditionalists, while media people tend to be left-wing innovators? While social policy and politics continue to be obviously hostile to lesbians, can it be true that a new radicalism has appeared in the media? Certainly, a brief and superficial glance at the way lesbians have been represented in the heart of the British mainstream in the past few years suggests that significant change is afoot. That *Vanity Fair* cover and article on kd lang[11] did not simply spring out of nowhere. Rather, they were part of what appeared to be an entire genre in glossy magazine journalism, the 'Lesbian Curiosity' article. In the UK, for example, *Cosmopolitan* ran an article in October 1992 entitled 'Women in love: are you going through a lesbian phase? (Or is it the Real Thing?)'. This was followed in January 1993 by an article in *New Woman*, 'Do lesbians have more fun?', and even the staid *She* magazine carried an article in January 1995, 'How lesbians feel about love, sex and motherhood'. Meanwhile, the hint of lesbian innuendo has been spicing up fashion photo shoots since at least the 1960s.

Women's magazines are a particularly important source of insights into mainstream culture and its understandings of sexuality and the erotic. These magazines provide the principal public space for women to talk about sex, sexuality and gender. Since *Cosmo* hit the stands and dragged the women's magazine out of the realm of recipes and knitting patterns, the discourse on sex in these publications has become ever more explicit and penetrating. Yet it is a discourse which, for all its liberal posing, remains locked within a very tight and proscriptive framework. For example, as Janice Winship points out, *Cosmo*'s frank promotion of sexual freedom for women is restricted to promoting *heterosexual* freedom:

> the ... less constructive side of *Cosmo*'s obsessive attention to heterosexuality is its relatively minimal attention to other relationships ... noticeable by its conspicuous absence as an acceptable practice and identity [is] lesbianism. When the rare article about lesbianism appears it is addressed, somewhat voyeuristically, to heterosexual women and expresses and urges a liberal tolerance rather than a feminist understanding.[12]

Since this was written, in 1987, articles about lesbianism have become noticeably less 'rare' in glossy women's magazines generally, but the unquestioning assumption of a heterosexual readership continues. This assumption, combined with the overwhelmingly energetic and active promotion of heterosexuality in the main body of these magazines, is deeply problematic. The 1992 *Cosmopolitan* article dealt, in fact, with 'the invisible thousands who come out temporarily': in other words, straight women who have a brief lesbian affair and then return to men. Their lesbian affairs are presented as aberrations from a 'proper' heterosexual path. You can almost hear the sighs of relief as the three women discussed in the article come back to their senses:

'Kate': My boyfriend used to get off on the whole thing and was quite encouraging. I was allowed to get involved with Anna and still see him as long as I told him about it in lurid detail. ... It stopped because I got scared about the idea of being a dyke, that I might not get married. ... And also seeing lesbian relationships going horribly wrong and being much more vicious than when things go wrong for men and women.

'Maria': The person I slept with was an old friend and it lasted about eight months. Peculiarly, it enhanced my subsequent relationships with men. ... Because the sex was very good with her, it taught me how to play and have fun.

'Nicky': I didn't know if I was lesbian or bisexual and it didn't matter. It was only after the relationship [with my girlfriend] finished that it took on a greater significance ... when I finally succeeded in losing my second virginity[13] ... he was turned on by the whole thing, and flattered that it was his penis that had 'converted me'.

The message is clear: if you're thinking of trying lesbian sex, prepare to be hurt – after all, lesbian relationships are 'much more vicious' than heterosexual relationships when things go wrong, and you might 'become a dyke' and never get married – but take comfort from the fact that it will enhance your sex with men, and that they will be turned on and flattered by it. In other words, lesbianism is presented throughout the entire article *solely in relation* to sex with men. The article is actually 'about' heterosexuality, and about *men's* relationship to lesbianism.

The 1993 article in *New Woman* is even worse. Purporting to be written by 'Joy Legatte ... an optimistic gay woman', it asks: 'If men are such a problem, does the answer lie in a lesbian relationship?' The answer, unsurprisingly, is a resounding 'no!'. 'Are lesbian relationships any easier? The truth is, they can often be harder.' This optimistic gay woman tells us that not only do lesbians suffer discrimination, which 'can put a relationship into a hothouse environment', but their relationships are even more troubled and short-lived than heterosexual ones, and the 'limited choice of partners ... can make for relationship difficulties'. Finally, in case the curious reader is not convinced by the horror story which has been presented, there is the chilling prospect of double-barrelled PMS:

As if that's not enough, two women equals two menstrual cycles. ... So while mutual support is likely to be higher, so is the possibility of a double dose of PMS, with synchronised snapping and snarling. Every month. That single factor nearly wrecked Laura and Cathy's relationship.

Scared off yet? Far from enhancing the general perception of lesbians among their readers or attempting to understand lesbian oppression, such articles are clearly designed to reinforce the idea that men are the best sexual and emotional partners for women. They work hard to counteract the possibility that women might find the idea of lesbianism attractive, and function to maintain the supremacy of heterosex. They also, despite titillating titles such as 'Do Lesbians Have More Fun?', remain silent on the subject of lesbian *sex*. In a genre where explicit chatter about G-spots, clitoral orgasms and (hetero)sexual pleasure is the norm, the relative coyness about lesbian sex is significant. The fact that such magazines carry articles about lesbians must not detract from their active promotion of heterosex. Thus, they construct sexual pleasure *as heterosexual*. Straights have sex, lesbians have (difficult) relationships. The question of whether or not lesbians have more 'fun' is never answered.

Although the hidden agenda behind their apparent interest in lesbianism is particularly explicit, glossy women's magazines are a fairly accurate example of what mainstream culture in general is 'making of' lesbians. The content may be 'lesbians', but it is never *lesbian*. That is, lesbians and lesbianism are objects of curiosity, lacking a point of view worth listening to, and certainly never included in the assumed audience to which mainstream culture addresses itself.

Being in control: the machinery of representation

This is the first important point to note about the representation of lesbians in mainstream culture: the dominant point of view, the voice speaking *about* lesbians, remains solidly heterosexual. To tease out the implications of this requires a basic understanding of how the 'machinery of representation' operates in contemporary culture.

Representation is enormously important in the construction and maintenance of social coherence. In order for societies to function, certain sets of beliefs, understandings and meanings must exist which are shared by a majority, if not all, of its members. Such beliefs, understandings and meanings continually circulate through the social arena via media such as film, TV, video, newspapers, magazines, academic discourse, photographs, pop songs, radio, advertisements, books, etc. But meanings are not manufactured, distributed and consumed in a straightforwardly linear process. Rather, they undergo a *circular* process, because the act of 'consuming' or 'reading' a cultural artefact *gives it meaning*, literally *makes sense of it*. Different readings of texts may then re-enter the cycle themselves. The meaning, the sense of the text, which is made in the act of reading it, does not inevitably coincide with the meaning which the producer of the text (the writer, journalist, photographer, composer, etc.) intended. It is probably fair to suggest, for example, that a mischievous camp 'reading' of *Gone with the Wind* is very different from a straight reading, or that a black interpretation of the film is different from a white construction. Clearly, most authors of texts address their words/images/sounds to a particular audience, assuming a specific set of shared codes which will enable the reader to make sense of the text in the way the author intended. Readings may remain obedient to this textual address, but, equally, they might disobey it, constructing contradictory meanings and subverting the author's original intentions. This is what happens when advertisement hoardings are grafittied. When lesbian activists spray grafitti onto a Wonderbra advert, so that the deeply cleavaged woman is saying 'Hello girls!' rather than 'Hello boys!', the meaning of the text is being made through a disobedient reading, and the disobedient reading is then reinserted into the cycle in order to subvert the dominant meaning.

This happens continually, to a greater or lesser extent, with all cultural products, sometimes overtly (as in the case of grafitti), sometimes invisibly. As texts circulate, the meanings associated with them shift; they are negotiated, challenged and reversed, or reinforced and reproduced. Either way, they are continually transformed. This cycle, the 'hermeneutic cycle', is the most important factor in maintaining cultural consistency. Individuals are socialized by means of it; nations, groups and societies gain their sense of identity through it; social norms and mores are reflected and policed by it. This is why propaganda is recognized as such an important political weapon, and why political campaigns are becoming, in the postmodern world, incestuous affairs between political 'personalities' and the media.

But this means that texts are fairly unstable as 'containers' of meaning. There is never just one reading of a text, never just one meaning for an action or behaviour; rather many conflicting readings and meanings compete for dominance. Thus, for example, religion and science compete in some contexts over the meaning of such issues as abortion, contraception, homosexuality, etc. Consequently, in order to preserve its hegemony, a dominant group must control the machinery of representation, including the technology of print, broadcasting and cinema, the skills and resources required to exploit this technology, and the languages and semiotic codes used in various media, distribution networks and commercial outlets.

It is obvious that different groups have greater or lesser power to influence the meanings circulating in the social arena. This power relates to the degree to which different groups have access to the machinery of representation. The technology of video is now widely available in affluent communities, but simply making a video does not mean that you can get anyone other than your family and friends to watch it. If you want, for example, to make a film or video which changes the way lesbians are perceived, it is essential that the finished product should be distributed in mainstream cinemas or broadcast by a licensed TV channel. Unsurprisingly, in the industrialized West, this means that you must be white, wealthy and male. If you don't qualify, you will have to fight to be heard.[14]

As a socially execrated group, it might be assumed that queers are denied access to the machinery of representation, but this is not strictly speaking the case. Being gay can be a drawback, but it isn't always so. After all, you can hide the fact that you are gay, whereas you cannot (generally) hide the fact that you are black or female. As Eve Kosofsky Sedgwick wittily puts it, 'Has there ever been a gay Socrates? Has there ever been a gay Shakespeare? Has there ever been a gay Proust? Does the pope wear a dress?'[15] It is not just dead authors whose work is revered despite the fact that they were gay. Indeed, there is almost an expectation in the West that the creative or artistic temperament in a man may be accompanied by homosexuality. Gay men are so *sensitive*, runs the homophobic mythology. Merchant, Ivory, Ginsberg, Hockney, Isherwood, Cole Porter, Pasolini, Maugham, Coward, Britten, Wilde, Anthony Sher, Forster: the history of cultural productivity is teeming with the names of gay men whose work has been revered. The problems arise when gay men either come out, refusing to stay safely closeted, or when they want to produce work about or for gay men, or from an avowedly gay perspective. As 'gay', their access to the machinery of representation may be compromised, but as 'men', that access remains privileged.

Lesbians, however, are women. And women still have a fight on their hands to gain access to the machinery of representation. The representations of lesbians and lesbian sex which circulate in mainstream culture have traditionally been within the pornographic vernacular. From 'high art', such as Gustave Courbet's famous painting *Sleep*, to the democratization of pornography which the camera introduced in the nineteenth and twentieth centuries, images of lesbian sex have been for the most part made by heterosexuals (mostly men) for heterosexuals (mostly men) to further the interests of heterosexuals (mostly men). 'Lesbian' sex continues to form a staple genre of contemporary soft porn for heterosexual men, as a glance at the advertisements for telephone sex-lines in men's magazines suggests.

Entirely typical is a recent issue of *Knave,* which offers the following plethora of Sapphic seductions for the boys: '2 girls/1 dildo, Juicy Lucy and Randy Mandy live together, Two Girl Special, Dame Dyke Commands You, Naughty girls want a woman, Lady Loves a Lady and 2 girls fight for 1 dildo'.[16] Such pseudo-lesbian fantasies are addressed to an audience which is assumed to be heterosexual; the meaning of 'lesbian' is here simply reprocessed in order to fit into the dominant heterosexual dictat that women exist for men's pleasure and that the nature of female sexual pleasure is irrelevant. This easy (although, of course, at the same time *uneasy*) absorption of 'lesbian' sexuality into the codes of heterosex makes a mockery of any suggestion that the towers of heterosexual dominance are starting to crack at the foundations because lesbian sex is more visible. Heterosexuality is still the standard by which all else is judged (and found wanting). For example, in *that* article in *Vanity Fair,* Leslie Bennetts describes kd lang thus:

> At first glance she seems undeniably bizarre, but hers is a deeply subversive presence; after you watch her for a while you realize how warped your own stereotypes are. In the beginning you simply see her as unnatural. Her face is utterly bare, devoid of makeup. Her hair has been shorn with what appears to be complete disregard for how flattering the results will be.[17]

The 'you' addressed by this piece is quite clearly *not* a lesbian. The address assumes not only that the reader shares his 'warped stereotypes', but that they will share the (undeniably bizarre!) perception that a woman *without* make-up is 'unnatural'. Far from offering evidence that the hetero mainstream is shifting towards including lesbians, such texts simply indicate that a very visible lesbian like kd needs to have a careful eye kept on her. Partly voyeuristic, partly anxiously reaffirming the dominance of the heterosexual perspective, the increased attention which the mainstream media have been paying to dykes recently does nothing to shake the general cultural division into a heterosexual 'us' and a queer 'them'. In brief, lesbians have been the object, not the subject, of increased visibility. We have been looked at, not listened to. There is still no position within mainstream culture from which to *read* as a lesbian. Even when a newspaper or magazine invites a lesbian to write about lesbianism, the assumption is generally that she is explaining an alien community to those who do not share its norms. The tone is anthropological. Just as curious whites have always had the cultures of subjugated others explained to them – usually with the aim of justifying white supremacy – so curious hets now peer at lesbian culture. It is simple cultural imperialism.

Imperialisms and appropriations: lesbian culture and the mainstream

Fortunately, lesbians do not have to depend solely on the heterosexual cultural mainstream. Although the mainstream excludes lesbians, this exclusion in and of itself encourages the growth of a culture which lies outside of and is eccentric (in the sense of off-centre rather than weird or bizarre) to that mainstream. As Moe Meyer writes:

> Possession of social knowledge is not dependent on access to the apparatus of representation. It is the arrogance of the dominant, derived from ownership of the apparatus of representation, that creates belief in a monologic construction of social knowledge.[18]

Lesbian social knowledge, then, derives at least in part from lesbian cultural productivity in arenas other than the mainstream. One feature which characterizes the growth of self-consciously lesbian communities in the era of mass communications technology is indeed the development of a body of lesbian (sub)cultural production. Lesbians produce, distribute and consume our own books, newspapers, newsletters, magazines, academic journals, painting, jewellery, photography, music, theatre, film, video and dress codes. Within this *lesbian* arena we are in control of the representation of lesbianism and of lesbian sex. This cultural milieu is not, of course, hermetically sealed from the mainstream. The boundaries are permeable, and there is copious 'leakage' in both directions. We appropriate, rewrite and subvert the semiotics of the mainstream. The mainstream in turn appropriates, rewrites and subverts the semiotics of the lesbian subculture. 'Queer knowledge can then be introduced and incorporated into the dominant ideology because the blindspot of bourgeois culture is predictable: it *always* appropriates.'[19] (author's italics).

Currently, this appropriation of dyke culture by straights has a particularly high visibility. For example, lesbian dress codes, hairstyles and footwear (the faithful Doc Martens) have been widely adopted by straight women – even the fully shaved head previously seen only on fiercely lesbian shoulders is now sported by ultra trendy hetties. This emulation is both flattering and frustrating (at such times of style leakage it can become difficult to recognize the real lesbians), but is also problematic because, finally, it expresses not only a lack of respect for lesbian culture, but a disdainful trivialization of it. Thus kd lang, representing the acme of style and cool in lesbian terms, is re-presented for and by heterosexual reading as 'unnatural', with a 'complete disregard' for her attractiveness. From a lesbian point of view, lang *of course* has a complete disregard for her *heterosexual* attractiveness. The 'attractiveness' which lang cares about, as a lesbian, is attractiveness to other *lesbians*. This is too threatening, destabilizing or simply incomprehensible to heterosexuals trying to 'read' lang's persona, so it is rewritten within the semiotics of the heterosexual mainstream as simple unattractiveness *per se*.

Some lesbians have called for a lesbian semiotics which cuts all contact with the mainstream. Celia and Jenny Kitzinger, for example, want images of lesbian sex that are made by lesbians '*as lesbians* and from "a lesbian gaze"'[20] (authors' italics). But it is naive or disingenuous to suggest that a 'pure' lesbian culture, circulating only specifically *lesbian* codes and meanings and utterly disengaged from the mainstream, could exist. Language (in its broadest sense, including visual language, body language, the language of fashion and music, etc.) just doesn't work like that. Codes, images and signs, and the meanings which circulate by virtue of them, shift continually within and between different cultural groups. It is by the process of appropriating, rewriting and recirculating signs, codes and meanings that languages develop and that different social and cultural groupings coalesce, generate a sense of identity, and establish their relationship with the mainstream. This is not only true of subcultural groups: the relationship which some groups establish with the mainstream is to assert that they *are* the mainstream.

But this assertion is always contested, must always be defended and reasserted, and remains vulnerable. This is why the heterosexual mainstream is currently engaged in recirculating representations of lesbians and lesbianism. In particular, this is why lesbian *sex* remains so invisible in the midst of all this increased surveillance and voyeurism.

Look, don't touch

Foucault famously proposed that surveillance is a key element in the kind of disciplinary social control which he saw as replacing the brute control by force of earlier eras. Using the historical example of the panopticon (a nineteenth-century lunatic asylum which was designed around a central 'control tower' from which every room could be seen and a disciplinary eye kept on the behaviour of all the inhabitants), he pointed out the many ways in which individuals subject not only others but also themselves to surveillance and policing. In a very real sense, the whole process of socialization is nothing more nor less than the internalization of that disciplinary gaze (perhaps in Freudian terms the super-ego). So, for the heterosexual mainstream, it is important that the troublesome and disruptive presence of homosex remains under scrutiny, in order to contain it and subject it to disciplinary power. While this is true of men's homosex, it is still more the case in women's homosex. Lesbian sex is extremely threatening to the anonymous 'watchers in the tower'.

The radical feminist critique of heterosex points out that heterosexuality, as it is currently socially constructed, both assumes and decrees that men and women, masculinity and femininity, stand in very different relation to matters of sexuality and the erotic. Indeed, as 'opposite sexes', they stand at polar extremes in relation to sexuality. 'Masculinity' as a construct contains a specific set of meanings about sex and the erotic which 'masculinity' as a performance expresses and enacts. This set of meanings revolves around the idea of a male sex 'drive' as powerful, selfish, goal-orientated and concerned with *conquest* rather than with emotional contact, reproduction or even pleasure. 'Femininity', on the other hand, embodies a set of meanings to do with *reproduction* and the establishment of a family: emotional intimacy, a desire for long-term and stable relationships, responsibility (for everything from contraception to sexual safety to ensuring maximum pleasure for her male partner) and selflessness. It is important to remember that, until very recently, women's sexuality was believed to *consist in* the desire for offspring, not for her own pleasure.[21]

It is not hard to see that this set of meanings operates in the interests of controlling female sexuality. Men are supposed to be 'naturally' locked in a constant struggle to channel the overwhelming physical force of their sex drive, while it is assumed that women are 'naturally' interested in sex only in so far as it will enable them to produce children. Women may therefore be kept in line by the threat of the sexually predatory male, and any desires which they might experience will be interpreted as not 'properly' feminine and hence pathological and to be rejected. Of course, the very fact that lesbians exist threatens to send this precarious sandcastle toppling. Lesbian sexuality is, by definition, *not* premised on the desire to reproduce. The mere fact that women may seek out other women as sexual partners makes it clear that there is such a thing as female *sexual* desire, and that there are women who are motivated by the desire for sexual pleasure uncomplicated by the possibilities of conception. This is why lesbian *sex* is so threatening, and hence so invisible in mainstream culture.

Ironically, there seems to be general agreement among lesbian/ feminist commentators that lesbian sex is not radical *per se*. Sara Dunn is fairly typical in her trivialization of the radical potential of lesbian sex:

> Lesbian sex is neither reactionary nor subversive – it can be either, just like all other sex. ... The privileging of sex and sexual representation as the site of women's oppression is misguided at best. But the privileging of sex and sexual representation as the site for radical impulses, for voyages of the Valkyries, comes perilously close to the same thing.[23]

But Dunn is wrong. Lesbian sex is not 'just like all other sex'. If it were, it would have a very different position in relation to mainstream culture, history, politics and feminism. Mainstream women's magazines are not publishing articles trying to prevent women having any old sex, but they *are* publishing articles trying to prevent women having lesbian sex. And the representation of lesbian sex is of particular importance here, since the desexualization of lesbianism is demonstrably a significant component of the repression of lesbians and of women more generally.

Within mainstream discourse it is perfectly acceptable for lesbianism to be rewritten as a pathology (a mental or physical illness) or as a 'lifestyle choice' akin to adopting the latest fashions in clothing or soft furnishings. It may be presented (as in the *Cosmopolitan* article referred to earlier) as a useful adjunct to heterosexuality, or as something so unpleasant (as in the *New Woman* article) that it should elicit pity rather than curiosity or envy in the straight woman reader. Most cleverly of all, it may be represented as 'normal' femininity – with its emphasis on emotions and relationships and its inherent dislike of sex itself – taken to extremes. What lesbianism may *not* be represented as is a *sexual* practice, since to recognize the sexual/erotic aspect of lesbianism is to recognize sexual/erotic aspects of *women* which are anathema to the mainstream ideology of heterosex.

The inescapable conclusion is that lesbian representations of lesbian sex do indeed constitute a radical challenge to lesbian oppression (and to women's oppression more generally). Yet representations of lesbian sex are policed more closely within lesbian communities – particularly lesbian-feminist communities – than anything else which lesbian artists, writers, photographers or film-makers do. It appears that panopticism is also a tool of *feminist* disciplinary power.

Good girls are seen and not heard: safer sex and lesbian sex

But sex and sexual practices have adopted an entirely new social and cultural position since the beginning of the 1980s, making some of the familiar debates anachronistic. There is a whole new conversation about sex going on at every level, from the individual to the national and from the local to the global, a conversation that was made necessary by the HIV pandemic. The fact that the virus may be transmitted by some sexual practices and not by others urgently required that entire societies begin to talk in explicit detail about sex. For innumerable reasons to do with religious belief, social mores, cultural norms, ideologies of gender, morality and simple political expediency, this apparently straightforward task has proved enormously difficult for most. Gay men in 'first world' urban environments, whose subculture was grounded in an explicit, varied and already politicized repertoire of sexual acts, and who were accustomed to talking about sex and sexuality, were able to develop an extraordinarily sophisticated language (both verbal and visual) in response to the virus which was devastating their communities. Lesbians, being queer too, might be expected to have done the same thing. Yet, as images of gay male sex have proliferated in the public domain in direct response to the demands of safer-sex education, images of lesbian sex are only now beginning to appear. The reasons for this say much about the position of lesbian sex in relation to gay male sex as well as to the heterosexual mainstream.

From the start of the epidemic, long before the virus had been identified, urban gay men's communities recognized the need for safer sex. Indeed, safer sex is an idea which began in these communities. Gay men, active both in the fight against the virus and against the entrenched homophobia which exploited the epidemiology of the epidemic to launch a new offensive against homosex, insisted that safer-sex educational materials must be erotic and exciting if they were to be effective.[23] As I write, fifteen years since AIDS came to the attention of medical science, there is a wealth of erotic, explicit safer-sex information for gay men. Yet, despite the now well-recognized fact that gay men are not the only sexual group at risk from HIV (worldwide, heterosex is responsible for the overwhelming majority of transmissions), they remain the only group for whom such materials are generally available. Moreover, the imaginative community initiatives developed by gay men – the jack-off parties, the safe-sex mandate in porn videos, the play-safe back rooms, etc. – have no equivalent among other sexual constituencies.[24]

Safer-sex educational material targeted at heterosexual men is largely non-existent, and that addressed to heterosexual women is copious but dramatically unerotic, concentrating on such matters as household hygiene and pregnancy to the almost complete exclusion of sexual pleasure, and often reinforcing the construct of 'woman' as a creature offended by or resistant to sex.[25] And lesbians? Largely neglected as a target audience by statutory health educators and voluntary AIDS service organizations alike, lesbians have been obliged to produce our own safer-sex educational materials. For example, it was not until 1985–86 that the San Francisco AIDS Foundation 'decided to do what became the first brochure on safe sex for lesbians'.[26] Similarly, the Terrence Higgins Trust in the UK, which has produced a wealth of high-quality erotic safer-sex information for gay men, has to date produced *one* eroticized image to promote lesbian safer sex – an image of two naked young women embracing in a shower, which the Trust has repeatedly recycled from poster to leaflet to booklet format. The body of safer-sex educational material developed to date, far from constituting any kind of radical 'new' discourse of the erotic, simply replicates the familiar constructions: gay men are excessively and recreationally sexual, while heterosexual men represent the invisible 'norm' whose sexuality is so absolutely proper and right as to resist problematization; heterosexual women are maternal, responsible and erotophobic, while lesbians remain insignificant or simply non-existent.

It might be argued that this is not a problem. After all, gay men in the UK, some other European countries, Australia, New Zealand and the USA still represent the group most at risk for contracting the virus. On the other hand, the sexual transmission of HIV between women is extremely rare – some doubt whether it is even possible – which puts 'lesbian sex' at the low-risk end of sexual encounters. The most risky 'body fluid' which an individual can take into their body is semen, leading one safer-sex activist and AIDS writer, Cindy Patton, to summarize safe-sex advice as 'Don't get semen in your anus or vagina'. Of course, lesbian *sex* doesn't involve semen. However, lesbians can and do have sex that does. In some communities, for example, it is seen as very Queer for lesbians and gay men to have sex with each other. Moreover, being a lesbian doesn't protect you from the risks associated with sharing injecting equipment, selling sex, being raped or having been heterosexual/bisexual at some point in your life. All this means not only that lesbians require information about AIDS but also that there are lesbians who are living with HIV/AIDS who need trustworthy advice on the kinds of sex they may safely have with partners and lovers. Lesbians have been demanding effective safer-sex education since the early days of the epidemic, but our demands have generally met with resistance, both from straight men who insist that lesbians don't have much sex anyway and from gay men who angrily reject the suggestion that the degree of risk to lesbians warrants any attention at all. Indeed, the misogyny of Western gay men's communities plumbed new depths in the late 1980s when a number of gay men publicly accused lesbians of 'virus envy'.

The insistence on maintaining silence about lesbian sexuality in the AIDS educational arena is curious for another reason. Imagine that a deadly new virus suddenly appears which infects everyone except swimming-pool attendants. The resources of scientific medicine would, sensibly, be mobilized to find out *why* pool attendants were not at risk, and what other people might learn from them in order to reduce their own level of risk. Now tell me why legions of heterosexuals and gay men are not queueing up demanding to know the secrets of lesbian sex so that they can learn how to reduce their own risk? This is not a facetious question, and it is impossible to answer without under-standing the oppressive and offensive construction of lesbian sex by non-lesbians. For cultures accustomed to dismissing or denigrating lesbian sex as inadequate, deviant, pathological, immature or simply not 'real' sex, the sudden recognition that lesbian sex is the safest sex you can have is not just intolerable, it is unthinkable.

AIDS health education has become a gay men's 'pornutopia'. The proliferation of the virus through the human population has been paralleled by a proliferation of glorious, life-affirming, sex-affirming images of gay men having sex in every way imaginable. A kind of joyous plague of erotica is set against the dreadful pandemic which has brought with it such grief and suffering. From the exquisite to the crude, from the self-consciously tasteful to the equally self-consciously tasteless, images of homosex are saturating a range of cultural arenas. From being the love which dare not speak its name, sex between men has become the most voluble sex in human history.

This volubility is in part the legacy of homophobia. Because homo-sexuality has been stigmatized and despised, gay men have responded by developing an affirmative identity based upon homosex itself. HIV turned out to be transmitted through the very sex which was already celebrated as the core of a gay *sexual* identity formed in defiance of homophobia. In addition, the whole AIDS 'gay plague' rhetoric threatened a return to repression and persecution which had to be fought on the terrain of homosex. This unique historical combination of social factors made possible and necessary the celebration of homosex in safer-sex materials.

In contrast to the articulate and extensive vocabulary of gay male sex, lesbian sexuality has always been inarticulate. Indeed, the inarticulacy of lesbian sex is well on the way to becoming a lesbian-feminist truism along with the idea of lesbian invisibility, as these extracts suggest:

> Gay male sex, I realize, is articulate. It is articulate to a degree that, in my world, lesbian 'sex' does not remotely approach. Lesbian 'sex' as

I have known it most of the time I have known it is utterly inarticulate. Most of my lifetime, most of my experience in the realms commonly designated as 'sexual' has been prelinguistic, noncognitive. I have, in effect, no linguistic community, no language ...'[27]

What it really felt like [discussing safer sex with lesbians] was that even lesbians didn't know what it was that lesbians did in sex ... there never seemed to be a perceived baseline of what lesbian sexuality was. ... I think that it does get down to the fact that lesbian sexuality exists in a kind of void.[28]

Why, as lesbians, do we rarely talk about sex? ... We can proclaim our identity and our politics, but to be publicly passionate is another matter![29]

There has been much discussion about why lesbians 'rarely talk about sex'. It seems to me that the wrong question is being asked, because quite clearly lesbians *do* talk about sex, in prose, fiction, poetry, painting, film, video, photography and song, as the many works discussed in this book demonstrate. However, this conversation is a restricted one. It continues to be difficult for lesbians to publish in the first place, since the machinery of representation is dominated by men and access to print and broadcast technology is controlled by male gatekeepers. Once published, lesbian work with a sexual content suffers from severe restrictions on its distribution. There are legal and commercial pressures which make it unlikely that many mainsteam bookshops, cinemas, galleries, etc. will take lesbian work, especially with an openly sexual content. Moreover, far too many lesbian and gay or feminist bookshops refuse to stock explicitly sexual lesbian books and cards. On another level, talking about sex within lesbian communities is made risky by the unspoken existence of a range of community 'norms', some (but not all) rooted in feminist orthodoxies of one kind or another. The question I think we should be asking is not 'why don't lesbians talk about sex', but 'why is talking about lesbian sex *forbidden*?'

It has become only too clear with the proliferation of sexual speech in the time of AIDS that *lesbian* sexual speech remains a prohibited tongue. Beth Schneider points out that 'With nearly obsessive public attention to the sexual practices of gay men, lesbians were largely ignored as sexual beings and as members of the lesbian and gay community.'[30] This refusal to recognize lesbian sexuality is not restricted to the USA, but is depressingly common throughout the world. For example, an Australian women's AIDS team comments that 'Denial, silence and misinformation about lesbians, HIV transmission and woman-to-woman sex has created confusion, anger and fear for some of us.'[31]

Safer-sex education is funded and produced by a variety of sources within the statutory sector (government health departments etc.), the private sector (condom manufacturers for example) and the voluntary sector (most AIDS service agencies, such as the Terrence Higgins Trust in the UK, RFSL[32] in Sweden or Gay Men's Health Crisis in the US). The refusal to recognize the HIV/AIDS-related needs of lesbians extends right across sectorial boundaries and incorporates every level of AIDS activity, from the clinical to the educational. There is still no adequate research into woman-to-woman sexual transmission or into the epidemiology of HIV among lesbians, and opinions still differ on what safer-sex advice should be given to women who have sex with other women.

Recently, some lesbians have succeeded in producing erotic safer-sex educational materials, although such initiatives remain few and far between. Gay Men's Health Crisis in the US has produced a stylish booklet on safer sex for lesbians, the AIDS Council of New South Wales (ACON) Women's Team published a 52-page pocket-sized illustrated guide, *Lesbian Sex,* in 1994, and in the UK Laura McGregor produced a series of eight explicit safe-sex postcards (see plate 5) for the Leicester Lesbian, Gay and Bisexual Communities Resource Centre.[33] Clearly lacking the financial resources which have been made available for gay men's safer-sex materials, current lesbian-produced safer-sex images reflect both the disregard for lesbian sexual safety within the AIDS community and the prohibited nature of lesbian sexual speech. The ACON booklet, while containing a wealth of useful information couched in fairly explicit language, tends to adopt a rather embarrassed cheerful tone, exemplified by their approach to lesbian pregnancy: 'The biological clock is ticking, you're feeling maternal and your desire is to be with child (*Well, buy another dog!! Just kidding*)'. The booklet is illustrated throughout with photographs, including some of the *tiniest* images of lesbians I have ever seen (most measure 2 cm by 3 cm), but almost all are of two dykes clowning around in what appears to be a sports hall, resolutely having *fun* rather than sex, and there is nothing which could be called an explict representation of lesbian sex. Indeed, the *only* full-page explicit image shows a needle injecting a vein (and, rather curiously, a fairytale castle in the background), giving recreational injecting drug use much more prominence than sex. Moreover, the booklet is addressed to 'anyone who identifies as a woman', and contains advice for post-op transsexuals. Is it over-cynical of me to suspect that a booklet like this is only possible if it serves men in some way? I should add that, for all my criticisms, this is an excellent publication in terms of availability and the amount of information it covers.

In 1992 professional photographer Steven Meisel produced the 'Safe Sex is Hot Sex' postcard series for the New York Red Hot and Dance group, depicting a range of sexual couplings including two lesbian couples. A comparison of these images, with their slick professionalism and confident rewriting of traditional pornographic iconography, with lesbian-produced safer-sex images suggests that lesbians have a lot of catching up to do. Perhaps surprisingly, given the British reputation for sexlessness, Laura McGregor's postcards are the most explicit and erotic lesbian safer-sex materials I have (yet) seen produced by lesbians.

In sight, out of mind?

The notion that lesbians have become increasingly visible in the cultural mainstream is only partly correct. What has become more visible is the *heterosexual idea* of lesbians and lesbianism, and it is an idea which denies or marginalizes the role of the erotic. Lesbian desire, lesbian sexual agency, lesbian sexual behaviour, remain prohibited topics of speech, while lesbians continue to be systematically denied access to the machinery of representation. The speaking-about-lesbians which goes on in the mainstream is in a heterosexual voice and is addressed to a heterosexual ear. There is still no space allocated for a lesbian reader or audience. A widespread assumption exists that lesbians simply don't talk about sex (or write about it, or make pictures of it). This (as we will see in later chapters) is simply not true. Yet the cultural arenas within which lesbians can and do produce representations of lesbian sex are closely policed, restricted and often closed. There is undoubtedly an active and often innovative conversation about lesbian sex going on, but it is far from easy for most lesbians to gain access to what is being said.

The policing of lesbian sexual speech is exacerbated by pro-censorship lesbian feminists, and the effects of this have been profoundly damaging. It is, however, important to remember that this censorship is of an entirely different order from the political, social and legal censorship wielded by the heterosexual establishment. Indeed, it is clear that the repressive straight majority have other weapons besides straightforward censorship. Part of the response from the heterosexual community to increased lesbian activism, both from lesbian feminists and from the new queer activism, has been to incorporate lesbianism into mainstream culture in order to re-present it as inadequate, unpleasant or (in the case of kd lang's make-up-free features) 'unnatural'.

All is not lost however! For the burgeoning of lesbian culture has been dramatic, and it is simply not possible to keep this new culture safely cordoned off from the mainstream. The assimilation of lesbian codes into Madonna's songs and into *Sex*, into the Paris fashion houses, TV soaps, the straight media and straight lifestyles may yet prove to be a powerfully destablizing presence in the field of gender and the erotic. While increased lesbian visibility is not necessarily a positive step, there is now far more lesbian cultural activity than ever before, and this inevitably produces more confident, less easily manipulated lesbian communities. There is a central place for sex in this lesbian cultural productivity, and many dykes are enthusiastically taking advantage of this unique historical moment to reaffirm a diverse and exciting lesbian *sexual* identity.

Notes

1. The Institute of Contemporary Arts did hold a 'drag king' competition in 1995. However, this was a first, and widely perceived as a perverse intervention into an established tradition. There are drag striptease shows in some lesbian clubs in the USA, and a historical tradition of 'passing women', but none of this compares to the longstanding phenomenon of male drag queens. The history of drag queens is related to the history of keeping women out of the theatre for religious and moral

reasons. Anyone interested in finding out more should read Marjorie Garber *Vested Interests: Cross-Dressing and Cultural Anxiety*, (Harmondsworth: Penguin, 1992), or one of the many books on drag currently available.

2. Michel Foucault, *The History of Sexuality: Vol. 1: An Introduction*, (Harmondsworth: Penguin, 1976, trans. 1979).

3. Anna Marie Smith, 'Resisting the Erasure of Lesbian Sexuality: A challenge for queer activism' in Ken Plummer (ed.), *Modern Homosexualities: Fragments of Lesbian and Gay Experience* (London: Routledge, 1992), p. 207.

4. Adrienne Rich (1981), 'Compulsory Heterosexuality and Lesbian Existence', reprinted in Rich, *Blood, Bread and Poetry: Selected Prose 1979–1985* (London: Virago, 1987). Rich has been criticized for the 'desexualization' of lesbianism which her invention of the 'lesbian continuum' in this article seems to imply. I believe such criticisms are justified, but the essay remains extremely important for its recognition of the political nature of lesbianism and in particular for its problematizing of heterosexuality.

5. *Ibid.*, p. 27.

6. *Ibid.*, p. 24.

7. For a detailed analysis of this failure, see my chapter 'Queer Subjects: Lesbians, Heterosexual Women and the Academy' in Mary Kennedy, Cathy Lubelska and Val Walsh (eds.), *Making Connections: Women's Studies, Women's Movements, Women's Lives* (London: Taylor & Francis, 1993).

8. The relationship between lesbian sexuality and feminism is discussed in much greater detail in following chapters.

9. All statistics taken from *Ms* Vol.VI, No. 2, September/October 1995, p. 14.

10. Beth's life was far from dull. Having killed her abusive father and buried him in the back garden, she had a painful adolescent affair with a girlfriend, followed by a fling with one of her (female) lecturers at college, and went on the run with her family when her father's body was dug up. A dramatic trial resulted in Beth and her mother being sent to prison, where the stress led to her sudden death from a previously undetected heart disease before her appeal could be heard. Thousands of British lesbians went into mourning.

11. Leslie Bennetts, 'kd lang Cuts It Close', *Vanity Fair*, Vol. 56 No. 8, August 1993, pp. 46–51.

12. Janice Winship, *Inside Women's Magazines* (London: Pandora, 1987), p. 116.

13. She means when she finally got fucked by a man.

14. This is why a TV company like Britain's Channel 4, with a mandate to serve minority groups and with a (small) budget to finance the production of independent films, is so important. It is also why the deregulation of British TV is potentially so disastrous. For a more detailed discussion of these issues, see Penny Florence, 'Portrait of a Production' in Tamsin Wilton (ed.), *Immortal, Invisible: Lesbians and the Moving Image* (London: Routledge, 1995).

15. Eve Kosofsky Sedgwick, *Epistemology of the Closet* (Hemel Hempstead: Harvester Wheatsheaf, 1991), p. 51.

16. *Knave*, vol. 24 no. 9 (all sic).

17. Bennetts, 'kd lang Cuts It Close', p. 50.

18. Moe Meyer (ed.), *The Politics and Poetics of Camp* (London: Routledge, 1994), p. 17.

19. *Ibid.*

20. In Gabrielle Griffin (ed.), *Outwrite:*

Lesbianism and Popular Culture (London: Pluto Press, 1993), p. 20.

21. For further discussion of this point, see p. 108.

22. Sara Dunn, 'Voyages of the Valkyries: Recent Lesbian Pornographic Writing', *Feminist Review*, No. 34, Spring 1990, p. 169.

23. See, for example, Simon Watney, *Policing Desire: Pornography, AIDS and the Media* (London: Methuen, 1987).

24. The attempt to introduce 'jill-off' parties for lesbians has not met with success.

25. For a detailed account of the representation of sex and gender in safer-sex materials, see my forthcoming book *En/Gendering AIDS: Sex, Texts, Epidemic.*

26. Sue O'Sullivan, 'MAPPING: Lesbians, AIDS and Sexuality: An interview with Cindy Patton, *Feminist Review*, No. 34, Spring 1990, p. 120.

27. Marilyn Frye, 'Lesbian 'Sex'' in Judith Barrington (ed.), *An Intimate Wilderness: Lesbian Writers on Sexuality* (Portland, Oreg.: Eighth Mountain Press, 1991), pp. 5–6.

28. Patton, 'MAPPING', pp. 121–22.

29. Diane Richardson, 'Constructing Lesbian Sexualities' in Plummer (ed.), *Modern Homosexualities* p. 188.

30. Beth Schneider, 'Lesbian Politics and AIDS Work' in Plummer (ed.), *Modern Homosexualites*, p. 160.

31. AIDS Council of New South Wales Women's Team, *Lesbian Sex* (safer-sex booklet funded by the AIDS and Infectious Diseases Branch of the NSW Department of Health, Sydney, 1994).

32. Actually the national Swedish lesbian and gay rights group, not an AIDS organization, but they have produced the bulk of voluntary sector AIDS material in Sweden.

33. These are available for a small charge from the Centre (Tel: 0116-254 7412).

THE
JOURNALS OF
BETH JORDACHE

4
A CHANNEL
FOUR BOOK

BR☰☰KSIDE

B☐XTREE

BASED ON CHANNEL FOUR'S
TOP-RATED TV SHOW

Beth Jordache, Channel 4's lesbian soap sensation.

Pseudo-lesbian images have long been a staple of porn aimed at heterosexual men.

Right: A typically explicit and erotic representation of gay male sexuality in safer-sex promotion. Terrence Higgins Trust.

safer sex

for gay men

Hot stuff for the girls!
A typically unerotic
HIV/AIDS brochure
addressed to women.
Terrence Higgins Trust.

HIV
AND
AIDS
INFORMATION FOR
WOMEN
The Terrence Higgins Trust ♡

Home-grown safer-sex
education. One of Laura
McGregor's postcard series
for the Leicester Lesbian,
Gay and Bisexual
Communities Resource
Centre.

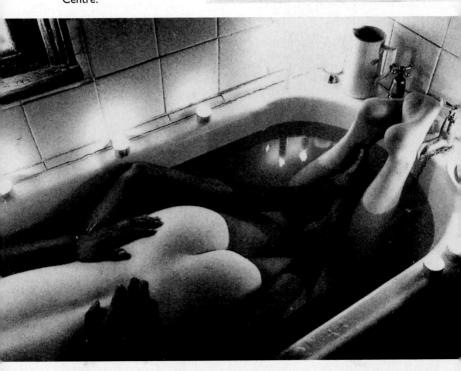

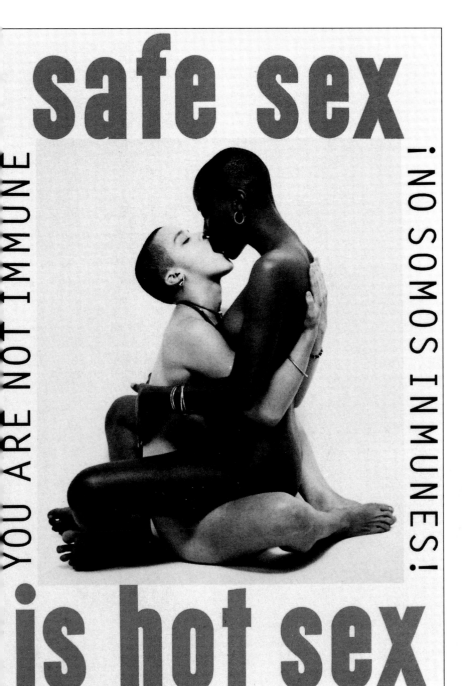

safe sex

YOU ARE NOT IMMUNE

¡NO SOMOS INMUNES!

is hot sex

Hot lesbian sex from Steven Meisel's 1992 postcard series, 'Safe Sex is Hot Sex',
for the New York Red Hot and Dance group.

'Triad' by Della Grace, from the 'Xenomorphisis' series.

Right top: One of Tee Corinne's 'Yantras of Woman Love'.

Right: Laurence Jaugey-Paget's comment on dyke voyeurism, 'Sin in the Cinema'.

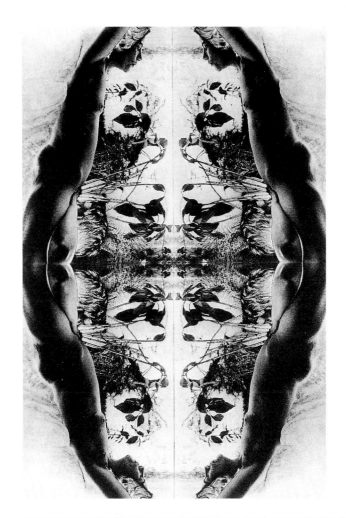

The Kiss and Tell exhibition
Drawing the Line in action. This
card, from their postcard
book, is for the reader to use
to send further comments to
the artists c/o their publisher.
Photograph © Isa Massu
1991.

One of the images from Kiss
and Tell's *Drawing the Line*
exhibition and postcard book.
Models Persimmon and
Lizard, photographer Susan.

Voices in the Wilderness?
Lesbian Sex Gurus

What is a lesbian sex guru, what do they do and do we need them? Are they just another version of the controlling mother, telling us how to have sex, or the gatekeepers to sexual liberation? Are some feminist bookshops right to refuse to stock their books, or should this decision be seen as moralistic censorship?

Images of heterosex saturate contemporary Western culture. An extraordinary range of cultural artefacts – from mail-order fashion catalogues to the Yellow Pages, from feature films to toothpaste commercials, from elite art to pop music videos – carry images of heterosexuality. An important feature of the claim that heterosex is morally, spiritually and socially superior to homosex is the naturalization of heterosex. Heterosex is constructed as 'natural' according to the (man-made) 'laws' of nature. In order to construct homosex as unnatural, appeals are made to zoology, 'animals don't do that' (they do, of course, as any well-informed zoologist knows), to physics, 'opposites attract' (which is fine with electromagnetism, but in what sense can male and female be thought of as *opposites*?), and somewhat desperately to religious law, 'God made Adam and Eve, not Adam and Steve' (fine, but what about David and Jonathan, Naomi and Ruth?). Yet heterosexuals, thoroughly programmed as they supposedly are by the laws of physics, biology and God, and immersed in a culture which rains images of heterosex onto their heads, still need books to tell them how to do it.

As we have seen, in contrast to the cultural overkill of heterosex, lesbian sex remains largely hidden. If heterosexuals, as the dominant group, still need information and instruction about sex, how much greater then is the need among lesbians. It is easier than it has ever been for confident and street-wise baby dykes growing up in the metropolitan centres of the West to get information about lesbians and (if they are in the right place at the right time) to find out about lesbian sex. It's not so easy for those lesbians growing up in rural areas, in minority ethnic or immigrant communities, or in communities still dominated by fundamentalist religious dogma. Even in a town large enough and liberal enough to support an alternative or feminist bookshop, feminist activism against 'pornography' or 'violence towards women' is often sufficient to ensure that these shops will not, or cannot, stock sexually explicit lesbian material.

The need for accurate and positive information about lesbian sex and sexuality is great. However, it is clearly not enough simply to provide that information. Recounting her experiences of homophobia and political lesbianism, Joan Nestle writes: 'I now had a sense of what I faced – the Lesbian-feminist antipornography movement on one side, and the homophobia and antisex mentality of some straight people on the other.'[1]

Any lesbian seeking access to explicit material about sex must run the gauntlet of this two-pronged assault. This may be relatively straight-forward, so much so that the obstacles between the lustful dyke and the lesbian sex book may seem no more than archaic horror stories from the distant past. In London, Edinburgh, Chicago, Boston, Auckland or Melbourne this may be so. In Port Talbot, Fort William, Santa Cruz, Echuca or Launceston[2] it is a different story. This is why there is such a great need for lesbian sex gurus.

To qualify as a lesbian sex guru you have to do more than write a 'how to do it' book on lesbian sex. The women whose work is discussed in this chapter – Pat Califia, Joan Nestle, JoAnn Loulan and Susie Bright (aka Susie Sexpert) – certainly educate us about lesbian sex and sexuality, but they are more than simple technical advisers. To begin at the beginning, however, there is no doubt that technical advice is valuable: manuals of advice and instruction in the techniques of love-making have been produced in many cultures for many centuries. From ancient texts such as the Hindu *Kama Sutra*, written by Vatsyayana between the first and fourth centuries CE,[3] or the Islamic *Perfumed Garden*, penned by Sheik Umar ibn Muhammed al-Nefzawi in the sixteenth century, through Marie Stopes's 1918 classic *Married Love*, up to the blockbuster success of modern manuals such as Alex Comfort's *The Joy of Sex*, there has always been a market for instruction manuals. Indeed, this demonstrable and widespread need to be told how to have sex is a very direct indication of our folly in asserting that human sexual behaviour is somehow 'natural', extra-social, the last refuge of animal instinct in an over-civilized world. As Leonore Tiefer comments, 'Human sexuality is not a biological given and cannot be explained in terms of reproductive biology or instinct.'[4]

There has been an extraordinary shift in recent years, with the publication of explicit manuals for lesbians, gay men, sadomasochists and other erotic minorities, but the one event which has most radically transformed the discourse of sexual instruction is the HIV pandemic, which necessitates the widespread democratization of explicit sexual speech. Of course, just because the epidemic *necessitates* the democratization of sexual speech doesn't mean that this meets with no resistance. Events in the time of AIDS show only too clearly that many people will go to great lengths to keep sexual speech as the prerogative of a political, religious or moral 'elite'. However, the effects of AIDS on sexual discourse have been nothing short of seismic. The HIV emergency already troubles the entire social superstructure of sexual relations at a global level. The anxious Victorian sexual mythology, to which so much of the post-colonial West is heir, stands exposed as not so much an inadequate fiction but an active threat to the health and safety of individuals and groups. The most successful safer-sex instruction is one which recognizes that behaviour is socially located, that individual changes in sexual technique need the support of a transformed social framework for the erotic (and for gender relations).

This is not new. Sex is always inevitably socially located, and the discourse of sexual instruction is always inevitably implicated in the social and political structures of its time. Thus, every writer in sex instruction begins by addressing the socially constructed reservations which his/her reader may bring with them to the text. As long ago as CE 100–400 Vatsyayana was obliged to reassure his readers that *kama* – 'the enjoyment of appropriate objects by the five senses' – was an appropriate subject for study:

> Some learned men say that ... Kama being a thing which is practised even by the brute creation, and which is to be found everywhere, does not want a work on the subject. This is not so. Sexual intercourse being a thing dependent on man and woman requires the application of proper means by them, and those means are to be learnt from the Kama Shastra.[5]

One important social function of sexual instruction manuals is to counteract contemporary prohibitions on explicit discussion about sex or on specific forms of sexual behaviour/pleasure, and to allay the feelings of guilt or shame which some readers may feel in consequence. However, such manuals are not in some way located *outside* the social world, so they also carry a responsibility to reinforce certain prohibitions in line with hegemonic social and political constructions of 'proper' sex. Sexual instruction manuals, therefore, are always *political instruments*. In the case of lesbian sexual instruction manuals, this political function is overtly recognized, a characteristic which distinguishes them from their heterosexual counterparts, whose political function generally remains covert or unrecognized.

The political function of lesbian sex manuals is to recognize and validate the sexual desire, activity and pleasure which takes place between women, in opposition to the cultural message that it is not 'real' sex, that it is sick, unsatisfying, neurotic, narcissistic or immature. In contrast, the history of the traditional sex instruction manual in the UK and the USA demonstrates a political imperative to control women by controlling sexuality. In particular, such manuals act to reinforce compulsory heterosexuality and attempt to reassert male control over women in response to the periodic success of feminist demands, as the rigorous feminist critique of this body of work demonstrates.

This discourse of control took many forms. It was suggested that women's health was put at risk by failing to have intercourse with a male partner:

> after twenty-five, the woman who has neither husband nor lover and is not under-vitalised and sexually deficient, is suffering mentally and bodily – often without knowing why she suffers; nervous, irritated, anaemic, always tired, or ruthlessly fussing over trifles.*

The political struggles for women's emancipation were blamed for unhappy marital sex lives and for the breakdown of the family. Influential sexologist Havelock Ellis was explicit about his 'desire to breed a firmly-fibred, clean-minded, and self-reliant race of manly men and womanly women', and identified feminism as attempting to contradict the biological basis which he claimed for this distinction between the sexes:

Those who propagandised this now rather antiquated notion of the 'equality' of the sexes ... were justified in so far as they were protesting against that superstition of the inferiority of women which has proved so influential. ... But the banner of Equality under which they fought ... had no biological foundation.[7]

The idea that feminists were responsible for the destruction of marriage and the family received 'official' sanction in 1952 when Joseph Brayshaw, representing the Marriage Guidance Council, proclaimed that 'in truth it is the new equality of women with man that has led inevitably to the disruption, for the present, of stable marriage and family life'.[8]

In response to the perceived threat from feminist activism, sex instruction manuals reaffirmed and renaturalized the construction of female sexuality as masochistic and principally maternal, and insisted that it was a woman's duty in marriage to perform her sexual duties properly. Thus, Havelock Ellis insisted on a gendered division of labour in sexuality, and declared that men's (supposed) delight in inflicting pain and women's (supposed) delight in receiving it, were both 'natural':

the primary part of the female in courtship is the playful, yet serious, assumption of the role of the hunted animal who lures on the pursuer, not with the object of escaping, but with the object of being finally caught. ... When in men it is possible to trace a tendency to inflict pain ... on the women they love, it is still easier to trace in women a delight in experiencing physical pain when inflicted by a lover, and an eagerness to accept submission to his will. Such a tendency is certainly normal.[9]

A 'marital advice' manual of the 1950s pointed out the wife's duty to ensure that her sexual mechanism was functioning smoothly:

If she does not enjoy her marital relations fully after a reasonable apprenticeship, she ought to take stock of the situation. ... She then owes it both to herself and her husband to find out exactly which part of her emotional clockwork [sic] is out of gear, have it repaired and put into smooth running order as soon as possible.[10]

It was not only men who saw the emancipation of women as a problem for domestic heterosexual happiness. In 1957 Judith Hubback, 'a graduate of Cambridge University and mother of three young children', wrote *Wives Who Went to College*, an attempt to identify and remedy the negative effects which an educated female might have on her future household. Hubback shares the belief, generally accepted at this time, that female sexual desire is founded on a reproductive urge, and suggests alternative outlets for this urge in the educated woman:

> Having borne the number of children she and her husband agreed upon ... she must consciously foster in herself an attitude on the emotional side of sex which is somewhere between the purely male and the purely female ... in future she will try to prevent the creative aspect of sex from featuring in her reactions. If she is wise she will direct her remaining creativeness into other channels. ... Many forms of creative work of varying degrees of permanence are possible, from minor activities such as cake- or jam-making, through knitting and house-decorating to the more permanent types of craft and art.[11]

If nothing else, this passage casts fresh light on the popularity of handicraft magazines among some women! This controlling discourse, however, did not end with the benighted years of the 1950s. Indeed, Helen Gurley Brown's best seller *Sex and the Single Girl*, widely regarded in the early 1960s as risqué if not actually immoral, instructed women to keep every aspect of themselves firmly under control in order to attract the sexual interest of men. Their movements should be restrained, and they were to remain as silent as possible: 'Being able to sit still is very sexy. Smiles are sexy. ... Talking all the time about *anything* is unsexy. Sphinxes and Mona Lisas knew what they were doing'.[12] Thus heterosexual female attractiveness depends on women not moving and not speaking! It is against this historical background that the emergence of the lesbian sexual instruction book and the work of the lesbian sex gurus must be seen if it is to be fully understood.

How to do it – sex instruction for lesbians

The two social factors hostile to the sexual pleasure of lesbians in the West have been the oppression of lesbians by the heterosexual main-stream and (since the 1970s) a powerfully anti-erotic strand of radical lesbian feminism. Other issues, including institutional and personal racism, anti-Semitism, class and disability oppression, exert additional pressure on specific groups of lesbians. In the early days of the homophile movement, in the USA in particular, publishing explicit information about what two women might do to share sexual pleasure was a radical and oppositional response to the anti-lesbianism of the mainstream. Lesbian sexuality, so often denied, belittled or simply rendered invisible, was incorporated into the political agenda of the struggle for lesbian rights. Thus early lesbian texts, now classics, such as Del Martin and Phyllis Lyon's *Lesbian/Woman*[13] or Ginny Vida's *Our Right to Love*[14] included forthright information about lesbian sex. There were early lesbian sex instruction manuals, including the Nomadic Sisters' *Loving Women*.[15]

The growth of lesbian feminism, and the close and dynamic interaction between the second wave of the WLM and the ongoing fight for lesbian liberation, gave rise to two problems in terms of lesbian sex. The first was that, in their eagerness to challenge the homophobic rhetoric which dismissed lesbians as sex-crazed and regarded lesbianism as a sexual perversion, lesbians were keen to downplay the erotic aspects of lesbian life and lesbian identity, and to foreground other issues which were more easily chracterized as 'political'. The second was the rise of political lesbianism (a lesbian-feminist identity which specifically rejected the idea that sexual activity between women was necessary for those who wanted to call themselves lesbians) and the growing feminist attack on many aspects of traditional lesbian and gay culture (such as drag, butch/femme roleplay, etc.), which were declared to be woman-hating and anti-feminist.

The problematic interaction between lesbians and feminists resulted in the desexualization of lesbianism on the one hand, confronted by a rebellious reaffirmation of lesbian sexuality on the other. Fairly typical of the political-lesbian position is British revolutionary feminist Sheila Jeffreys, who proposed a specifically feminist sexual practice. Unfortunately, her proposal is not backed up with detailed instruction. She describes feminist lesbian sex as: 'an adventure in the total transformation of sexuality with the object of eliminating sexual violence and the objectification of women ... it is ... intense and astonishing, a real adventure that takes courage'.[16] I would like nothing better than the chance to explore an 'intense and astonishing' lesbian sexual experience, but Jeffreys is selfishly keeping to herself the explicit instructions which I need in order to take up her proposal. Since so much lesbian sexual activity is forbidden in the revolutionary lesbian-feminist vision of sex – vaginal or anal penetration, the use of sex toys, s/m, butch/femme role-play, 'objectifying' women's bodies – Jeffreys's intense and astonishing experience may involve previously unknown activities. As Kathryn Harriss comments, 'The reader is left with the impression of some transcendent experience, but how do you get there, and what exactly are you meant to do in bed?' I think we should be told.

Most mainstream lesbian-feminist books are not going to tell. Yet, for every text which ignores, denies or erases the sexual nature of lesbians, another reaffirms and celebrates dykes' desire. Alongside books like *Woman Plus Woman, Sappho Was a Right-On Woman* and *Woman-Identified Woman,*[18] none of which accorded lesbian sexuality a more than cursory mention, came books like *Lesbian Sex* and *Sapphistry: The Book of Lesbian Sexuality,*[19] which enthusiastically foregrounded it. And, just as heterosexual sex gurus adopted a more public stance, offering first the televised clichés of Dr Ruth and later the full-blown multimedia spectacle of post-porn modernist Annie Sprinkle, lesbian sex gurus too began to adopt personas which were as much performative as didactic. Not only did they inform and educate, they celebrated.

This transformation was in tune with shifts in the wider culture: gone was the gloomy, medicalized paradigm which constructed sexual pleasure as valuable *because of something else* – because it cemented holy matrimony, relieved tension, maintained appropriate gender roles or defused revolutionary tendencies. In its place was a hedonistic paradigm, subtly informed by the human potential movement, which constructed sexual pleasure as an intrinsically worthwhile goal.

As with any aspect of lesbian culture, lesbian erotic instruction partakes of such shifts and transformations in the wider culture. The defence of lesbian sexuality was certainly in part a reaction against its erasure within the hegemonic feminist politic, but it was also shaped by a complex collection of social factors – the postmodern commodification of the body, the HIV pandemic, developments in contraceptive technology, dramatic changes in ideologies of gender, the globalization of culture and the rise of moral relativism – which were working a sea change on sexuality in general. A figure like Annie Sprinkle, sex worker turned media star, polymorphous perverse high priestess of fantasy, would not have been comprehensible in the relatively recent past. For a 1970s feminist, the idea of an entertainer encouraging audience members to photograph her cervix while she held her vagina open with a speculum, or masturbating on stage with an enormous vibrator as the (literal, or at least convincingly simulated) climax to a spectacular show, would have been simply incomprehensible.[20]

Four lesbian sex gurus

The four lesbian sex gurus whose work is discussed here, JoAnn Loulan, Pat Califia, Joan Nestle and Susie Bright, represent very different approaches to sex, and to the business of teaching lesbians about lesbian sex and sexuality. They are all American. I have no plausible theories about why the UK has not produced a lesbian sex guru! British lesbian culture is as saturated with material from the USA as any other section of the market, and this applies equally to books, so perhaps we have just not needed to write our own. However, feminist and community bookshops have often refused to stock books by Nestle, Califia and Bright – Loulan has always been regarded as politically correct, for reasons which will become clear below – with the result that many lesbians are denied access to their work.

The various approaches taken by these four writers are informed by the other work which they do, and their reasons for writing about sex. Loulan is a lesbian counsellor, Nestle a lesbian writer, Bright a bisexual sex educator and journalist, Califia a writer, journalist and founder member of the lesbian s/m group SAMOIS. All are white. All share a commitment to challenging racism and other oppressions founded on 'difference', although Joan Nestle, as 'a Jew, a lesbian, working class, a feminist femme' speaks most clearly about the intersections between privilege, oppression and sexuality. They differ in their relationship to feminism, but all of them express clear rejection of those feminists who attempt to control lesbian sexuality.

Unsurprisingly, their work shares many key themes in common. All are self-consciously political (although the details of their political agendas differ), all reject sexual guilt, all are informative about the explicit details of lesbian sex (although they differ greatly in their presentation of this information), most are as concerned with pleasure as with information, often producing texts which are in themselves erotic, and all of them are (to varying degrees) self-revelatory. This last characteristic sets them firmly within the established tradition of feminist writing. Sexologists and sex 'experts', such as Alex Comfort, Havelock Ellis and Marie Stopes, noticeably fail to tell their readers what turns them on. You could wade through shelves full of mainstream heterosexual sex instruction manuals and come away thinking that they are mostly written by celibates. The feminist recognition that 'the personal is political', the rejection of 'objective expert opinion' as a mere synonym for 'what men think', together with the experiences of CR groups organized around respectful listening to women's personal accounts, resulted in a new privileging of the self-revelatory authorial voice. Writing rooted in personal experience is valued by feminists, and has become characteristic of feminist or feminist-influenced writing. This is reinforced for some women by their experiences with the human potential movement, with various forms of counselling or co-counselling, or with twelve-step programmes dealing with addiction, all of which validate the expression of intimate feelings. Thus, although Loulan remains silent about her sex life, we learn that she is from an alcoholic household, and that she has had to learn not to take care of people.[21]

However much Califia, Loulan, Nestle and Bright have in common, each has her own distinctive approach, demanding separate discussions.

JoAnn Loulan – the tyranny of orgasm and the inner child.

JoAnn Loulan is the only lesbian sex guru whose books are generally stocked by feminist bookshops in the UK, although her third book, *The Lesbian Erotic Dance*, is still regarded as problematic by some because it seems to advocate butch/femme role-play. Loulan is a practising counsellor, and her writing on lesbian sex is interwoven with threads from astrology, twelve-step philosophy, the human potential movement and traditional American self-help. Although she recognizes the political nature of lesbian sex, and acknowledges social factors which may influence or structure individual sexuality, her proposed solution for lesbians troubled by sexual issues is fundamentally individualistic/pop-psychological. This makes her approach very seductive. Loulan identifies powerful political and social pressures on lesbian sex, and suggests that, by following her programme of psychodynamic exercises and by employing the right counsellor/therapist, each one of us is able to overcome these large-scale problems at the level of our individual selves. She suggests that the ways in which male control has been exerted over women restrict and control lesbian sexuality:

> For centuries now sex has been defined by men. How sex should be done, with whom and how often has been determined by men's sexual needs. Women have never been consulted about what in sexuality makes sense to us. It is no accident that our voices have been unheard; it is the result of sexism.[22]

Loulan asserts that homophobia and sexual trauma are as significant as sexism in blocking lesbian sexuality, and suggests that lesbian-feminist attempts to control lesbian sexual behaviour collude with the very homophobia which they claim to be fighting: 'Some members of the lesbian community foster homophobia by trying to establish "politically correct" ways in which lesbians may express their sexuality.'[23] The combined forces of sexism and a judgemental lesbian community effectively silence lesbian speech about sex:

> The hardest topic for lesbians to talk about when we discuss sex is what we actually do in bed. ... It is scary partly because there is so much judgement within the lesbian community about what we do. Every possible sexual activity is judged by someone. ... Some people

think that lesbians have to have sex a particular way to be lesbians. Nonsense! Lesbian sex is *anything* two lesbians do together. Monitoring our own and others' sexual behaviour is in no one's interests but our oppressors.[24]

This forthright rejection of the lesbian sex prefects, especially when it comes from a professional counsellor and a feminist, offers powerful reassurance to lesbians bruised and confused by the sex wars. Ironically, having recognized that it is so difficult for lesbians to talk about 'what we actually do in bed', Loulan continues: 'I will only cursorily describe what we do in bed as there are entire books on the subject. If you want to know about any particular activity ... see the bibliography.'[25] Any lesbian who buys a fluorescent pink book called *Lesbian Sex*, and turns to the chapter headed 'What We Do In Bed' is going to be disappointed when the author merely refers her to a bibliography listing three books on lesbian sex (two of which are out of print) and fourteen books on addiction/alcoholism. In fact, Loulan received feedback from readers expressing this disappointment, as she recounts in her second book, *Lesbian Passion*:

> After reading my last book, *Lesbian Sex*, some people said to me, 'There wasn't enough juice in it. Don't just tell us that lesbians have oral sex and kiss a lot – we know all that stuff. Tell us something new that can spice up our sex lives.'[26]

Loulan's response is five pages of rather alarmingly coy information about dildos, butt plugs ('If you're afraid of poop, you might be interested to know that the poop usually isn't right down there near the anus ...'), wearing dildo harnesses and 'soft restraints'. She refuses outright to discuss s/m: 'There's serious controversy in our communities over any act that might be considered sado-masochism. I'm not going to touch that with a ten-foot pole.'[27] There is, I suggest, a problem here, even within the counselling paradigm that Loulan constructs. How far can a lesbian trust the support and strength of a counsellor who rejects the notion that the community has the authority to control lesbian sexuality and yet promptly submits to that control herself?

Despite the upfront titles on her books, Loulan is not, in fact, a lesbian sex guru. She is a lesbian *relationships* guru. *Lesbian Sex* and *Lesbian Passion* contain advice on disability, motherhood, sobriety, ageing, self-esteem, celibacy, eating disorders, self-injury, incest and maintaining long-term relationships. Her goal is not to maximize lesbian sexual pleasure, nor to celebrate lesbian lust, but 'healing the child within.'[28] Sexuality is simply the medium which she chooses to use to help lesbians do this.

There is no doubt that this approach has been very useful to many women. Loulan's books sell well and she is a regular guest on radio and TV. Indeed, she is busy enough to employ a ghost writer. The issues Loulan confronts are experienced by many lesbians, and we are often marginalized, pathologized or rendered simply invisible in the self-help literature in these areas. Yet the paradigm which Loulan constructs and works within – a 'healing' paradigm, fundamentally spiritual and indi-vidualistic – is of painfully limited use to lesbians who want information about lesbian sex. A good example is her approach to disability.

Although it is admirable of Loulan to give space to Jill Lessing to write about disability and lesbians, a discussion about social responses to impairment, followed by a brief exercise on 'self-love' is of limited use to disabled lesbians trying to find the kind of practical information which they are too often denied. Moreover, to suggest that disabled lesbians should work on 'enhancing your own level of acceptance of your body' and reassuring your inner child is to hand responsibility firmly back to them. At a time when disabled activists promote a social model of disability and insist that the (currently) able-bodied main-stream take responsibility for the exclusionary and oppressive practices which *dis-able* people with impairments, this self-love approach on its own is reactionary and dis-abling. There is a practical section in which Loulan discusses specific impairments and incorporates accounts from disabled lesbians, but for some reason it is relegated to an appendix, an unfortunate reinforcement of the idea that this is a subject best kept in the background.

This apolitical, individualistic approach typifies Loulan's construc-tion of lesbian sexuality. I find it disturbing, because it verges on a pathologization and medicalization of lesbian sex which is all too common in mainstream sexological discourse. Loulan's model simply replaces the male view of sex with an alternative norm. 'We are', she suggests, 'in the midst of redefining for ourselves what sexual desire is, what the "*normal*" amount of sexual activity is, what our *natural* rhythms of sexuality are'[29] (my italics). Once there is a norm, once there is an idea of what is natural, then individuals may be labelled 'abnormal' and 'unnatural.' It really doesn't matter if our failures are ultimately due to patriarchal oppression, it is still our responsibility to 'heal' and to 'recover'. Loulan's language makes clear her unspoken belief that there is 'healthy' and 'unhealthy' lesbian sex. She asks her reader to follow a programme of exercises for sexual and emotional health: 'Take off all your clothes and look at yourself in a mirror for fifteen minutes a day. At the end of a week look at yourself for one hour. Yes, one hour.' Then the reader is instructed to 'Write a letter to your sexual response. Tell it how dissatisfied you are', or to 'Draw a picture of your genitals. Colour them in and make the colouring elaborate.'[30] I am not suggesting that such exercises are unhelpful; however, I do think that they are problematic, for two reasons. Firstly, Loulan's focus is on *emotional health*, not on 'sex'. Of course, lesbians need emotional support as much as anyone else, but writing a book about spirituality, recovery and healing the inner child and calling it *'Lesbian Sex'* is cynical and dishonest. It is no different from using sex to sell cars, computers or instant coffee, and moreover it reinforces the anti-lesbian myth that lesbians are more interested in relationships than in sex, and that lesbian 'sex' is not real sex.

Secondly, Loulan's metaphors of healing and recovery, her involvement with, and advocacy of, twelve-step programmes (and an addiction model for sex) and her presentation of a very restricted sexual repertoire all construct a primarily medical model of lesbian sexuality. If there is 'healthy' lesbian sex there must, by definition, be 'unhealthy' lesbian sex. The medicalization and pathologization of lesbian sex has been a powerful force in lesbian oppression (and in the oppression of women generally). It is no less oppressive in the hands of another lesbian. 'The master's tools', as Audre Lorde famously remarked, 'will never dismantle the master's house.'[31] Finally, it is no small matter to assume that all lesbians have the time, resources and privacy to enable them to stand naked in front of a mirror for an hour!

Joan Nestle – the hard-won struggle for pleasure

Anyone who wants to know just how fascistic feminists can be should read Joan Nestle's autobiographical account, 'My History With Censorship.'[32] Nestle's approach to lesbian sexuality is that of a historian. She founded the Lesbian Herstory Archives in New York, and as well as writing personal accounts of lesbian history in the USA from the 1950s to the present has offered other butch/femme lesbians a space from which to speak by editing a collection of their accounts.[33] The most self-revelatory of lesbian sex gurus, Nestle intersperses narrative accounts of her own emotional and sexual life with discursive pieces on censorship, prostitution and her involvement in anti-racist activism. She experienced anti-Semitism and the terrors of McCarthyism at first hand, and this direct knowledge informs her refusal to tolerate the offensive tactics of the feminist sex prefects. In 1981, Nestle wrote 'Butch-Femme Relationships: Sexual Courage in the 1950s',[34] a ground-breaking account which reclaimed traditional butch/femme relationships and identities from the feminist misreading of them, and celebrated the courage and radicalism of butch and femme lesbians in those dangerous days. 'Butch-femme relationships as I experienced them', she writes, 'were complex erotic statements, not phony heterosexual replicas'. She goes on to suggest that this history has been misrepresented within feminism: 'We Lesbians from the fifties made a mistake in the early seventies: we allowed our lives to be trivialized and reinterpreted by feminists who did not share our culture.'[35] The strength of Nestle's position is that she speaks about the disrespectful feminist treatment of lesbian culture from a feminist perspective, acknowledging her own debt to feminism:

> because I shared both worlds, [I] know how respectable feminism made me feel, how less dirty, less ugly, less butch and femme. But the pain and anger at hearing so much of my past judged unacceptable have started to rise.[36]

Not only was Nestle the first lesbian to validate butch/femme relationships, but her work incorporated a degree of class consciousness generally missing from feminist lesbian debate. Nestle is a working-class woman, and is in no doubt that the unacknowledged class privilege of many lesbians remains an important issue in the theory and practice of lesbian sex. The response to her outspokenness, however unsurprising, remains shocking:

> That year marked for me the second McCarthy period in my life. Only this time, many of the holders of truth were women.

They called the organizers of conferences where I was speaking and told them I was a 'sexual deviant', labeling me as a dangerous person who betrays the feminist cause. The place where I earn my living ... was visited by a member of Women Against Pornography who saw it as her duty to warn a group of students and professors about me. 'Don't you know she is a Lesbian? Don't you know she practices S&M? Don't you know she engages in unequal patriarchal power sex?'[37]

Nestle outlines with chilling clarity the political implications of such tactics, and the cost to lesbians of being excluded from the community of lesbian feminists. 'Some Lesbian-feminists', she concludes, 'will turn us in and feel they have made the world safer for women by doing so. ... I almost think I have lived too long when I see Lesbians become members of the new vice squad.'[38]

In the transgressive university of lesbian sex, Joan Nestle is not a technician or a biologist. She does not write how-to-do-it manuals, nor does she travel the country giving instruction on sexual technique. She is a sex historian. Her work celebrates a lesbian erotic culture in defiance of concerted attempts on the part of patriarchal homophobes and of political lesbians to eradicate it. She honours the erotic choices of working-class lesbians, women sex workers, Jewish and 'third world' lesbians and butch/femme lesbians with as much passion as she devotes to chronicling their struggles against oppression. But as well as offering a political framework for their lives, her stories turn women on and the point is that both are important. Her femme/butch reader *The Persistent Desire*, a collection of stories, discussion, poetry, interviews and photographs, encapsulates the riches of a community despised by the heterosexual mainstream and betrayed by feminism.

Pat Califia – 'a very peculiar sort of lesbian'[39]

Recently the Women's Studies librarian at my university was approached by a woman student who demanded that Pat Califia's book *Sapphistry* be removed from the shelves because the author 'promotes violence against women' (her request was refused). For the same reason my local community bookshop refuses to carry anything by Califia (although, in the interests of economic survival, and in the time-honoured tradition of the dirty-raincoat school of sexology, they will order any book you want and keep it behind the counter for you to collect), and I am well used to Women's Studies students who – without ever having read her work – vocally denounce her as a pornographer who endorses racism and woman-hating. Strange qualifications for a guru?

Agony aunt for the leading American gay news magazine the *Advocate* for more than a decade, founder member of lesbian-feminist s/m group SAMOIS and author of lesbian erotic stories, Califia has frequently clashed head-on with political lesbians. She has a degree in psychology, but her work steers well clear of the pop-psychological path taken by Loulan, and her Mormon upbringing seems to have left her with little tolerance of guilt-tripping or of fundamentalism in any guise. It is to Califia that a dyke may turn for the most explicit and inclusive information about sexual practices. Her sex instruction manual, *Sapphistry: The Book of Lesbian Sexuality* is far and away the most informative lesbian sex book currently available, and has the added bonus of Tee Corinne's historically inspired illustrations. *Sapphistry* and the *Advocate Adviser*, a collection of her correspondence during her time at the *Advocate*, show Califia in her element in her role of sex instructor, and she is also a skilled writer of s/m erotica.

If s/m can be seen 'as a blasphemous parody of feminism, a black mass of the women's movement,'[40] then Pat Califia is the Antichrist. Like Joan Nestle, she knows at first hand the pain of being rejected by a vocal group of lesbian feminists, and like Nestle, she is well aware of the costs of that exclusion:

> in the absence of government agencies and institutionalized religion, lesbians have developed their own social and cultural mores. The opinions and traditions of our own subculture can acquire more power over our behaviour than the larger society. After all, if we become outlaws within our own community, where will we go?[41]

For a lesbian-feminist Antichrist, Califia has oddly acceptable credentials. There is that degree in psychology, the fact that she surveyed over 300 lesbians before writing *Sapphistry*, and that she incorporates material on communication skills developed at the Resource Center for Human Relationships in Oakland, California. All of which sits rather uncomfortably with her demonization. Yet, although she seems to work from the same intellectual foundation as the most respectable of lesbian feminists, the conclusions she reaches are anathema to the political-lesbian doctrine.

In common with the majority of political lesbians, Califia's work is powered by anger. She has a radical-feminist political critique which recognizes the role of the erotic in the subordination of women, and in turn privileges the erotic in developing a feminist oppositional strategy. But there the similarity ends. Many radical feminists construct sexuality itself as an inherently masculine praxis, and therefore reject desire, fantasy and pleasure as politically suspect or outright reactionary and counter-revolutionary. Ti-Grace Atkinson is typically forthright in her rejection of all things sexual *on behalf of* the 'true' feminist:

> Feminists are on the fence, at the moment, on the issue of sex. But I do not know any feminist worthy of that name who, if forced to choose between freedom and sex, would choose sex. She'd choose freedom every time. ... By no stretch of the imagination is the Women's Movement a movement for sexual liberation.[42]

She goes on to suggest that a feminist who has done her political work properly will either not have sexual fantasies at all, or will have New Improved ones: 'It has been of interest to feminists that as we have asserted ourselves increasingly in the political arena, our sexual fantasies – in so far as we still have any – no longer have that earlier masochistic character.'[43]

Califia's radical feminism leads her to a very different conclusion. Against the archetypal heroine of hegemonic radical-feminist discourse – the political lesbian who has Risen Above Sex – Califia pits *her* feminist heroine – the Slut. Taking the 'feminist cliche that women are divided into virgins and whores' out of the safe realms of the symbolic, and setting it firmly in the material world, she denounces 'respectable' feminists for colluding in the abuse of the slut:

> There is no mention in anti-porn rhetoric of how much the hatred voiced by 'respectable' women puts the slut in danger, how much 'nice' women's jealousy and fear of being identified with her isolates the slut and makes it possible for her to be exploited and abused.[44]

Califia goes further. Within this radically oppositional paradigm, the slut, far from being the ultimate victim of patriarchy, embodies the excessive power of female sexuality which resists male control: 'The slut is, in Dworkin's parlance, male property – a victim of male violence – a woman who accepts male definitions of her sexuality. Instead, I believe that she is someone men hate because she is potentially beyond their control.'[45]

This is why Califia's work is so exciting. Unlike Loulan, she does not simply criticize political-lesbian ideology for putting a damper on 'healthy' lesbian sexual expression. Rather, like Nestle, she recognizes the subversive potential inherent in an active, desiring lesbian sexuality outside male control. Moreover, in opposition to the political-lesbian feminist ideology which mandates an extreme degree of control over sexuality in the interests of the political struggle, Califia proposes *integrating* the exploration and validation of sexual pleasure into her feminist agenda. Thus, her efforts at giving pleasure to the readers of her erotic fiction are an integral part of her liberationary agenda. And, in contrast to the 'juicy wetness' school of most lesbian erotic fiction, Califia is skilful (and effective) as a writer of erotica, 'topping' her reader with a masterly hand.

From this sex-positive perspective, the burden of guilt and shame which are associated with sexual desires, acts, feelings and fantasies in many women's experience are implicated in the male control of women. 'It seems as if it doesn't matter what we feel bad about,' she writes, 'as long as we feel bad about something.'[46] In attributing a wider social-control function to the regulation of women's sexuality, Califia follows well-established feminist practice. Ironically, she belongs to the tradition of precisely those American radical feminists who are most likely to be labelled 'anti-sex' – Angela Dworkin, Catherine MacKinnon and Susan Brownmiller – all of whom identify *sexuality* as the cornerstone of patriarchal oppression.

Dworkin and MacKinnon claim that the pornographic representation of female sexuality controls women by promoting an ideology of heterosex as something done by men to women, and Brownmiller suggests that sexual violence and the threat of sexual violence is used to control all women. The two clearly intersect: in this analysis, sexual violence and pornography are mutually interdependent. Together they construct a feminist vision of the erotic which is bleak indeed. Sex itself becomes inevitably oppressive, dangerous, politically loaded. The only politically appropriate tactic for feminists was to withdraw from sex altogether, or to reconstruct sexuality *in reaction to* the constellation of behaviours and desires which constitute heteropatriarchal sex. Sheila Jeffreys, Julia Penelope and others are attempting just such a reconstruction. The central problem with this strategy (apart from the significant difficulty that purging sex of all behaviours rejected by this analysis effectively removes much of its pleasure and excitement), is that a vision of sex which is constructed in reaction to the patriarchal model is, *by definition*, still controlled by that model. If, in order to do politically revolutionary feminist sex, you have to spend more time in bed thinking about what *men* do (so that you can refuse to do it) than you spend thinking about what your girlfriend loves, surely you are prioritizing men over women *even in the act of doing lesbian sex*. Since political lesbianism claims lesbian sexuality as a magical space outside male control, this is powerfully ironic.

A little touch of Califia in the night?

I can almost hear the howls of rage which will greet my next proposal. For, if the radical-feminist model of sexuality is flawed by its neglect of pleasure and by the degree to which it is forced to depend on masculinity for its meanings, how can this be remedied? I suggest that, in order to develop a truly woman-centred, radical and transformative politics of the erotic, we must turn to the macho slut herself. It is precisely Califia's perspective on the subversive potential of sexual pleasure which is missing from the traditional radical feminist critique of the erotic.

Califia certainly offers us a politics of pleasure. She writes, in the introduction to *Sapphistry*:

> The majority culture controls us by limiting our vision and denying us all possible images of the women we might become. This book carries a subversive message. ... It is difficult to combat misogyny on a large scale if it flourishes within us. We can confront our internalized hostility and heal the damage done by a society that fears and hates the body.[47]

According to this utopian vision, it is through sexuality that liberation may be achieved; not by instituting still more repression and control in the name of feminism, but by refusing repression, losing control *in the name of feminism*. For Califia, it is precisely the energy of the erotic which motivates and fuels rebellion:

Our sexuality can be a source of pleasure, nourishment and strength. This book is an attack on the repression and colonization of women's sexuality. It is intended to strengthen us and prepare us for a long, difficult struggle for liberation.[48]

It might be objected that this is simple sexual libertarianism: that Califia is spoon-feeding her readers the simplistic, apolitical utopianism of a Reich, with his orgone energy, or a Marcuse. Indeed, the most frequent criticism levelled against Califia by lesbian feminists is that she represents the old, familiar libertarian line which has been so effectively exposed by feminists. Yet the characteristic which distinguishes Califia from the libertarians, and indeed from the bulk of political lesbians, is the fact that her approach is firmly located in the *social*. She incorporates a materialist analysis which, although somewhat unsophisticated, stands in marked contrast to the extreme symbolic nature of much radical-feminist discourse (in which sexual penetration equals colonization, the sexual exchange of power is equivalent to the entire Third Reich, etc.).

Thus, when Califia offers guidance to disabled lesbians in *Sapphistry*, she seeks the advice of lesbians with impairments and sets her practical and explicit chapter firmly in the body of the book. When writing about older lesbians, she recognizes that 'Older people need more than sexual freedom. Their economic problems have yet to be solved. The typical nursing home is not a warm, comfortable environment for anyone ...'.[49] Moreover, her recognition of social and material factors enables her to challenge the overdetermined symbolism of much radical feminism. Responding to feminist anti-s/m activists, Califia maintains respect for their position and acknowledges the legitimacy of some of their concerns, while pointing out the weaknesses in their final position. It is instructive to contrast her willingness to engage thoughtfully with this contentious debate with the frankly irrational hostility of many anti-s/m writers:[50]

Anti-S/M feelings among feminists have some legitimate sources. We are still fighting an entrenched psychoanalytic concept that says women are naturally masochistic and passive. This concept is used to justify the sexual, social and economic exploitation of women. The ugly idea that women encourage, cooperate with, and secretly enjoy rape or sexual abuse is a companion piece of misogyny.[51]

While recognizing – and echoing – the legitimate concerns of anti-s/m feminists, Califia reminds her readers that sexual game-playing and economic exploitation are activities of a different order. Enjoying s/m is not the same as enjoying socio-economic oppression:

> having an S/M fantasy and dealing with second-class status in a male-dominated society are very different things. Women work at low-paying jobs because they must survive and those jobs are often all that is available. An S/M fantasy is a choice made out of a field of possible erotic themes. Saying 'yes, mistress' to a lover who has you beside yourself with pleasure is not the same thing as saying 'yes, sir' to a boss.[52]

This reintroduction of the material and the social into the feminist debate on sexuality, coupled with her insistence that women's exploration of sexual pleasure constitutes an act of resistance to patriarchal control, make Califia's account of lesbian sexuality both more positive and more pragmatic than the dominant radical-feminist position allows for. As the Lucifer of lesbian feminism, cast out of the heaven of political correctitude for fomenting rebellion, she represents, ironically, probably the most effective way of transforming the impasse between lesbian feminists and non-feminist lesbians, and of developing a transformative theory of lesbian sexuality. She is also – for dykes whose interest in transformative theories of lesbian sexuality is minimal – the lesbian sex guru who is most likely to show you how to have a great time in bed.

Susie Sexpert, postmodern postqueer chic chick

Susie Bright is as deeply involved in the business of lesbian sex as Pat Califia, and has had a varied career as a sex guru. A former editor of lesbian sex magazine *On Our Backs*, she worked for a while reviewing 'blue' videos for straight men's sex magazines *Penthouse* and *Forum*, made a cameo appearance as her 'Susie Sexpert' persona in Monica Treut's 1988 film *Virgin Machine*, and packs theatres around the USA and Canada with her video presentations, lectures and safer-sex demonstrations. Her sex guru persona is as different from Califia's as it is possible to be. Califia's self-consciously performative persona is that of the lesbian pervert, the leather daddy dyke. The author's photo on the cover of *Macho Sluts* shows her crouching in full leathers, half-smiling at the camera from behind dark glasses, and she writes self-mockingly about her efforts in maintaining this image:

> Naturally, I was wearing nothing but black ... I felt I had to hold up the side for pervs, even if that meant people frequently asked me, 'Are those the same clothes you wore on Monday?'. I was sulking because the ventilator shaft was blowing cold air on me, and I secretly suspected I had ruined by tough image forever by complaining bitterly about its effect on my delicate sinuses ... [53]

Bright, on the other hand, comes across as a perverse Girl Guide or cheerleader. Her persona is relentlessly wholesome and cheerful, an impression emphasized by her entertaining descriptions of the impact motherhood has made on her life. For the covers of her books she poses in a skin-tight latex mini dress, studded belts, handcuffs and unkempt hair, or lies, sphinx-like, against a background of spotty fabric which vaguely references the iconographic cliché of leopard skin. Pornographic paraphernalia notwithstanding, her cheery grin and forthright eye contact undermine any suggestion of eroticism. This is perversion at its most unthreatening: dress-up play that erases or conceals the darker side of sexuality. In *Virgin Machine,* a resolutely wholesome Susie Sexpert, sporting determinedly sensible glasses and dangly earrings that spell out 'PEACE', introduces the heroine, Dorothee, to her suitcase full of dildos. A less likely dildo enthusiast than this high-school head-girl figure is hard to imagine.

Like Califia, Bright is outspoken in defence of sexual freedom. Unlike Califia, she trashes lesbian-feminism unreservedly, dismissing what she terms 'vice-squad feminist babbling',[54] although she does recognize that there is a range of opinion within feminism. Declaring herself to be 'hopping mad over the biggest lie ever told since the world was proclaimed flat: lesbians don't have sex,'[55] she pulls no punches in her criticism of the biological essentialism which she perceives to be the foundation of lesbian-feminist moralism:

> Lesbian-feminist sex theory reduced itself to purging anything aggressive, vicarious, and non-oval-shaped from its erotic vocabulary. The mainstream lesbian media mouthed sexist cliches about the 'nature of men and women' that could have come out of a

fundamentalist pulpit. ... These theoretical premises created the opportunity for traditional right-wingers to use conservative feminist rhetoric to seduce liberals and naive bystanders into fighting the 'evil' of pornography.[56]

The politically disastrous consequences of feminist anti-pornography activism are not the only reason for Bright's wrath. She is, in common with all the lesbian sex gurus, concerned about the damage suffered by individual lesbians. 'Even lesbians who weren't indoctrinated by feminism', she writes, 'too often had their sexual lives ruled by secrecy and shame.'[57] Her conclusion, shared with others such as Gayle Rubin, is that feminism is an effective intellectual and political structure for understanding gender, but that it is inadequate when faced with the erotic, and she shares Califia's refusal to tolerate the feminist tendency to elide socio-economic oppression and sexual fantasy:

The real question is: How can feminist ideology incorporate *your* desires? As helpful as feminism has been in explaining gender differences, it has not yet developed as a philosophy that explains sexuality, or the erotic.

Understanding why you are making fifty-nine cents to every man's dollar is hardly the jumping-off point to determining the source of your lust.[58]

Where Califia might concede that economic oppression may well have an influence on the 'source' of lesbian lust, Bright – less thoughtful and more impatient of feminism – demarcates the erotic from the social with an unsophisticated certainty. Her refusal to engage with radical-feminist critiques of the erotic leave her firmly situated in a traditional libertarian position. Describing a conference of booksellers, Bright compares the 'local feminist author who ... said she wouldn't attend unless *On Our Backs* and other sexually explicit literature were taken off the shelves' to the group of concerned Christian citizens who demanded that the shelves be cleared of '*Playboy* ... all the astrology, tarot, and Eastern religion books'. Her libertarian approach leaves her no alternative but to lump both interventions together and dismiss them as evidence of hypocritical moralism: 'Put all censors on notice that I consider their efforts totalitarian piggery, and their horror of explicit sexuality a thin veneer for their own ignorance and hypocritical morality.'[59]

Reducing feminists and religious fundamentalists to 'totalitarian pigs' is mere name-calling. However understandable Bright's rage in the face of these attempts to control what others may read, it does not offer a way of understanding and challenging what are, in fact, very different forms of repression.

As a sex educator and performer, Bright is active in the front line of sexual politics. In the USA, it is a front line which is more dangerous than anything which has (yet) been seen in the UK, and the dangers which she has confronted are frighteningly immediate: 'In Northampton, Massachusetts, a police escort advised me not to eat out for fear of an anti-porn sniper attack. I was so angry and tearful – I didn't want to die for lesbian porn in western Massachusetts.'[60] Her agenda is broad, her interests catholic. She discusses everything from fist-fucking to Camille Paglia, from her own bisexuality to the struggles of women living with HIV and/or AIDS to 'heal their sexuality'. Like Califia and Nestle she is extraordinarily self-revelatory, but, like Annie Sprinkle, she takes self-exposure one critical stage further, to the point where it becomes exhibitionism and blurs into performance. Bright describes in detail her experiences masturbating with Chinese Healing Balls; what it was like having her labia pierced ('I did discover a surprising sound effect the first time I used my vibrator'[61]); how she dealt with the pain of childbirth by eroticizing the sensations; and how she ended up giving a public demonstration of using dental dams for cunnilingus – with the campus Lutheran minister as her volunteer guinea pig.

Bright is probably the most proactive sex instructor among the lesbian sex gurus. She shares with her fellow gurus the determination to dispel the myth that lesbian sex happens 'naturally': 'Oh sodomy. ... It doesn't come naturally just because you're gay. We stumble and fumble and watch dirty movies for tips, but there's a lot to lesbian sex that doesn't get talked about.'[62] But, where Loulan or Califia are happy to publish instruction manuals, Bright takes the teaching business that characteristic stage further. Not only does she offer written instruction on sexual technique – interspersed with entertaining anecdotes – she actually goes out and shows you what to do. She has given public demonstrations of fist-fucking, safer-sex techniques, how to locate your G-spot and the uses of a variety of sex toys. Then, instantly increasing the teaching potential of each workshop, she publishes accounts of what took place in *On Our Backs* and in her books.

There can be little doubt that Susie Bright and Susie Sexpert between them have had a beneficial effect on many lesbians' sex lives and self-esteem. But her oversimplistic approach does lead to problems. In her eagerness to ditch the guilt-inducing moralism of lesbian feminism, Bright too often confuses mouthing-off with political analysis. Her version of 'the personal is political' sometimes elides personal revelation and simple exhibitionism, and her sexual libertarianism is too restricted a perspective to enable her to realize a vision of lesbian sexuality which is anything other than good clean *fun*. In Bright's world, anything which gets in the way of her pleasure risks being labelled politically reactionary. This may be a useful strategy for reclaiming sexual pleasure, but it is lousy politics. And, since Bright does not hesitate to proclaim her approach *political,* despite the rudimentary nature of her political analysis, it too often results in a kind of dishonest, manipulative game-playing which is hard to stomach.

A prime example is the defensive article in *Sexual Reality* where she comes out as bisexual. Detailing a painful history of losing her girlfriends to men and then dumping her own girlfriend for a man, she shamelessly manipulates the political language of both feminism and Queer to justify her behaviour:

> I understand now that a mouthful like 'heterosexual privilege' doesn't have anything to do with the luxury or honour of bedding down with my oppressor – or my mentor. It's just an academic way to describe the flat-out devastation of losing your woman to a man.[43]

No, Susie, it isn't! To reduce the feminist critique of the institution of heterosexuality to simple jealousy is as underhand and silly a piece of childishness as any anti-lesbian propaganda the boys on the right have ever come up with. Bright continues by detailing her guilt at ditching her girlfriend for a man:

> My shame at leaving my girlfriend, who had fucked me in the ass with her arm, who had tasted every fluid in my body, who had ... loved me so well – how could I do this to her? Just watch me – and then watch yourself follow in my footsteps.[44]

And this is, finally, what Bright's libertarianism comes down to. We all, inevitably, behave badly. Sometimes it is fun to behave badly – when 'behaving badly' means breaking the rules of repressive governments and repressive feminists – and that is liberation. At other times, it hurts to behave badly, and that's just human nature.

Sexperts and gurus – towards the future

The combined forces of mainstream homophobia, misogyny and a particular brand of puritanical feminism – all determined to bring disobedient lesbian sexuality firmly under control (if not to eradicate it altogether) – exert a political, social and cultural pressure on lesbian sex which is unique. No other sexual minority is subject to the same degree of remorseless and judgemental scrutiny. Caught between the anxious masters of heterosexual ideology, who proclaim lesbian sex to be immature, inadequate, inauthentic and insignificant and the domineering mistresses of political-lesbian ideology, who declare that authentic lesbian sex must be egalitarian, purged of suspect association with desire, lust, pleasure or other manly attributes, lesbian sex has needed its gurus urgently.

It is perhaps unsurprising that it is in the USA, with its alternative culture of personal growth, twelve-step programmes and the kind of intimate self-exposure exemplified by guests of Oprah or Donaghue, that the lesbian sex guru has emerged. In the UK we may have (briefly) nurtured *Quim*, the most stylish lesbian sex magazine of them all, and there are certainly plenty of lesbian feminists prepared to speak out against the repressive tactics of the heterosexual mainstream and political lesbianism, but we have as yet produced no lesbian sex gurus. Nor is there a British equivalent of Dr Ruth or Annie Sprinkle.

The sex wars have had a lasting effect in the UK, with many feminist and community bookshops refusing to stock explicit books on lesbian sex, and many feminist publishers unwilling to take the risk of publishing them. A notable exception has been the feminist publishing collective Sheba, which took the bold step of publishing the first British collection of lesbian erotic writing, *Serious Pleasure,* in 1989. Sheba were called pornographers for doing so, but the anthology sold well enough for them to follow it up with *Serious Pleasure Two.* 1995 saw the publication by Pandora of the first British Lesbian sex manual, Zoe Schramm-Evans's *Making Out: The Book of Lesbian Sex and Sexuality.* In a radical break from the time honoured (and money-saving) tradition of illustrating lesbian sex manuals with drawings, *Making Out* is graced with full-colour and half-tone photographs by Laurence Jaugey-Paget, a regular contributor to *Quim*. It might be called the first lesbian coffee-table sex book.

The lavish production values of *Making Out* are simply out of the financial reach of small lesbian or feminist publishing houses. Pandora is an imprint of the large mainstream publisher HarperCollins, and the publication of *Making Out* marks the increasing respectability and profitability of the lesbian market for such commercial publishing houses. Adopting a liberal and *laissez-faire* tone, the book attempts to appear encyclopaedic, with an alphabetical structure covering Anus to Vanilla. Activities from scat to s/m, enemas to group sex are briefly discussed in a non-committal and detached tone which is a million miles away from the self-revelatory intimacy of Califia, Nestle or Bright. The book is undoubtedly useful: practical advice in the sections on sexual health, sex in pregnancy and sex gear is not easy to come by in mainstream sex manuals. When feminist and community bookshops refuse to stock lesbian sex manuals from the American small presses, such as Califia's *Sapphistry*, the large mainstream bookshop chains like Waterstones and Blackwells are unlikely even to have heard of them or, if they have, to think it worth their while importing them. A slick, full-colour publication from an established publisher is a different matter. For this reason alone, *Making Out* is likely to be far more accessible to lesbians than other lesbian sex manuals.

Schramm-Evans is, however, no lesbian sex guru. The cover blurb refers to her 'direct, informative and no-nonsense style', and if that makes her sound like your PE teacher at school, that's fairly accurate. Perusing *Making Out* leaves the reader with the impression that lesbian sex is a collection of rather jolly activities open to any woman who is a good sport. Schramm-Evans manages to make rimming, getting fucked by a man and s/m sound like activities a Girl Guide might be awarded a badge for. No doubt such determined demystification of lesbian sex offers support to the anxious or curious lesbian novice, but the result is unnervingly clinical and tame. Moreover, the superficial tone of the text denies or conceals the conflictual and complex social, cultural and psychological factors which shape lesbian sexuality and sexual practice.[65] The ugly history of the struggle over lesbian s/m is reduced to a minority political *taste*: 'While many people may find the notion of sexual slavery politically incorrect or distasteful, the fact is that it has always been a part of the general sexual fantasies of both women and men,'[66] while the highly theoretical argument about penetration is referred to so obliquely that anyone unfamiliar with the terms of the debate would be thoroughly confused:

> Surely, anything that two women do together can only be inherently lesbian, even if they were consciously to imitate heterosexual activity? ... questions of the 'correctness' of a behaviour seem at last to be fading away in favour of pleasure for its own sake and for many women, penetration can be supremely pleasurable.[67]

These and other comments make it clear that Schramm-Evans is addressing a highly specific audience – young assertive, urban dykes who are integrated to varying degrees into queer culture – and her book reflects and reproduces *as hegemonic within lesbian subculture* the values of that group.

Many other lesbians who write about lesbian sex share this tendency: they write as if the values of their peer group were *the* values of *the* lesbian community. Thus, while Julia Penelope takes it completely for granted that 'real' lesbians abhor s/m and lesbian pornography, JoAnn Loulan assumes that her models of addiction, recovery and healing may be generally applied to all lesbian relationships. These are women who think they have access to a privileged truth. Joan Nestle and Pat Califia, on the other hand, know that there is no such thing as a 'truth' about lesbian sex. As working-class women, and as women who have had to fight other lesbians for the right to have their sexual choices recognized, Califia and Nestle know full well that there are many truths to be spoken about lesbian sex, and that there are no 'right' choices. They therefore work hard to construct a space in which *other women's voices* may be heard. In this they are very different from those lesbian writers who speak from the position of privileged truth-telling, and who construct, in consequence, a monolithic model of lesbian sex.

Whereas Penelope's monolithic model of lesbian sex is the archetypal politically correct feminist version, Schramm-Evans adopts the archetypal *laissez-faire* libertarian model (which is, of course, simply political correctness of a different order). Purged of conflict, uncertainty or complexity, just as surely as political lesbian sex is purged of anything male-identified, woman-hating or heterosexual, this model is just as unreal and equally tyrannical. It's foundational ideology (basically, 'anything goes' liberalism) is simply inadequate to the task of constructing a complex, textured understanding of sexuality, and it also results in an oversimplification which is often unhelpful. For example, where feminist-identified lesbian sex instructors take great care to pay more than cursory attention to the needs of disabled lesbians, Schramm-Evans allocates an insultingly brief three paragraphs. In contrast to the (superficially) explicit detail in the rest of the book, there is nothing here about the practicalities of sex for lesbians with impairments, just a vaguely liberal sermon about stating your needs, sharing with a partner and the need to 'believe ourselves to be lovable'. She concludes:

> Disabled women give as well as receive and can be a source of calm and reassurance. We are all part of the same body, sick and healthy, old and young. We can ignore this fact only at the cost of diminishing ourselves.[68]

This limp pseudo-mysticism is not only naff it is insulting to disabled lesbians who are entitled to expect more from a book on lesbian sex than pious assurances that they can give as well as receive. In the light of ongoing political activism on the part of the disability rights movement, these three saccharine paragraphs represent a refusal to recognize and engage with this increasingly vocal section of the lesbian community. You don't get to be a lesbian sex guru by confining your words to any kind of elite.

Virtual sex gurus? Towards the future

As lesbians, we have needed our sex gurus to help make sense of a chaotic babble of voices all determined to tell us what lesbian sex *really* is. They have fought hard, against what has sometimes seemed to be an invincible army of religious bigots – the right wing, the lesbian sex prefects, the press and media and the mainstream political establishment – to carve out a space for lesbian desire and pleasure. It is hard to imagine what the role of the lesbian sex guru might be in the future, and who will emerge as the next generation of gurus. Technological developments such as the internet, with its queer bulletin boards and dyke link-ups, or virtual reality sex with headsets, electronic gloves and computer-generated images seem to promise a hedonistic utopia. Who will control your fantasies as you surf the internet or conjure up

Martina, kd and/or Jody to partner you in virtual lovemaking?

Well, that's the problem. The technosphere is controlled by the boys, and it costs money. Lesbians, being among the poorer groups in the developed West, are ill-equipped economically to dictate the development of new technology. Women are certainly getting involved in the design and development of these new toys, but it remains a male-dominated sphere. Silicon valley may be crawling with Digital Queers (and certainly Michelangelo Signorile tells us it is[69]), but it is the queens, not the dykes, who have their fingers on the keyboards and joypads. (Speaking personally, I've never managed to get beyond level 1 of *Sonic the Hedgehog*, so the thought of getting hopelessly stuck trying to undo the virtual fly buttons on the lesbian computer sprite of my choice does not appeal!)

The sex wars may not be over – no peace treaty has been signed and there are still plenty of stray bullets flying around – but the fragmentation of lesbian community life means that it is at least possible to behave as if they had. The mainstream commercialization of lesbianism offers the seductive illusion that right-wing politicians and the lesbian sex prefects have crumbled in the face of the pink pound/dollar. The approach adopted by a new-style postmodern, postqueer, postfeminist lesbian sex manual such as *Making Out*, is an uneasy 'if we ignore them, they'll go away'. Yet for every glossy coffee-table sex book there is a Dale County Ordinance or a Section 28 to fight. For every lesbian sex magazine launched there is a preacher offering to 'cure' lesbians and gay men. We may be e-mailing hot erotica to each other across the planet, or grappling with Ripley in our personal rerun of '*Aliens on Lesbos*', but you can bet your plug-in modem that somebody will be trying to stop us. With the current rapid transformation of technology, and a future that remains so unpredictable, I'm not going to hazard a guess about what we will all be doing in ten years' time. But I suspect we will still need lesbian sex gurus in one form or another.

Notes

1. Joan Nestle, *A Restricted Country: Essays and Short Stories* (London: Sheba, 1987), p. 148.
2. Launceston, Cornwall or Launceston, Tasmania, either will do. And I'm willing to bet there's a Launceston or two in the USA too.
3. I use Common Era (CE) here rather

than the traditional Anno Domini (AD). CE is increasingly used as a non-eurocentric, non-Judaeo/Christian-specific historical measure.

4. Leonore Tiefer, *Sex Is Not a Natural Act and Other Essays* (Oxford: Westview Press, 1995), p. 6.

5. John Muirhead-Gould (ed.), *The Kama Sutra of Vatsyayana* trans. by Sir Richard Burton and F. F. Arbuthnot (London: Panther Books, 1963).

6. Stella Browne (1923), cited in Sheila Jeffreys, *The Spinster and Her Enemies: Feminism and Sexuality 1880–1930* (London: Pandora, 1985), p. 116. Although I disagree quite stringently with Jeffreys's political position, her feminist deconstruction of traditional sex manuals is scholarly and insightful.

7. In Jeffreys, *The Spinster and Her Enemies*, p. 137.

8. In Sheila Jeffreys, *Anticlimax: A Feminist Perspective on the Sexual Revolution* (London: The Women's Press, 1990), p. 9.

9. In Jeffreys, *The Spinster and Her Enemies*, pp. 130–1.

10. In Jeffreys, *Anticlimax*, p. 28.

11. Judith Hubback, *Wives Who Went to College* (London: William Heinemann, 1957), p. 150.

12. Helen Gurley Brown, *Sex and the Single Girl* (New York: Bernard Geiss, 1962), p. 78.

13. Del Martin and Phyllis Lyon, *Lesbian/Woman* (New York: Bantam Books, 1972, reprinted 1995).

14. Ginny Vida (ed.), *Our Right to Love: A Lesbian Resource Book* (Englewood Cliffs, NJ: Prentice-Hall, 1978).

15. *Loving Women* (1976) is now out of print as far as I can gather, but excerpts from it are reprinted in Vida (ed.), *Our Right to Love*.

16. Sheila Jeffreys, 'Butch and Femme: Now and Then', *Gossip*, No. 5,

(London: Onlywomen Press, 1987), p. 90.

17. Kathryn Harriss, *What Is This Big Fuss about Sadomasochism? Lesbian Sexuality and the Women's Liberation Movement* (University of Kent at Canterbury, Women's Studies Occasional Papers, 1988), p. 9.

18. Dolores Klaich, *Woman Plus Woman* (Tallahassee, FL: Naiad, 1974); Sydney Abbott and Barbara Love, *Sappho Was a Right-On Woman: A Liberated View of Lesbianism*, (New York: Stein and Day, 1972); Trudy Darty and Sandee Potter, *Woman-Identified Woman* (Palo Alto: Mayfield, 1984).

19. JoAnn Loulan, *Lesbian Sex* (San Francisco: Spinsters Ink/Aunt Lute, 1984); Pat Califia, *Sapphistry: The Book of Lesbian Sexuality* (Tallahassee, FL: Naiad, 1980, revised 1983 and 1988).

20. For an account of Annie Sprinkle's performance, see Anna Douglas, 'Annie Sprinkle: Post Post Porn Modernist', *New Formations*, No. 19, pp. 95–109.

21. JoAnn Loulan, *Lesbian Passion: Loving Ourselves and Each Other* (San Francisco: Spinsters Ink/Aunt Lute, 1987).

22. Loulan, *Lesbian Sex*, p. 3.

23. *Ibid.*, p. 23.

24. *Ibid.*, p. 47.

25. *Ibid.*

26. Loulan, *Lesbian Passion*, p. 95.

27. *Ibid.*, p. 97.

28. *Ibid.*, pp. 7–20.

29. Loulan, *Lesbian Sex*, p. 3.

30. *Ibid.*, pp. 7–8.

31. Audre Lorde, *Sister Outsider: Essays and Speeches* (New York: The Crossing Press, 1984), p. 110.

32. In Nestle, *A Restricted Country*.

33. Joan Nestle (ed.), *The Persistent Desire: A Femme-Butch Reader* (Boston: Alyson, 1992).

34. Reprinted in Nestle, *A Restricted*

Country.

35. *Ibid.*, p. 103.
36. *Ibid.*, p. 106.
37. *Ibid.*, p. 146.
38. *Ibid.*, p. 150.
39. This is how she describes herself in Pat Califia, *The Advocate Adviser*, (Boston: Alyson, 1991), p. xii.
40. Mandy Merck , *Perversions: Deviant Readings* (London: Virago, 1993), p. 250. This is not Merck's own perspective on s/m.
41. Califia, *Sapphistry*, p. 54.
42. In Robin Linden, Darlene Pagano, Diana Russell & Susan Leigh Starr (eds.), *Against Sadomasochism: A Radical Feminist Analysis* (San Francisco: Frog in the Well Press, 1982), p. 91.
43. *Ibid.*, p. 92. Atkinson does not bother to clarify who exactly she is speaking for here, nor does she satisfy her readers' curiosity as to whether their fantasies became *sadistic* as a result of political involvement.
44. Pat Califia, *Macho Sluts* (Boston: Alyson, 1988), p. 19.
45. *Ibid.*, p. 20.
46. *Ibid.*, p. 11.
47. *Ibid.*, pp. xi–xiii.
48. *Ibid.*, p. xiii.
49. *Ibid.*, p. 95.
50. See above, pp. 41–73 for detailed discussion of the lesbian-feminist debates on lesbian s/m.
51. Califia, *Macho Sluts,* p. 119.
52. *Ibid.*, p. 119.

53. Califia, *Advocate Advisor,* p. ix.
54. Susie Bright, *Susie Sexpert's Lesbian Sex World* (San Francisco: Cleis Press, 1990), p. 14.
55. *Ibid.*, p. 11.
56. *Ibid.*, p. 13.
57. *Ibid.*, p. 14.
58. *Ibid.*, p. 30.
59. *Ibid.*, p. 58.
60. Susie Bright, *Susie Bright's Sexual Reality: A Virtual Sex World Reader* (San Francisco: Cleis Press, 1992), p. 14
61. *Ibid.*, p. 143.
62. *Ibid.*, p. 79.
63. *Ibid.*, p. 154.
64. *Ibid.*, pp. 155–6.
65. Please note that my criticisms here relate to the *text* of *Making Out*; Laurence Jaugey-Paget's photographs are something else altogether, and are discussed in some detail in Chapter 6.
66. Zoe Schramm-Evans, *Making Out: The Book of Lesbian Sex and Sexuality* (London: Pandora, 1995), p. 147.
67. *Ibid.*, p. 133.
68. *Ibid.*, p. 15.
69. Michelangelo Signorile, *Queer in America: Sex, the Media and the Closets of Power* (London: Abacus, 1993).

5

Seeing Dirty?
Lesbians and Pornography

Consider for a moment the meaning of the word 'homoerotic' as applied to the visual arts. If a painting, print, photograph or film is called homoerotic, it means that it represents *men* as objects of desire, objects of the desiring gaze. Think what this says about the relations of power which structure desire and the erotic in Western culture. Calling representations of men as objects of desire 'homoerotic' – literally, erotic to members of the same sex – covertly recognizes two (related) socio-cultural 'facts': first, that it is not possible for a woman to desire a man, or to look at a man's body with erotic pleasure; and second, that it is not possible for a woman to desire a woman, or to look at a woman's body with desire. If it were possible for women to turn a desiring gaze upon men, then there would be no need to call eroticized representations of men *homo*erotic; they could simply be *erotic*, the assumption being that women would find them erotic. If it were possible for women to turn a desiring gaze upon women, then there would be no need for the word 'homoerotic' at all. After all, if our assumption is that either men or women could find images of either men or women erotic, then Botticelli's *Birth of Venus* would be no more and no less *homo*erotic than Michelangelo's *David*.

The very difficulty of excavating the implications of homoeroticism as a concept exposes the degree to which our culture assumes that eroticism is unidirectional, and that it is utterly polarized along lines of gender. If eroticized images of men are *homo*erotic, then desire is something which men own and women arouse, the desiring gaze is something which is the property of men and which they turn upon women, and erotic pleasure is sought by men and provided by women. In short, the erotic is a realm of consumption in which men are the consumers and women are the product. Part of the stigma of male homosexuality lies in the fact that when the desiring male gaze lights on a body, these eroticized relations of power construct that gazed-upon body as feminized by the very act of being looked at with desire.

Clearly this paradigm does not reflect any intrinsic biological or psychological 'truth' about male or female sexuality. However, it does reflect a social, cultural and political truth. For the means whereby ideas are turned into texts, symbols and images have historically been controlled by men. In the binary relationship of 'artist and model', the artist is male, the model female. In addition, there is always an invisible third person in this equation – the one who pays for the art, who looks at it, consumes it, owns it – and that third person is also gendered male. Almost always he *is* male, since throughout history it has been men who have had the economic and social power necessary to employ artists, to collect paintings, to make and destroy artistic careers and reputations. So, in 'art', women's bodies have become a commodity commanding an exchange rate between men. It is also the case that it is white ruling-class men who have control over the machinery of representation, such that working-class people or people of colour have also been constructed as the object rather than the subject/owner of the gaze.

The importance of this analysis goes far beyond academic debates about the fine arts or equal opportunities issues in the art world – although these are all important, and feminist activists such as the Guerrilla Girls have developed a sustained critique of sexism in art. Textual practice (the making of books, films, paintings, prints, photographs, videos, plays, etc.) does far more than merely reflect the social reality of its time; it plays an active part in the construction of that reality. Living in a culture where pictures of naked women are called *erotic* and pictures of naked men are labelled *homoerotic* profoundly influences the development of a desiring, sexual sense of self for women and men. In a postindustrial Western culture saturated with visual imagery, gender identity and sexual identity must be negotiated in response to multiple (and proliferating) iconographies of sex. Pictures are not socially irrelevant decoration, they contribute to the cultural construction of 'reality'. As such, visual culture exerts a significant influence on the material world. This is the analysis which lies behind behind both the feminist critique of pornography and the assertion that the production of lesbian 'porn' is a political act. Yet despite this shared theoretical foundation, the two positions have become polarized, facing each other with intense hostility over a seemingly unbridgeable gap. The 'porn wars' are far from over, and their legacy has been incalculably damaging both for feminists and for queers. Moreover, a moderately rigorous unpicking of the arguments on both sides soon reveals that the apparent polarization of the two sides in this war is the result of misreading, theoretical sloppiness and a depressingly familiar tendency for feminists to score own goals.

The porn wars – a brief history of pro-censorship feminism

Early 'second-wave' feminism initially incorporated sexual experiment-ation for women into its political agenda. Germaine Greer wrote for the radical underground sex magazine *Screw*, and had a short stint as a sexual agony aunt for *Oz*, under the *nom de plume* 'Dr G.'. Feminists joined forces with other radicals in opposing censorship (or 'censorshit', as we called it in my radical hippy peer group) of all kinds. Yet this erotic enthusiasm could not survive in the face of steadily mounting evidence of the extent of men's sexual violence against women, as Marilyn French recounts:

> Those were days of innocence ... we did not yet know what twenty-odd years of feminism have revealed: the dimensions, cruelty and pervasiveness of men's unconscionable treatment of women in actual life, concealed behind the lace curtains of the home generations of male-supremacists called sacred.[1]

Women set about establishing rape crisis lines and refuges for battered women, fighting for revisions in the law on rape and assault and for changes in the way in which the police and the judiciary dealt with these crimes. But it was not (and is not) adequate simply to deal with the consequences of men's sexual violence; there was a clear need to account for it. The evidence is overwhelming: the sexual abuse of women by men is so commonplace as to be routine in the so-called 'first world.'[2] What is, as yet, missing is an *explanation*.

As feminists worked to relieve the symptoms of male sexual violence through the pragmatic activism of rape crisis lines and refuges, an urgent attempt was made to understand and prevent the *causes* of that violence. The focus fell on pornography, to the extent that it became *the* central issue for feminist activism in the 1970s and 1980s, a place it continues to hold for many feminists today. There is a tendency among some old-style liberal and socialist feminists to represent the pornography debate as a temporary, hysterical distraction from the real business of liberating women from material constraints. In 1984, Betty Friedan urged feminists to 'Get off the pornography kick and face the real obscenity of poverty',[3] while Carla Freccero writes that 'It seems astonishing, from the perspective of 1989, that pornography should have become so important in feminist movements and that it should have provoked such bitter animosities and deep divisions.'[4] Freccero's 'we've all grown out of that pornography stuff now' position is both a misrepresentation of the feminist *present* – pornography continues to constitute the primary arena of activism for large numbers of feminists – and a highly partial rereading of the feminist past. Lynne Segal, despite sharing Freccero's anti-censorship politics, is less inclined to rewrite history:

> Anti-pornography feminism is compelling because it makes intuitive sense. Much of pornography is at the very least complicit in some of the most offensive aspects of our sexist, male-centred culture: it appears to position men as active and powerful, women as commodified – objects, not subjects. ... Unlike liberals, concerned only with freedom of speech, untroubled by questions of whose speech is heard, feminists have always seen cultural production as a site of political struggle.[5]

Segal is one of the few socialist feminists who recognize that the ferocity of the feminist assault on porn was motivated by shock at the newly revealed phenomenon of routine sexualized violence against women and the desperate need to understand the roots of that violence. This dilemma, far from being a radical red herring, lies at the very heart of feminist politics. For, if the roots of male sexual violence are *innate*, as some feminists suggest, then feminism may only achieve women's liberation through the eradication of men. If, on the other hand, the violence of men's sexuality (and the sexualized nature of male violence) is a cultural and social artefact – if men are *made* violent by the same institutions and social structures that make women passive – then it is possible to change men (and women). Surely this is foundational, for a genocidal feminist politic makes no sense within its own terms, whereas a transformational feminist politic has a point!

When the new generation of 'second-wave' feminists delved into the jealously guarded male territory of rape, abuse and pornography, the truths they uncovered were monstrous. As Andrea Dworkin pointed out, the routine abuse and injury of women indicates that women are simply not recognized as fully human: 'What breaks the spirit of those fighting for women's rights is that one can never take for granted a realization that a woman is an actual human being who, when hurt, is hurt.'[6] From this perspective, pornography, the textual practice which most explicitly constructs and packages female sexuality in the interests of male pleasure, is always already a political practice.

Feminist anti-porn rhetoric is compelling, since the visual evidence is available to everyone. Moreover, many studies have shown that there was a measurable increase in representations of sadistic violence towards women in pornography during the height of the feminist critique, and it is clear that, to some extent at least, pornography reflects one aspect of the male response to feminist challenge. Dworkin certainly identifies sadistic porn as an attempt to punish women for resisting male power:

> Fascist propaganda celebrating sexual violence against women is sweeping the land. Fascist propaganda celebrating the sexual degradation of women is inundating cities, college campuses, small towns. Pornography is the propaganda of sexual fascism. ... Female rebellion against male sexual despotism ... is now a reality through-out this country. The men, meeting rebellion with an escalation of terror, hang pictures of maimed female bodies in every public place.[7]

It is in Dworkin's use of the word 'propaganda' that the complexities of the pornography debate lie. It is clear that male sexual violence against, and abuse of, women is commonplace. It is also clear that pornographic representations of women's bodies by and for men are equally commonplace. It is reasonable to suggest that both are cofactorial in some way in the wider social subordination of women, as a class, to men as a class. Indeed, on the evidence it is unreasonable to suggest otherwise. Yet the nature of the relationship between them – between the image and the act – remains indeterminate, as does the relationship between porn, male violence and male supremacy.

The feminist critique of porn incorporates four quite distinct theories of the relationship between pornographic images and the subordination of women. Some suggest that the consumption of pornography *directly incites* men to abuse women, others that pornography is complicit in the general cultural construction of gender relations and sexuality; some focus on the abuse of women during the making of pornography, while others insist that porn is an expression of male sexual *anxiety*, acting to assuage the psychic distress caused by the always already doomed attempt to embody phallic masculinity.

Anti-censorship activists, whether or not they speak as feminists, all too often reduce this complexity to a simplistic naivety. In their accounts, anti-porn feminists reduce male supremacy to sex, see pornography as the primary cause of women's oppression, and distort the available evidence to fit this argument. This anti-censorship position is exemplified by Carla Freccero, who concludes that 'relationships between cultural forms and consumers are mediated in ways far more complex than the anti-porn movement suggests.'[8] Yet this is to misrepresent the anti-porn agenda which, although it indeed incorporates individual accounts which suffer from gross oversimplification, constitutes on the whole a set of analyses which acknowledge and attempt to deal with the complex and often contradictory dynamic of the pornographic enterprise. It is only by paying insufficient attention to the multiple and shifting critique of anti-porn feminism that feminists such as Kate Ellis *et al.* are able to conclude that anti-porn feminists have simply scapegoated pornography for the wider ills of sexism:

> We believe that the frustration engendered by two decades of working against the most egregious expression of sexism, male violence against women, has led many women, often unfamiliar with pornography ... to scapegoat *sexual images* in their search for the real cause of this seemingly incurable social evil.[9] (my italics)

The use of 'sexual images' in this passage highlights a familiar and unhelpful strategy of anti-censorship discourse, to elide the pornographic and the merely sexually explicit in order to accuse anti-porn feminists of being 'against' *all* sexual imagery. Despite repeated statements from leading anti-porn feminists that it is *not* sexual explicitness *per se* which is problematic about pornography,[10] this misrepresentation remains central to some of the most vigorous attacks on their position. Examining the four key strands of the feminist anti-porn position in some detail will help to clarify the continuing importance of at least part of their analysis.

The idea that pornography is the direct cause of men's sexual violence towards women is hotly contested both between feminists and outside feminism. Legal hearings on pornography in the USA, such as those accompanying the Meese Commission or the Minneapolis Ordinance, have recorded the testimony of dozens of women who describe the direct part played by pornographic publications in their experience of rape and sexual abuse. It is unarguably the case that men have frequently forced women to carry out behaviours described or depicted in pornographic texts, or that they have used pornography to justify their behaviour. Yet this is not at all the same thing as claiming that pornography *causes* such abuse. As Canadian artists' collective Kiss and Tell comment, to hold pornographic imagery *responsible* for men's abuse of women ultimately results in absolving men and restricting women:

> Whatever happened to men being held responsible for their own actions? The shift in assigning the responsibility for rape to sexual imagery, rather than actual people, is chilling. To say that a woman shouldn't explore her sexuality (the hard parts as well as the sweet parts) because it might incite men to rape is an old, old line.[11]

It is difficult to imagine how a direct causal relationship between the consumption of pornography and sexual violence on an individual level could ever be finally proven. There is plenty of circumstantial evidence linking the two, but correlation is not the same thing as causation. The best conclusion which may be drawn from the evidence as it currently stands is that the men who rape and abuse women are often consumers of pornography, and that they most certainly do force women against their will to submit to practices depicted in that pornography.[12] But pornography is an enormous industry – among the largest in the developed West – and it must be concluded with some certainty that the men who do *not* rape and abuse women are the majority of its consumers, simply because the consumers of pornography constitute such a massive social cohort. Given that this is the case, it is as logical to claim that consuming pornography *prevents* men raping and abusing women as it is to claim that pornography *causes* these behaviours.

In fact, it is only possible to claim that consuming pornography leads to violence in the context of a model of male sexuality which sees it as intrinsically violent. Some radical feminists, including Andrea Dworkin, do use such a model:

Pornography does not exist to effect something as vague as so-called erotic interest or sexual arousal; it exists specifically to provoke penile tumescence or erection. In male-supremacist sexuality, the penis is a carrier of aggression, a weapon, the standard-bearer of male identity, the proof and the measure of masculinity. ... The use of the penis to conquer is its natural use.[13]

If erection is the prelude to the 'natural' act of aggression against women, then of course anything which provokes erection can be seen as inevitably resulting in such violence. Why, then, bother with feminism at all? Such essentialism is a theoretical and political dead end, and makes feminism a necessarily androcidal (or at least, castrating) enterprise.

So, the argument that pornography provokes individual men to acts of sexual violence against women is both tenuous and politically unhelpful. The more sophisticated perspective argues that pornography is an especially powerful agent in the hegemonic cultural construction of gender and of sexualities. Many anti-censorship feminists reject the idea that pornography contributes in any way to the oppression of women; this position is generally held by socialist feminists who have a materialist analysis of women's oppression. A typical approach is that of Anne McClintock who insists that 'Demonizing porn as a genre offers too easy a scapegoat for women's ills, and does little to alter the real conditions of women's lives.'[14] While few would disagree that 'demonizing' *any* practice is unhelpful, a deconstructive analysis of porn does, in fact, offer very useful material with which we may begin to alter the 'real conditions of women's lives'.

The weakness with materialism is that it cannot explain the origins of male supremacy in a satisfactory way. Thus Lynne Segal, summarizing the position of Feminists Against Censorship in the UK, writes that 'They believe men's cultural contempt for and sexualization of women long predated the growth of commercial pornography and is a product of the relative powerlessness of women as a sex.'[15] Not only is this a rather extreme misrepresentation of anti-porn feminism (even the most outrageous anti-porn propaganda does not claim that men's contempt for women started with commercial pornography), it is a surprisingly naive perspective on cultural production. To suggest that the codes of pornography (which Segal somewhat confusingly summarizes as cultural contempt and sexualization) are the result of women's 'relative powerlessness ... as a sex' is to naturalize that powerlessness and, more importantly, to fail to understand the dialectical relationship between culture and cultural product. Cultural texts do not simply reflect the culture which produces them, they have an effect on it. They may reproduce and hence reinforce its dominant values – as in the case of tabloid newspapers, TV soaps, advertisements, etc. – or they may challenge and try to undermine those dominant values, setting up a discourse which is *oppositional* to the mainstream. For example, most lesbian-authored books, music, works of art, films, videos, theatre performances, etc. are engaged in contributing to an oppositional discourse around questions of sex, gender, desire and identity.

So, while it goes without saying that commercial pornography did not *originate* men's contempt for women, or the sexualization of women's bodies, that particular discourse inevitably influences wider cultural beliefs, attitudes and behaviours. If pornography represents women as sexually passive, for example, that provides additional reinforcement to an already dominant set of beliefs held by both women and men. Moreover, most Western societies tend to enforce silence about sexual matters. Individual sexual 'problems' are seen as the proper business of medicine, especially psychiatry, and the question of sexual desire and pleasure is largely confined to the pages of pornography/erotica. Professor of psychiatry Leonore Tiefer comments:

> The societal message is that you *have* to be sexual, you have to *want* to be sexual. ... Yet there's no tradition of sexual coaching or intercourse training or masturbation training or honest feedback ... I and clinicians like me have become the friendly expert – which is ridiculous when you think about it in terms of cost, availability and the medical model context of therapy.[16]

This means that not only is pornography one discourse among many which contribute to the cultural construction of sexuality and gender but that it is a very powerful discourse. In the midst of a cultural silence about the doing of sex, the voice of explicit pornography is loud and clear. When Andrea Dworkin says that 'in a sex-polarized society men ... learn about women and sex from pornography',[17] she is right. Moreover, given that pornography both *reflects* pre-existing social reality and *reproduces* that reality, MacKinnon's analysis is right too:

If pornography is an act of male supremacy, its harm is the harm of male supremacy made difficult to see because of its pervasiveness, potency, and success in making the world a pornographic place. ... Women live in the world pornography creates.[18]

The second argument of the feminist critique of pornography thus holds good. And, since lesbians share the social position of women, this particular 'harm' of pornography is of concern to lesbians, whether or not pornographic images specifically represent 'lesbian' sexuality. But what about the third argument, the degree to which women are abused during the making of pornography? This again seems a difficult question to resolve. The most extreme example cited by feminists as evidence that women are abused during the production of pornography is the snuff movie: the claim being that women are actually tortured to death on screen in order to provide the ultimate in sexual entertainment. The films in question were popularly supposed to come from South America – 'where life is cheap', as the promotional material claimed – and to have been seized by American police when imported into the USA. The film *Snuff*, which apparently depicted a script girl being sliced to pieces and disembowelled, was made by 'slasher' filmmakers Michael and Roberta Findlay to capitalize on such rumours. As Harriett Gilbert suggests, whether or not the actresses were slaughtered in the making of snuff films 'may not be the important point (except, of course, to the actress concerned)'. For, as Gilbert points out:

> The fact remains that people paid to watch what they either believed to be, or thought *might* be, a woman being tortured and killed for their entertainment. Were they all insane? Or were they merely, as many women are quite convinced, enjoying the usual, sadistic heterosexual male pleasure, but magnified?[19]

The other key example of the abuse of women in the making of pornography is the often cited case of Linda Marchiano. As the porn actress 'Linda Lovelace' Marchiano starred in *Deep Throat*, and then went on to write a book entitled *Ordeal*, in which she describes how she was enslaved, tortured, battered and raped by her abusive husband. Catherine MacKinnon cites *Ordeal* as evidence of the abuses women suffer at the hands of pornographers. Yet, as Anne McClintock notes, it was marriage, not the porn industry, which was the cause and location of Marchiano's suffering: 'What is important ... is that while Marchiano became involved in porn only through [her husband's] coercion, it was the making of *Deep Throat*, her fame and renewed confidence that finally empowered her to escape her abuser.[20] In Linda Marchiano's own analysis, it was her new porn-star self which gave her the strength to escape: 'Linda Boreman and Linda Traynor never managed to get away from Chuck; it took a Linda Lovelace to escape.'[21] From this reading of Marchiano's account, it was working in pornography that gave her the courage to *escape* from appalling abuse. Ironically, although she in no sense claims to have enjoyed the work itself, and concludes that she is 'ambivalent' about her time as a porn actress, pornography became in some sense her lifeline.

Some of the most virulent and hostile attacks on feminists have come from those with a vested interest in defending pornography. From their perspective, the idea that women may be coerced into working for pornographers is simply evidence of feminist arrogance or stupidity:

> the desperate belief that women can only participate in pornography if they have either been forced or tricked in some way ... takes most models and actresses for fools, and is typical of a feminism which is endlessly searching for new ways to disavow the actual complexity and diversity of female sexuality ... [22]

This construction of feminism as a repressive project 'endlessly searching' to deny female sexuality is part of the familiar defensive male reaction to feminist criticism which seeks to disavow the actual complexity and diversity of women's oppression and of feminist activism. But what truth is there in this critique? Is the very idea of women being coerced into working for pornography a myth promulgated by deluded feminists?

Unsurprisingly, the evidence is contradictory. There are autobiographical accounts which make it clear that many women are indeed coerced into acting in pornographic photographs, videos and films, and that their experiences have been abusive in the extreme. Moreover, there are well-documented cases that have come before the courts, in which adult men videotape or photograph their sexual abuse of children.[23] But there are also other autobiographical accounts written by women who have worked in pornography which insist that their experience was not one of direct coercion or abuse. However, very few of these accounts present an unambiguously pleasurable experience. Rather, they reveal that the women chose the work because they needed the money and had no other way of earning it, and they retain a deep ambivalence towards the experience:

> I'm not glad I contributed to the pornography industry. ... I've read a lot of feminist theory, however, and I feel disloyal when I say that my movie experiences were not brutal and degrading. ... The last thing I want is for some young woman to read my essay and say, 'See? It's perfectly okay to be a porn model – it sounds like fun.' But does that mean that I should ... invent a brutality I didn't experience?[24]

A tiny minority of women working in porn do so from explicitly *feminist* principles. One such is Nina Hartley who believes that her work as a porn movie actress constitutes a positive imagery campaign:

> If the media can have an effect on people's behaviour, and I believe it does, why is it assumed that sex movies must always reinforce the most negative imagery of women? ... From my very first movie I have always refused to portray rape, coercion, pain-as-pleasure, woman-as-victim, domination, humiliation and other forms of non-consensual sex. ... I consider myself a reformer.[25]

The question of whether or not women are directly abused in the making of pornography is not an open question. There is ample evidence that many are, and this is criminal and abusive behaviour which cannot be sanctioned, whichever side of the 'porn wars' you happen to be speaking from. Moreover, as lesbian sex artist Susan Stewart cautions, the difference between abusive and non-abusive can be very subtle when making erotic photographs of women, simply because abuse and photography are so closely linked for many women:

> Without sensitivity the very act of *taking* a picture or *shooting* a scene can sometimes border dangerously on abuse. Many women can recall very harrowing encounters with photography, ranging from childhood abuse and coercive studio sessions to finding images of themselves displayed in exhibits or published without their knowledge or consent.[26]

Making pornography may be abusive to the women involved in many different ways. Working in porn is not, however, *necessarily* abusive. It is clear from some women's accounts that it can be a choice, and that it can even be politically motivated. This is a problem for a simplistic feminist critique of pornography, in that it foregrounds the troublesome truth that working in pornography may be functional for some women. Equally, many women are indirectly forced into various forms of sex work because they have to feed their children, pay medical bills or finance their way through education, and other ways of earning money are closed to them. In such a situation, the effective feminist solution is the transformation of women's economic position, not the eradication of pornography or attacks on women sex workers. In fact, anti-porn feminists have 'shown scant concern for the women and men who work in the sex industry', as McClintock's account of one episode shows:

> To their disgrace, WAP [Women Against Pornography] in New York teamed up with the boys at the League of New York Theater Owners and Producers and the 42nd Street Redevelopment Corporation, taking money and office space to help 'clean up' Times Square and coerce sex workers out of sight, out of mind and out of pocket.[27]

At such times it is hard not to conclude that some anti-pornography feminists express their concern for women sex workers in rather strange ways.

But what of the final argument, that pornography, rather than being an expression of male sexual power, constitutes an attempt to assuage male sexual *anxiety*? It has become something of a truism in gay men's thinking about sexuality that gay porn offers an antidote to the anxiety and self-loathing which may result from simply being a gay man in a homophobic culture.[28] It does this in two ways: first, by representing gay sex as positive, pleasurable and usual; and second, by reasserting the *masculine* nature of gay men's desire and sexuality in opposition to the wider cultural derogation of male homosexuality as effeminate and feminizing. It celebrates sexual masculinity by offering, in Tim Edwards' words, 'the simultaneous eroticisation and valorisation of masculinity.'[29] Many gay men, however, are troubled by the heavy socio-cultural burden borne by gay porn, recognizing its roots in circumstances not of their choosing:

> It's a curious situation in that our 'subculture' is positively defined in terms of its porn production, because it is to do with self-image.

News magazines carry sexual imagery, not because we're all sex-obsessed, but because we define ourselves positively by it. We're almost obliged to find our positive definitions *there*, as a resistance and response to the dominant's reduction of us to a sexual preference.[30]

Gay men, accustomed to problematizing their sexual praxis, have little hesitation in acknowledging that porn functions to reinforce gay masculinity, but few feminist or heterosexual male theorists suggest that the same may be true of straight men's porn. Anne McClintock, in her thoughtful critique of anti-porn feminism, engages with the work of some male writers who have defended pornography. She comments: 'I expected a volley of virile defensiveness, I was startled instead by the tone of male insecurity and sexual distress. ... Women are seldom privy to how much men are unmanned by desire.'[31] From the perspective of men 'unmanned by [heterosexual] desire', hetero porn is represented as fulfilling a similar function to gay men's porn. McClintock reads this account from a feminist position and reinscribes a feminist critique onto this pathetic scenario of damaged, yearning men:

> Porn, they claim, offers men a dream vacation from sexual scarcity, staging the delirious spectacle of erotically demanding women who 'freely surrender their powers of rejection'. Porn theatres are the body shops of society where men beat their egos back into serviceable shape. But is it any wonder, then, that women voice unease at the spectacle of our sexual agency managed on male terms for male affirmation?[32]

The suggestion that men, whether gay or hetero, turn to pornography to heal the cultural wounds of phallic masculinity does not absolve porn of harming women. As McClintock points out, it manipulates and mis-represents women's sexuality in the service of men's. However, it does indicate that the gendered pornographic relations constructed within mainstream feminist discourse – with men as the masters and women as the victims – is too monolithic and fails to take account of what may be a contradictory relationship between *men* and pornography.

But all this has concentrated on pornography made by men, gay or hetero, and on pornography as a practice which exemplifies and reinforces men's power over women. I am impatient to get back to lesbians. What effects have the porn wars had on dykes, and what can be said about lesbian 'porn'?

Anti-porn is the theory, violence the practice: feminist dirty tricks

If the feminist debates about pornography remained in the realm of theory, few could object. But the practical consequences of feminist anti-porn activism have been widespread and damaging in the extreme, ranging from the by now familiar tactic of stripping women of their feminist title to outright violence. The violence, particularly in the USA, has been extraordinary. In 1982, a direct-action group calling itself the Wimmen's Fire Brigade were jailed after admitting they were responsible for bombing three shops in the Red Hot Video chain in British Columbia.[33] Andrea Dworkin cites this incident approvingly, together with a catalogue of violent direct action carried out by feminists against pornography:

> In Ohio, Sisters of Justice destroy adult bookstores in lightning attacks. In Minnesota, a few hundred women savage an adult bookstore and destroy the stock. ... In Canada, feminists are jailed for bombing an outlet of a chain that sells video-pornography. In Massachusetts, a woman shoots a bullet through the window of a closed bookstore that sells pornography.[34]

These are the familiar strategies of anti-abortionists, of racists, of homophobes. It is chilling to witness an influential feminist writer like Dworkin applauding their adoption by anti-porn activists. The only possible outcome of these tactics is a rein of terror, whereby feminist and community bookshops simply cannot risk the possible consequences of stocking material which anti-porn campaigners are likely to label 'pornographic'. This is not the way to win the debate, it is not a political victory. Those who suffer most are not the mainstream porn industry but the beleaguered pioneers of lesbian, gay and queer cultural production.

The familiar strategy of announcing that any woman who disagrees with you is thereby not a feminist runs throughout feminist anti-porn discourse. Introducing her wildly rhetorical essay 'Why pornography matters to feminists', Andrea Dworkin dismisses her critics as *masquerading* as feminists: 'I haven't seen any defense of pornography by

anyone *posturing as a feminist* that addresses even one point made in this piece'[35] (my italics). Apart from its straightforward inaccuracy – feminists have engaged in heated debate over almost every one of the (contentious) points presented as facts in this piece – Dworkin's outrageous suggestion that women somehow disguise themselves as feminists in order to defend pornography renders 'feminist debate' on the issue oxymoronic. If one side are always only *pretending* to be feminists, there can be no feminist debate. It also undermines Dworkin's own position, since the implication is that she finds it so difficult to engage with other feminists on this issue that she has to resort to denying that they are feminist at all. This is convenient, but remains a self-defeating strategy in the long term. If to be a feminist is to be against pornography the only outcome is a drastically reduced number of 'feminists', where 'feminism' becomes a dictatorship, with all the intellectual and political infantilism which dictatorships inevitably engender. And Dworkin is absolutely clear that her position is unarguable: 'Also: the acceptance of pornography means the decline of feminist ethics and an abandonment of feminist politics; the acceptance of pornography means that feminists abandon women.'[36] There is no attempt in this piece to explain what is meant by these assertions, no recognition of the slippery and contradictory nature of arguments about sexualized imagery, no acknowledgement that a feminist ethics of pornography may be complex. This is debate at the level of the play-ground.

It has become depressingly common for anti-porn feminists to resort to this kind of ideological bullying rather than engage in debate. All too often it is lesbian publications which offer a soft target: after all, the publishers of *Mayfair* and *Playboy* won't really mind if you tell them that they're not feminists, but a feminist-identified readership is crucial to the survival of small, independent lesbian and/or feminist publishers. Gillian Rodgerson describes the treatment which one small British publisher received at the hands of anti-porn feminists:

> Despite a solid feminist reputation, Sheba was ... the target of attacks by the pro-censorship lobby [for publishing *Serious Pleasure*, a collection of lesbian erotica]. Sheba's editors are convinced that, through pro-censorship attacks, they have lost the support of many erstwhile readers. Hostile reviews alone have convinced some feminists that the collection was purveying pornography and impugning feminist moral integrity.[37]

Because they took the decision to publish the first British collection of lesbian-authored erotic stories for a lesbian audience, Sheba found their right to call themselves feminists under attack: 'Because of *Serious Pleasure* we are now referred to as Sheba 'Feminist' Publishers, in inverted commas.'[38]

Members of the British group Feminists Against Censorship (FAC) were subject to a vitriolic smear campaign, and to invasions of their lives which can only be described as bullying:

> We are frequently charged with being in the pay of the pornography industry; individual members who are involved in publishing sexually explicit lesbian/feminist written and visual material have been publicly abused as 'peddlars of pornography'; there has been a worrying suggestion that opponents of our position have approached employers about our views – a tactic used against women involved in the fight against antipornography groups in the United States.[39]

Both the direct-action violence and the ideological bullying tactics adopted by some anti-porn feminists cause much greater damage to lesbians than to the male-owned, multi-million pound/dollar mainstream porn industry. Such informal attempts at imposing censorship in flagrant disregard of community debate have had directly anti-lesbian consequences. But still greater damage is caused by more formal attempts to institute *legal* censorship.

Anti-pornography feminists have worked in close association with senators, members of Parliament and government bodies in the UK, the USA, Australia and Canada to impose legal restrictions on 'porno-graphic' material. This despite earlier declarations on the part of key anti-porn figures that censorship is not the answer. Catherine MacKinnon (ironically one of those most closely involved in drafting later legislation) wrote that 'pornography cannot be reformed or suppressed or banned. It can only be changed.'[40] Writing in 1974, Robin Morgan rejected censorship because she predicted that the likely consequences would be damaging to women's interests: 'I'm aware that a phallocentric culture is more likely to begin its censorship purges with books on pelvic examination for women, or books containing lyrical paeans to lesbianism, than with 'See Him Tear and Kill Her'.[41]

Despite such clear warnings many feminists have formed alliances, with politicians on both the right and the left and with political groups both radical and reactionary, in order to impose legal restrictions on sexual imagery. In the USA, such alliances have usually been with the right, the natural home of sexual repression. In the UK, where Labour MP Clare Short, the National Union of Students and (briefly) the National Council for Civil Liberties (now Liberty) have all been recruited to the censorship cause, feminists have worked with the traditional left.

Morgan's cynicism has been more than validated by subsequent events. Legislation which feminists have lobbied and campaigned for, have been involved in drafting or have supported in committees and commissions has been used with particular enthusiasm against lesbian and gay imagery. Feminist anti-porn rhetoric has been employed to justify a range of attacks against lesbian and gay cultural products, publications and community services.

In the UK, during the Thatcher administration, there was no need for feminists to instigate or collude with the harassment of lesbians and gay men. Customs and excise officers stepped up anti-lesbian and gay activity in response to a general political climate of overt homophobia:

Lavender Menace (now West and Wilde) in Edinburgh regularly had shipments from the US destroyed and, to a lesser extent, Gay's The Word bookshop in London was targeted. Then, in the notorious 'Operation Tiger', Gay's The Word was stripped of much of its stock and its workers and directors were charged with 'conspiracy to import offensive material'.[42]

What is noticeable, however, is that few feminists spoke out against this harassment, failing to draw any conclusions about the implications of such actions for women in general or for lesbians in particular.

In Canada, many feminists supported the 1992 Supreme Court ruling, known as the Butler decision, which changed the definition of 'obscenity' from a moral one to one based on the notion of harm. The legal definition of obscenity is now 'images of sex with violence or sex which degrades or dehumanizes any of the participants'. This brings the law very much into line with Catherine MacKinnon's feminist definition of pornography. But, as Persimmon Blackbridge warns, a seemingly feminist legal definition is not much use when the law is still administered by the same patriarchal institutions:

> ... who gets to decide what is violent, dehumanizing, and degrading? Our friends the police? Our friends the courts? Our friends the Customs agents? How can the wording be specific enough, or vague enough, to prevent mainstream authorities from using the law to target people who challenge their values?[43]

The Butler decision has, indeed, been used to harrass lesbian and queer communities. As Blackbridge points out, there are issues of class and sexual orientation at work here which are completely ignored in anti-porn feminist rhetoric:

> A few days after the Butler decision came down, the police busted Glad Day Books in Toronto for selling the noncommercial, lesbian-produced sex magazine *Bad Attitude*. There was nothing in the seized magazine that isn't in Madonna's book *Sex*. The courts judged *Bad Attitude* obscene, but *Sex* has never even been hassled. Money changes everything. Being straight helps too.[44]

Clearly anti-pornography feminist activism has resulted, both directly and indirectly, in attacks on lesbian cultural production. This may, of course, be justified. If ridding the world of pornography will significantly improve the position of women, and if the production of lesbian erotic material stands in the way of that goal, then the loss of our materials, the attacks on our community bookshops, the denigration of individual lesbians and the rejection of debate in favour of terrorism and bullying are a price well worth paying. But if this is *not* the case, then such behaviour is inexcusable.

Do bad girls go to heaven? Lesbian porn

The feminist argument against pornography is that, in complex and multiple ways, it reinforces the social, psychological and cultural infrastructure which gives men power over women. According to both Dworkin and MacKinnon, 'Pornography is the sexualized subordination of women'[45] and 'institutionalizes the sexuality of male supremacy, which fuses the eroticization of dominance with the social construction of male and female.'[46] Moreover, the dismissive counter-argument, which holds that pornography does not contribute to men's power because the roots of that power are material/economic, is based on a failure to understand the relationship between representational practice and the material world. For example, Leonore Tiefer writes as though men's power and women's power were incomparably distinct: 'Antiporn campaigns say that porn gives men power. But in fact, men already have power. Explicit sexual materials and performances can contribute to women's sexual power.'[47] But you can't have it both ways. You cannot claim that explicit sexual materials can contribute to women's power, while at the same time claiming that they do not enhance men's power simply because 'men already have power'. So pornography certainly can, and does, contribute to men's power. But the specific detail of this critique is important to the development of strategies which may refuse that power to men while giving women access to it.

MacKinnon sees porn as institutionalizing 'the sexuality of male supremacy': in other words, a complementary male/active, female/passive sexuality. In Dworkin's model, pornography is *male* speech which depends on female *silence*.[48] In their submission to the Supreme Court of Canada in support of the Butler decision, the feminist Legal, Education and Action Fund (LEAF) insisted that 'Pornography is made to produce male sexual excitement, erection and masturbation. ... It is not made to further any search for truth.'[49] How does this clarity square with labelling Sheba's collection of *lesbian* erotica 'pornographic'? Summarizing the feminist anti-porn position, Persimmon Blackbridge identifies its denial of *women's* desire and cultural productivity:

> Pornography is assumed to be made by men and for men. Sexual images by and for women are never mentioned. It's such a familiar erasure of our lives. It leads to a law where what is assumed to be true about men is by default assumed to be true about women.[50]

This is, of course, true for all women, but Blackbridge is writing as a lesbian, and she is concerned with the damaging consequences of feminist anti-porn activism for lesbians. If you want to know what sexual silence looks like, cast an enquiring eye over the history of homosexuality in Western art. Emmanuel Cooper's classic study *The Sexual Perspective*[51] resonates with a richness of homoeroticism – that is, *male* expressions of erotic feeling for men's bodies – reaching back to the late nineteenth century and tracing its roots back to the Renaissance and beyond. Gay desire and sexuality is not simply acknowledged and celebrated, it is explored in all its troublesome complexity. Compared to this many-layered profusion, the lesbian images in the book – Cooper takes care to allocate lesbian art a fair share of space – barely whisper of sex at all. Were it not for Della Grace's photograph 'The Three Graces' and Mandy McCartin's painting *Force Field*, lesbian desire would be all but invisible here. Anne McClintock is right when she comments wryly that sexual starvation has been the traditional lot of women: 'Women's desire ... has been crimped and confined to history's sad museum of corsets, chastity belts, the virginity cult and genital mutilation. Alongside women's erotic malnourishment, men's sexual scarcity looks like a Roman banquet.'[52]

To point out that pornography commodifies women for male consumption is only half the story. It also denies, silences, erases *female* desire. In so doing, the very practice of pornography (not just its content), contributes to the control of female sexuality by men, and to the cultural construction of gendered sexuality whereby men are sexual subjects, women sexual objects. A blanket policy of censoring erotic texts simply contributes to this cultural gagging of women's sexual speech.

If pornography *is* the sexualization of male supremacy, then 'pornographic' does not mean sexually explicit, or erotic, or sexually arousing. Many anti-censorship writers (mischievously?) refuse to make such a distinction, eliding 'pornographic' and 'sexually explicit' and claiming that the feminist critique of pornography would result in the banning of sex-educational materials or safer-sex promotional leaflets.[53] Pro-censorship feminists too often fail to distinguish between lesbian-produced sexual imagery and mainstream heterosexual porn. Blanket condemnations of *all* erotic imagery, or legislative strategies based on generalized notions of obscenity, degradation or harm, inevitably fail to distinguish between those images which are likely to contribute to the social control of women and those which may empower women:

> That pornography causes harm is such a sweeping statement. How does pornography *actually function*? Is it the same everywhere, for everyone? ... How does gay and lesbian porn function within *our* communities? Does it cause harm? How do geographical, cultural, racial and class differences affect the ways that porn functions in various gay and lesbian communities?[54]

Any debate on pornography requires that we define our terms. If the harm of pornography is located in its complicity with men's power to control women sexually (in the sense of both controlling women's sexuality and using sex to control women), then that meaning must somehow be incorporated into the word itself. Of course such meanings are *already* present in the word itself. The literal meaning of 'porno/graphy', a word constructed from Greek roots, is 'pictures of prostitutes'. I suggest that the etymology of the word offers a solution to its flagrant misuse by both sides in the porn wars. Prostitution is in many ways the exemplary institution of male supremacy. The fact that it is a market wherein women are the goods and men the customers[55] reflects a wider social structure where men have power and money and women do not, and where men are sexual subjects and women sexual objects. It also reinforces the belief that this social structure is 'natural', and inherent in heterosexuality. The fact that, of the millions of women around the globe who sell sex for a living, many have no other means of survival, reflects the ubiquitous extent of women's economic dependency on men – in other words, their economic *subordination* to men. Nor can prostitution be separated in any simple way from other forms of heterosex, since economic considerations generally underpin heterosexual relationships to a greater or lesser extent.

My definition of 'porno/graphy', then, is any textual practice which represents women's subordination to men as natural, proper or desirable, and which sexualizes that subordination. I use the slash to reinscribe the original meaning onto the body of the word – porno/whore, graphy/picturing.[56] This highly specific use of the word helps to disentangle the offensive and potentially harmful practice of porno/graphy from quite distinct practices, such as the making of lesbian or gay porn. It also makes available that useful word 'erotica'. Many people have argued that the difference between pornography and erotica is a class difference: the privileged classes have 'erotica', the working classes have 'pornography'. Although there is some truth in this when comparing 'high' art (say, Botticelli's painting *The Birth of Venus*) with 'popular culture' (for example, a Betty Page[57] pin-up magazine), it is a distinction which has lost much of its usefulness with the democratization of sexualized imagery. Cheap, high-quality erotic materials are now available to everyone who wants them; some are porno/graphic and some are not.

I strongly believe that the most useful strategy for shifting the gendered balance of power in the realm of the sexual is not the extermination of erotic texts but their proliferation. In particular, the proliferation of erotic materials produced by and for those groups which have traditionally been excluded from the porno/graphic scenario: lesbians, heterosexual and bisexual women, gay men and queers. Of all such groups, lesbians have the potential to be most radical, most transgressive of mainstream values, most disruptive of the porno/graphic narrative.

The mainstream heterosexual porno/graphic narrative constructs sexual agency as something which is the intrinsic property of men. It is men who own the desiring gaze, men who 'do' sex, men who control, produce, distribute and consume porno/graphy. Gay men's porn disturbs the conventions of porno/graphy by offering the troubling possibility of moving between subject and object while viewing one image. Far from offering simple mastery of the presented object of desire, gay male porn offers a choice between desire and identification. As Richard Dyer comments, 'I'm turned on by images of men by themselves. My reaction to these images oscillates between thinking I'd like to feel that man and I'd like to be that man. That oscillation is a unique element of gay porn.'[58] However, because gay porn remains a commodity which is produced, controlled, marketed and consumed by men, its challenge to male sexual power is limited.

Gay porn troubles gender in intriguing and complex ways, simultaneously complying with and disavowing the porno/graphic dictat that to gaze at a body is to feminize it. In this, it poses a threat to the coherence and hegemony of porno/graphic discourse. However, the continued dominance of the male sexual consumer means that gay porn remains obedient to the major structural rules of porno/graphy. It is only women who may radically transform erotica, and the most explosive challenge to the regime of porno/graphy yet mounted has been produced by dykes. The next chapter takes a closer look at this lesbian porn.

Notes

1. Marilyn French, *The War Against Women* (London: Hamish Hamilton, 1992), p. 168.
2. This is also the case, of course, in the countries of the former Soviet bloc and throughout the 'third world' – see Robin Morgan (ed.), *Sisterhood is Global: The International Women's Movement Anthology* (Harmondsworth: Penguin, 1984); Joni Seager and Ann Olson, *Women in the World: An International Atlas* (London: Pluto Press, 1986); Lesley Doyal, *What Makes Women Sick? Gender and the Political Economy of Health* (London: Macmillan, 1995), – but this is an account of what took place in the industrialized West at a particular point in time, and cannot be generalized to other cultures or historical moments.
3. Cited In Marianne Hirsch and Evelyn Fox Keller (eds.), *Conflicts in Feminism* (London: Routledge, 1990), p. 307.
4. *Ibid.*, p. 307.
5. In Lynne Segal and Mary McIntosh (eds.), *Sex Exposed: Sexuality and the Pornography Debate* (London: Virago, 1992), p. 5.
6. Andrea Dworkin, *Letters from a War Zone: Writings 1976–1987* (London: Secker and Warburg, 1988), p. 172.
7. *Ibid.*, p. 201.
8. In Hirsch and Fox Keller (eds.), *Conflicts in Feminism*, p. 316.
9. Kate Ellis, Barbara O'Dair and Abby Tallmer, 'Feminism and Pornography', *Feminist Review*, No. 36, p. 37.
10. Catherine MacKinnon, for example, is very careful to distinguish between the pornographic (which she believes is harmful to women) and the obscene (which she regards as generally harmless to women). She identifies 'nudity, explicitness, excess of candour, arousal or excitement' as belonging to the (patriarchal/legal) category of *obscenity*, and hence not the object of her critique. She defines pornography quite specifically as sited in the arena of gender, not the erotic (see MacKinnon, 'Pornography: Not a Moral Issue' in Renate Klein and Deborah Steinberg (eds.) *Radical Voices: A Decade of Feminist Resistance from Women's Studies International Forum* (Oxford: Pergamon Press, 1989), p. 145). The importance of a clear definition of pornography is discussed later in this

chapter.

11. Kiss and Tell, *Her Tongue on My Theory: Images, Essays and Fantasies* (Vancouver: Press Gang, 1994), pp. 79–80.

12. See, for example, cases cited in John Stoltenberg, *Refusing to Be a Man* (London: Fontana/Collins, 1989), pp. 148–50.

13. Dworkin, *Letters from a War Zone*, p. 241.

14. In Segal and McIntosh (eds.), *Sex Exposed*, p. 114.

15. Lynne Segal, 'Pornography and Violence: What the "Experts" Really Say' in *Feminist Review* No. 36, Autumn 1990, p. 32.

16. Leonore Tiefer, *Sex is not a Natural Act and Other Essays* (Oxford: Westview Press, 1995), p. 129.

17. Dworkin, *Letters from a War Zone*, p. 207.

18. MacKinnon, 'Pornography', p. 155.

19. Harriett Gilbert (ed.), *The Sexual Imagination from Acker to Zola: A Feminist Companion* (London: Jonathan Cape, 1993), p. 244.

20. In Segal and McIntosh (eds.), *Sex Exposed*, p. 129.

21. *Ibid.*

22. Simon Watney, *Policing Desire: Pornography, AIDS and the Media* (London: Methuen, 1987), p. 70.

23. See, for example, Susanne Kappeler, *The Pornography of Representation*, (Cambridge: Polity Press, 1986).

24. Jane Smith, 'Making Movies' in Frederique Delacoste and Priscilla Alexander (eds.), *Sex Work: Writings by Women in the Sex Industry* (London: Virago, 1988), p. 58.

25. *Ibid.*, p. 144.

26. Kiss and Tell (eds.), *Her Tongue on My Theory*, p. 33.

27. In Segal and McIntosh, *Sex Exposed*, p. 114.

28. See, for example, Watney, *Policing Desire*, essays in Edmund White, *The Burning Library: Writing on Art,* *Politics and Sexuality 1969–1993* (London: Picador, 1989), and Tim Edwards, *Erotics and Politics: Gay Male Sexuality, Masculinity and Feminism* (London: Routledge, 1994).

29. Edwards, *Erotics and Politics*, p. 86.

30. Mick Wallis in Simon Shepherd and Mick Wallis (eds.), *Coming On Strong: Gay Politics and Culture* (London: Unwin Hyman, 1989), p. 210.

31. Segal and McIntosh, *Sex Exposed*, p. 112.

32. *Ibid.*, p. 113.

33. Susan Cole, *Pornography and the Sex Crisis* (Toronto: Amanita, 1989), p. 53.

34. Dworkin, *Letters from a War Zone*, p. 206.

35. *Ibid.*, p. 203.

36. *Ibid.*, p. 204.

37. In Segal and McIntosh (eds.), *Sex Exposed*, pp. 278–97.

38. *Ibid.*, p. 279.

39. Gillian Rodgerson and Linda Semple, 'Who Watches the Watchwomen? Feminists Against Censorship', *Feminist Review*, No. 36 p. 21.

40. Klein and Steinberg (eds.), *Radical Voices*, p. 144.

41. Cited in Tiefer, *Sex Is Not a Natural Act*, p. 117.

42. Rodgerson and Semple, 'Who Watches the Watchwomen?' p. 20.

43. Kiss and Tell, *Her Tongue on My Theory*, pp. 77–8.

44. *Ibid.*, p. 85.

45. Dworkin, *Letters from a War Zone*, p. 248.

46. MacKinnon, 'Pornography', p. 147.

47. Tiefer, *Sex Is not a Natural Act*, p. 134.

48. Dworkin, *Letters from a War Zone*, p. 249.

49. Kiss and Tell, *Her Tongue on My Theory*, p. 82.

50. *Ibid.*, p. 80.

51. Emmanuel Cooper, *The Sexual Perspective: Homosexuality and Art in the Last 100 Years in the West*, 2nd edn. (London: Routledge, 1994).

52. In Segal and McIntosh (eds.), *Sex Exposed*, p. 113.

53. See, for example, Watney, *Policing Desire*, and essays in Segal and McIntosh, *Sex Exposed*.

54. Kiss & Tell, *Her Tongue on My Theory*, p. 84.

55. The provision of sexual services to women for money, whether by male gigolos or women sex workers, remains a tiny and insignificant practice. The provision of sexual services to men for money, mostly by women sex workers but sometime by boys and other men, is 'the oldest profession', and is common around the globe.

56. This is a commonly used etymological pattern: hence photo/light graphy/picturing, or litho/stone graphy/picturing.

57. Betty Page (aka Betty Mae) was a well-known model for soft-porn photographs taken by the brother and sister team of Irving and Paula Klaw. Something of a pin-up star and minor cult figure, she featured in many 'spanking' shots and in bondage sequences, generally with other women. An 'ancestress trouvée' for some British lesbians today, her photograph has graced the pages of *Quim*, and a London club, 'Betty's' has been named after her. Readers interested in finding out more are referred to Harald Hellman and Burkhard Reimschneider, *Betty Page: Queen of Pin-Up* (Cologne: Benedikt Taschen, 1987).

58. In Shepherd and Wallis (eds.), *Coming on Strong*, p. 202.

6

Grow Your Own: Lesbian Erotica

The porn wars succeeded in polarizing the lesbian-feminist community to the degree that it became very difficult to remain active in feminism if you did not wholeheartedly support the anti-porn, pro-censorship position. The results have been very damaging for feminism and for lesbians. Many lesbians who foreground desire and sex as the bedrock of lesbian identity, who produce and/or consume erotica or who believe that the harms of censorship are greater than the harms of pornographic imagery appear to have rejected feminism altogether. In the wake of the sex wars, in the light of the HIV pandemic, and in response to right-wing attempts to crush an increasingly confident homoculture, a new collectivity of sexual minorities in resistance has emerged and named itself queer. Membership of this exuberant new queer community is rooted in a self-consciously transgressive sexuality, which positions itself in opposition to *any* attempt to control, restrict or police sexual expression. As we have seen, those feminists who have attempted to control sexuality, by regulating 'pornography' and by attacking sado-masochists, have laid claim to being the authentic voice of feminism. It is hardly surprising then that, although the conditions for its development owe a great deal to feminism, the new queer culture tends to take this at face value and to represent feminism as erotophobic, puritanical and controlling.

For many in the new generations of lesbians, feminism is simply irrelevant. Yet feminism and queer should be political allies. Both are rooted in a will to destabilize and discredit the institution of gender itself. 'Gender', as the Queer Nation slogan has it, 'is apartheid'. Without a sexual activism which queers gendered sexuality, feminism remains limited amd limiting; without the power analysis of feminism which recognises that economic, political and cultural power is in the hands of men, queer cannot go anywhere. For lesbians, who are both queer and female, the stand-off between queer and feminism can mean that we are marginalized within both camps:

Before coming to the [Lesbian] Summer School, I called myself a lesbian feminist. But over the past four days I felt more and more outcast because of my political beliefs. I was told yesterday that I must be an SM dyke for thinking the way I do, and today, that I was 'a lesbian from the waist downwards'. I really resent this kind of labelling and patronisation from older lesbians which closed off discussion between the two 'factions'.[1]

It is not surprising that increasing numbers of lesbians ('older' lesbians as well as younger) just get fed up with this kind of offensive treatment and throw in their lot with queer. But the queer social and political milieu offers a different kind of offensive treatment, as this comment from *Quim* suggests:

There's a brand of boy around at the moment who reckon that just because you're a pro-sex dyke, maybe don a bit of leather, and talk brash and bold on occasion, that you have forgotten your feminism and they can get away with sexist put downs, anti-women jokes and all the rest of it. ... I've been in rooms, too often recently, with gay men who assumed, until set straight, that they could get snide about the 'feminist kind of lesbian' and I'd laugh along ... [2]

Some lesbians jumped into queer with both feet, naming feminism as one of the forces of repression and claiming 'an intellectual and theoretical need to ally with gay men around the politics of representation and sexuality which had been hijacked by radical lesbian feminists.'[3] But for many, there is no simple question of choice. Because there has been a close political relationship between lesbians and feminism, many lesbians work hard to bridge the political divide between feminism and queer. Tori Smith, for example, insists that the feminist groundwork behind the new queer activism should be acknowledged: 'One thing I hope as a historian is that the fact that feminists pioneered a lot of queer ideas doesn't get lost, so it becomes something that only grew up out of ACT UP or men's ideas.'[4]

It is no coincidence that some of the most interesting work in the field of sexuality, gender, sexual representation and erotica is being carried out by lesbians who engage with both feminist and queer ideas. Cherry Smyth describes her pamphlet *Lesbians Talk Queer Notions* as 'situated firmly within feminism and queer politics, while expressing ambivalence towards both',[5] and the key figures of the new Queer Theory in the academy – Judith Butler, Elizabeth Grosz, Teresa de Lauretis, Eve Kosofksy Sedgwick *et al.* – are all lesbians whose work dismantling gender is informed by a specifically feminist recognition of male power.

What does this have to do with lesbian porn? Traditionally lesbian porn is precisely where the lines of battle have been drawn between feminism and queer. I would suggest that producing lesbian porn is not only queer, it is an important radical-feminist activity. I am not alone in this suggestion. Celia and Jenny Kitzinger, for example, both radical feminists, call for the production of explicit images of lesbian sex:

> we are loathe to accept that refusal of representations of lesbian sex scenes is the only viable political position. ... We want media images which address *lesbian* rather than simply female reality, and which do not erase the sexuality of lesbianism. Perhaps the answer is to write our own?[6]

However, their rejection of the desexualization of lesbianism is hampered by the extent to which their argument clings to a traditional anti-porn feminist analysis. In the end, what apparently starts out as a political validation of lesbian erotica retreats into an all too familiar attack on lesbian erotic imagery as porno/graphic. The anti-porn party line is not being queeried here, it is merely being repeated:

> What does concern us ... is this. If we construct lesbian representations of lesbian sex, how do we know that we have done so *as lesbians* and from a 'lesbian gaze', as opposed to adopting a male gaze and utilising the conventions of male pornography? ... Lesbian pornography can also reinforce ... oppressive meanings. Many lesbians believe that it does.[7] (author's italics)

The Kitzingers go on to cite, as evidence of the offensiveness of lesbian porn, the fact that some British-produced lesbian erotica has been censored by a number of feminists:

> The feminist bookstore, Sisterwrite, in London, refused to stock *Love Bites* (a book of lesbian erotica by Della Grace, published by Gay Men's Press!) or the lesbian porn magazine *Quim* (which reproduces[8] Della Grace's photographs), because the material is 'violent and could cause offence to some of our customers.'[9]

They go on to attack *Quim*, the lesbian photography exhibition *Stolen Glances*, London lesbian nightclub *Venus Rising* and American lesbian sex magazine *On Our Backs* as porno/graphic. Indeed, not content with labelling them porno/graphic, they present lesbian porn as complicit with a whole catalogue of social evils including Nazism, compulsory heterosexuality, the slaughter of innocent animals (in order to produce leather and fur) and anti-feminism. This is a tired and offensive strategy. Simply mentioning Nazism and animal slaughter in the same sentence as lesbian porn – and their analysis does not go much beyond this – does not constitute a debate. What it does is to construct an entirely illusory agenda whereby anyone who abhors fascism or supports animal rights *must*, willy-nilly, abhor the work of large numbers of lesbian photographers and writers, sight unseen. This is done, moreover, in the interests of *controlling* the representation of lesbian sexuality.

The attack on 'lesbian porn' by feminists has, to date, not progressed beyond the most outrageously Orwellian propaganda tactics. Perhaps the commonest ploy is to selectively misrepresent the content of lesbian erotica, while at the same time presenting it as so dangerous, anti-feminist and contaminating that your readers are unlikely to buy any to check it out for themselves. Thus, the contents of *Quim* are described in the following terms:

> heavily reliant on the traditional pornographic paraphanalia [sic] of sadomasochism: whips, chains, studded belts, black leather boots, stiletto heels, corsets, Nazi-style caps, fists and pierced nipples. Far from 'transgressing' traditional representations, they reinscribe them: the dominatrix, the bound woman on a rack, the huge (albeit detachable) dick.[10]

When I first read this paragraph I had the uneasy feeling that the *Quim* which I had happily been burying my face in was not the same magazine described here. Armed with this list, I returned to the issues in question (Nos. 1 and 2) and trawled through the pages looking for evidence of debauchery. In seventy-two pages and eighty-nine photographs, my search unearthed the following:

- whips: one (in an advert for a club)
- chains: one (possibly two if you count jewellery)
- studded belts: two (one in a cowboy costume)

- black leather boots: none at all in *Quim* No. 1, three in *Quim* No. 2
- stiletto heels: two (although one of them was on one of the black leather boots and has hence scored twice on the filthometer)
- corsets: one (plus one in the club advert which featured the whip)
- Nazi-style caps: this is a difficult one, since there are no Nazi caps at all. However, if we include all black peaked caps (such as those worn by traffic and school crossing wardens, etc.), there are five (of which two are in adverts and two in one tiny shot of a club)
- fists: possibly two, although one of these is raised in greeting by a woman in a frock on 1988's Lesbian Strength March, and the other could only be called a fist if you were really determined to do so
- pierced nipples: one nipple in each issue
- bound woman on a rack: this is the product of a fevered imagination. There are no bound women on racks. There is a highly stylized sketch of a woman lying on a *table*, but if tables are to become politically incorrect, what are we going to eat off?
- huge detachable dick: one (plus its reflection in a mirror).

There was also a photograph of a plastic dinosaur. I think you should be told.

These two issues of *Quim* also contain images which can only be described as lyrical, affectionate, romantic and playful. In fact, the armoury of s/m paraphernalia which the magazine is supposedly 'heavily reliant on' is massively outnumbered by such gentle and romantic images, not to mention pictures of quite ordinary women with all their clothes on. There are also articles on safer sex (and there is precious little of this available for lesbians, as both myself and Jenny Kitzinger have written elsewhere), interviews, music and book reviews. Later issues contained articles on health problems such as RSI, endometriosis and ME, as well as discussions about butch and femme, the existence of a lesbian aesthetic, the effects of racism on black lesbians, the stereotyping of fat lesbians and advice on safe drug use. Also, importantly, the magazine provided a rare outlet for the work of lesbian photographers engaged in the crucial business of trying to find new ways of representing lesbian sex.

There is something happening here which lesbians and feminists need to think about very carefully: a kind of seeing-but-not-seeing, a readiness to judge from a position of adherence to dogma, rather than to question and challenge thoughtfully and respectfully. I don't pretend to know *why* a handful of artefacts was perceived in this instance as saturating an entire magazine, but I suspect that it results partly from the anxiety which sexually explicit imagery arouses in the context of feminism, and partly from the kind of selective seeing which stems from political certainty. In fact, the decision taken by Sisterwrite to ban *Quim* and *Love Bites* is far more offensive than anything contained in either publication, since it implies that the open exploration of lesbian sexuality is obscene and, moreover, that we should treat feminists like children and protect them from possibly disturbing imagery. Of course, it could be that Sisterwrite were simply not prepared to face the outrage of offended pro-censorship feminists. If this is the case, it is a sad indication of the extent to which the rule of dogma has been substituted for political dialogue in some feminist circles.

Why lesbian porn is important

The continued policing of women's desire and pleasure is not in the interests of any women, lesbian or non-lesbian. This is not to argue for the 'liberation' of some illusory authentic female sexuality: sexuality is always inevitably socially constructed, as the attempts to define a feminist sexuality demonstrate. It is to argue that, at this particular time and in the cultural context of 'first world' lesbian communities, it is politically and strategically necessary to resist the imposition of sexual norms on women. Leonore Tiefer is right when she suggests that 'What women need is not more "official" rules for how to be "normal" but the recognition that women's sexuality in the past has been constrained by patriarchal structures'[11] (although her assessment that such constraints belong in the past is over-optimistic). She goes on to insist that, within the terms of this analysis, the suppression of pornography – and she means *all* pornography here – is harmful to women:

> If we accept that women's sexuality has been shaped by ignorance and shame and is just beginning to find new opportunities and voices for expression, then now is exactly the wrong time to even think about campaigns of suppression. Suppressing pornography will harm women struggling to develop their own sexualities.[12]

In the context of a general exploration of women's sexuality and erotic voices, lesbians occupy a very special position. Our sexuality has been subject to the most brutal suppression, with contradictory results. For, while images of lesbian sex have been scarce or non-existent, the very fact that our oppression hinges upon defining us as a *sexual* people forces questions of desire, practice and pleasure into the foreground. Lesbians are old hands at questioning our sexuality.

Few would deny that lesbian sex has been conspicuous by its absence from dominant Western culture. As Jenny and Celia Kitzinger point out, 'Until 1961, the US Production Code specifically forbade representations of lesbianism or male homosexuality [in film]. ... Explicit lesbianism is still censored today'. They go on to identify a specific silencing of lesbian sex which continues, even in the context of a more liberal climate in the media: 'Even when lesbianism is acknowledged in the media, lesbian *sex* is not.'[13] Yet the very ubiquity of this erasure, this silencing, can provoke creativity, as Kiss and Tell comment:

> We love making representations of our own sexuality. What we don't love is how state censorship denies our rights and threatens our queer culture. Yet this very censorship stimulates us to think of devious and delightful ways to challenge these prohibitions.[14]

In 'a world where lesbians are both invisible and hated',[15] the production of images and texts which explicitly and unapologetically represent lesbian desire and sexual pleasure, which depict a wide range of lesbian sexual practices, and which explore lesbian sex and how to represent it in all its complex and troublesome variety is not only an affirmative act in resistance to anti-lesbianism, it is an urgent political necessity in feminist terms. Moreover, as Cindy Patton points out, lesbian desire destabilizes the foundations of heterosexual dominance: 'lesbian desire always and insistently subverts dominant sexuality. Lesbians are not simply women who love women, but women whose daily sexual practice is a resistance to the cacophony of heterosexual anxiety.'[16]

The representation of lesbian sexuality is both a powerful weapon against the heterosexual oppression of lesbians and a key strategy in the feminist struggle to end women's subordination. It is also important at the most basic level of lesbian survival in a hostile world:

An important element of lesbian images is the ways in which they build community. ... There is a tremendous demand and need for self-representation by a community whose psychic survival depends on the sure knowledge that there are others like ourselves.[17]

Given the radical-feminist analysis of porno/graphy as the institutionalization of male supremacy, and since male supremacy depends on controlling women's sexuality within (and by) patriarchal constructions of 'proper' femininity, lesbian porn cannot, by definition, be porno/graphic. Given the ways in which lesbian-produced erotica destabilize heterosexual supremacy – 'even the most recalcitrant heterosexual male cannot help but be disturbed by his exclusion from lesbian-produced representations'[18] – and given that its production and consumption contributes to the strength and survival of lesbian communities, lesbian porn is a powerful political tool and community resource. The refusal of feminist bookshops to sell lesbian erotica is not only offensive, it is politically counterproductive.

A brief herstory of dyke porn

Eroticized representations of women having sex with each other are not new; they have appeared with greater or lesser frequency at different times throughout the history of Western culture. It makes no sense to think of the majority of such representations as 'lesbian', not only because they were seldom produced by or for lesbians but because the word 'lesbian' signifies a very particular set of meanings which are culturally and historically specific. Even figures from recent history, such as Gertrude Stein or Radclyffe Hall, would mean something very different by the word 'lesbian' than a post-Stonewall dyke in a San Francisco leather bar.[19] And *her* meaning for the word will be very different from that of the revolutionary lesbian separatist, the queer theorist, the lesbian mother fighting for custody of her children, the male-to-female transsexual who identifies as lesbian ... and so it goes on. Thus, *lesbian* erotica as such is only a very recent phenomenon, and certainly did not exist before the nineteenth century.

Most representations of women having sex with each other were produced to turn men on. Any comprehensive survey of European fine art includes many such images: from eighteenth-century mythological paintings by Boucher to the decadent perversity of Rops or Klimt in the nineteenth century; from the lush sensuality of Courbet's famous depiction of *Sleep* to the brittle and intricate pen and ink drawings of Beardsley. Such representations were truly porno/graphic, in that they represented an attempt to recapture lesbian sexuality for male pleasure, incorporating lesbians into the economy of desire where men are the consumer and women the product on sale. Yet contemporary cultural theory tells us that 'meaning occurs during viewer engagement',[20] so there remains the tantalizing possibility of a re-recapturing of such images. Sticking a postcard of *Sleep* to the fridge in a lesbian kitchen does not alter its conditions of production, but it does undermine the relations of power in which the painting has been located by re-presenting it as a delightful image of lesbian sexual satiation.

Until the second wave of feminism, such acts of piracy, the reading against the grain of heterosexual texts and images, was the only option for most lesbians.[21] As Susan Stewart acidly remarks, 'Some of us have been reading against the grain for so long that our eyes have splinters.'[22] One of the immediate consequences of the resurgence of feminism in the 1960s and 1970s was that women began to explore their sexuality in the context of resisting male power. Women made use of the visual arts, in particular photography, to explore questions of gender and sexuality. In itself this marked a radical departure from the traditional conventions, where the visual arts were produced by men, and women were restricted to the roles of model or muse. This self-consciously feminist art turned a female gaze on the bodies of women and men, and offered the possibility of an openly desiring *lesbian* gaze. Photography, as a fairly democratic visual art medium which required no art-school training or investment in expensive materials, was especially important in this context, and continues to be so today. Indeed, women have been taking photographs, and taking photography seriously, since the birth of the medium in the nineteenth century.

At first, the lesbian possibilities in this feminist explosion of women's photography remained inchoate and hidden. Early collections – such as *Women See Women* or Cynthia MacAdams's *Emergence*[23] – contain many potentially erotic representations of women but make no reference to lesbian desire or, indeed, to the fact that lesbians exist. MacAdams went on to publish *Rising Goddess*,[24] a book of 118 nude photographs of women in natural surroundings. The women bathe in rivers, hot springs or the sea, lie about on mountains, in deserts, beneath trees and in sand dunes. Several are intertwined in sensual embrace, and many are powerfully eroticized by MacAdams's tactile and sensuous vision. Set side by side with Della Grace's *Love Bites*, the photographs in *Rising Goddess* exude a lasciviousness and erotic charge that Grace's more self-consciously 'transgressive' images cannot match.[25] Yet the word 'lesbian' is not mentioned, either in Kate Millett's preface or Margaretta Mitchell's introduction. According to Millett the women are 'mysterious, awesome ... utterly unafraid, unashamed. ... Women warriors, dancers, priestesses, sages. ... Wonderful fearless creatures'; according to Mitchell they represent 'The symbolic content of the Goddess image ... the image for woman of her spiritual wilderness'. Although much of this rhetoric is fairly transparently coded in the lesbian vocabulary of the time, the lesbian sexual response is here resolutely denied. *Rising Goddess* may be spiritual, wild or symbolic – indeed, anything but one-handed reading matter for the lustful lesbian.

Ironically, it is with the intensification of the pornography debate within feminism that the production of deliberately and avowedly erotic images of, and for, lesbians begins in earnest. It would be a mistake to suggest that this new productivity was only, or even principally, in reaction against the worst excesses of feminist anti-porn activism, although clearly such considerations played an important part. Many lesbians in fact accepted the accuracy of the feminist critique of heterosexual porn, but they also recognized the extent to which the silencing and erasure of lesbian erotica was part of what feminists were supposedly fighting. Women such as Pat Califia, Joan Nestle or Kiss and Tell do not call themselves anti-feminists, nor do they present their erotica as an attack on feminism. On the contrary, they insist that they are feminists, and that the production of lesbian erotica is a feminist enterprise.

What's going down ... some lesbian 'pornographers'

At the time of writing, there is a veritable explosion of productivity in lesbian erotica. Every country with a lesbian community has, it seems, its lesbian sex magazine. From the well-established *On Our Backs* in the USA or *Wicked Women* in Australia, to newer publications like *Lezzie Smut* from Canada, it seems there is more lesbian-produced erotica than at any time in history. These magazines provide space for discussion of safer sex, sexual/gender politics and theory, serve as noticeboards for community events and publish the work of lesbian erotic photographers and writers. The best-produced, most innovative and most exciting to date was Britain's very own dear *Quim*, which weathered censorship, feminist hostility and the oppressive right-wing climate of Thatcherite and post-Thatcherite Britain from 1989 to 1994, during which five issues came out. The fact that lesbian communities are succeeding in publishing quantities of lesbian erotica in the teeth of hostility from all sides (the political right, religious fundamentalism, pro-censorship feminism, various 'pro-family' groups and campaigns) indicates that desire and sexuality are very important to lesbians! Indeed, Lizard Jones identifies lust as the foundation of queer culture and communities:

> It is my theory that lust and sex are the building blocks of lesbian and gay culture. Just lusting after someone of the same sex is a risk, and I live in a community of queer people who have taken this risk in order to follow their desires.[26]

The proliferation of lesbian sex magazines has contributed to an internationalization of lesbian community and culture which insists on the centrality of sex and desire, and which has initiated a trans-global lesbian conversation about sex, lust, desire, representation, theory and politics. Well aware of the historical erasure of earlier material, the Lesbian Herstory Archives in San Francisco maintains a collection of lesbian sex magazines, thus ensuring a degree of safety for these still threatened voices. (Although, in sad contrast, the British Lesbian Archive does not accept 'pornography'!)

There are extraordinary differences between lesbians who produce lesbian erotica. Della Grace, for example, whose reference point is queer culture, and who states that her resistance is to 'the Lesbian and Gay "community", who ... has [sic] little tolerance for members who transgress current "acceptable" modes of behaviour',[27] has little in common with Kiss and Tell, whose politics developed from working in feminist anti-porn campaigns and who maintain a close relationship with feminist theories of representation and sexual politics. Whatever their politics, their theoretical position, or their success in turning women on, lesbians who produce 'sex art' do not have access to the kinds of close critical scrutiny which any artist needs in order to develop. You have only to think of the critical attention – both mainstream and gay – paid to the work of gay artists such as Robert Mapplethorpe or Tom of Finland to recognise that *no* lesbian artist gets taken this seriously. Partly, this is a question of technical virtuosity: there are substantial material reasons why lesbian draughtswomen or photographers have not (yet) achieved the technical skill of Tom of Finland's masterly drawings or Mapplethorpe's stunning photographs. But critical accounts of Tom and Mapplethorpe do not foreground their technical skill. Critics focus on their subject matter. There have been a few critical assessments of Della Grace's work – they have been embarrassingly mediocre for the most part – but there is almost nothing about the work of Kiss and Tell, Tessa Boffin, Laurence Jaugey-Paget, Tee Corinne, Lola Flash, Pelot Kitchener, or Ingrid Pollard.

I am going to devote some space here to an all-too-brief discussion of the work of four lesbian 'sex artists': Della Grace (because she is currently so centre-stage), Tee Corinne (because she crosses the OK/not OK boundary in traditional feminist terms), Laurence Jaugey-Paget (because she is part of the new generation of lesbian photographers) and Kiss and Tell (because their work is so innovative and engages so directly with theories of representation).

From Titian femme to bearded lady: Della's progress

Della Grace is probably the best-known lesbian photographer working in the UK today. Which is not to say that she is the best, the most adventurous, or even the most productive. But her pictures are everywhere: on cards, illustrating articles in Quim, being deconstructed in scholarly journals, adorning (ad nauseam) the front cover of lesbian and gay socialist magazine *Rouge*, popping up in the trendy lefty mainstream press, on book jackets, in exhibitions from London to Helsinki, Della's pictures proliferate. How long before 'Pussy-Licking Sodomite' (a personal favourite of mine) appears on a lesbian box of chocolates?

In part, all this attention comes from the fact that Della makes sure that her lifestyle, as much as her work, is packaged for public consumption. Well aware of the benefits of whoring for the media circus, she exploits the current straight voyeuristic interest in queer culture to the hilt, and that section of the straight press which likes to pose as dangerously liberal loves her. In July 1995 the *Weekend Guardian* carried a feature article on her goatee beard, complete with full-colour bearded self-portrait on the front cover and a selection of her photographs inside, including a full-page reproduction of 'Cyclops'. The straight press particularly love 'Cyclops', a black and white portrait of a nude peroxide blonde wearing a leather chest harness buckled around her breasts and a leather dildo harness partly obscuring her face. The picture got its name from the direct one-eyed gaze through the straps of the dildo harness. The woman's shoulders are pulled back in a way which suggests that her arms are tied and which offers her breasts to the gaze; her gaze is stern, almost threatening, and serves to trouble – in a somewhat limited way – the degree to which she is surrendering autonomy by being presented to the gaze in this fashion. *New Formations*, a trendy academic 'journal of culture/theory/politics', featured 'Cyclops' on the front cover of their special 'Perversity' issue,[28] while the *Guardian* article commented that the picture's 'sado-masochistic trappings serve to emphasize the aggressive femininity of the model.'[29]

It is regularly suggested that Grace's work has been compared to that of Robert Mapplethorpe, stylish American photographer of the rich, famous and trendy, of beautiful women, beautiful flowers, and of the hardest edge of the gay s/m scene. Sarah Kent, writing in the London listings magazine *Time Out* about the publication of Grace's book *Love Bites*, comments that 'West coast photographer Della Grace has been compared with Robert Mapplethorpe for giving a public profile to a group which legally does not exist [sic] – the lesbian subculture'.[30]

Yet another of the intriguing half-facts which coalesce around Della, this comparison with Mapplethorpe seems a particularly unhelpful and peculiarly heterosexual thing to do. It is also an immensely unfair burden to dump on Grace. Mapplethorpe was one of the most important art photographers of his generation. His technical skill and his aesthetic vision were both extraordinary, and he would certainly have been a great photographer even without the s/m images or the sensuous male nudes which mark him as the most uncloseted gay artist yet, and one imbued with an uncompromising refusal to deny his own desires and the subculture in which he enacted them. His work is, above all, characterized by an almost chilling honesty. From the beginning, he took as many risks in exposing his own body to the gaze as he did in photographing those who sat for him, risks which he continued to take right up to his death from AIDS. His often terrifying photographs of cock torture speak eloquently of the conflictual relationship which (some?) men have with their sexuality and with the penis itself, and the s/m scenes which he recorded could not be dismissed by anyone as harmless fun or play-acting.

Della Grace's work is almost the opposite of all this. She is technically competent, at times highly skilled, but far from brilliant. Some of her work is aesthetically exciting, but much of it is fairly routine; she does not, I think, have the self-discipline or the aesthetic rigour needed to be an important art photographer. The s/m scenes she depicts are stage-managed, and speak more of the desire to shock than of any exploration grounded in her own desires. As she admits, 'The SM lesbian community does not have much to do with sado-masochism. It's more an exploration ... playing without guilt'.[31] She has recently taken a leaf out of Mapplethorpe's book and begun to employ self-portraiture in her work: the *Guardian* article reproduced a self-portrait of her (clean-shaven) engaged in sex with her lover, taken from her 1995 series 'Hermaphrodyke', a work 'dominated by a series of studies of Grace and her girlfriend Simo Maronati having sex'.[32]

To compare Grace with Mapplethorpe is therefore both unfair and inappropriate. By treating her as if she were purely an 'art photographer', it also deflects attention away from her importance as a *lesbian* photographer. I have written elsewhere[33] that the two key genres in lesbian photography appear to be 'doc phot and erot phot': documentary photography that investigates and records the lived experiences of lesbians and our communities, and erotic photography which explores the representation of lesbian sex and sexuality. Della Grace does both. *Love Bites*, for example, includes photographs of marches – Lesbian Strength, Lesbian and Gay Pride, Stop the Clause, Gay Freedom Day – in London and San Francisco, and shots of club and bar scenes. We need all the lesbian documentary photographers we can get, to record our activism, our celebration and our play. No straight photographer is going to bother (and would we want them to, anyway?) and, without images such as these, key moments in our history will be lost. But it is as a sex photographer that Grace is best known, and it is her work in this area which concerns us here.

As one of the mainstays of *Quim*, and as the woman responsible for *Love Bites*, Grace's sex photography has moved through several stages. In the beginning was the provocative and theatrical playfulness of *Love Bites*: using a dressing-up box of props and costumes, the women in the staged scenarios camp it up in high style, cocking a snook at the grown-ups. In 'Cold Store Romance', two dykes, Robyn and Angie, clown around in tutu, docs, black net and leather, making a game of the whole thing. In the now familiar series 'The Ceremony', mix-and-match gender games are played between a leather-capped, bare-breasted 'groom' and flirtatious femme 'bride' in corset, PVC gloves, studded wristband and white net veil. Thanks (I suspect) to the peaked leather cap, 'The Ceremony' has been subject to the familiar lazy thinking which damns it by association with fascism. This is seen most clearly in Louise Allen's review of *Stolen Glances*, a book about lesbian photography which included three shots from 'The Ceremony':

> this set of images causes a dilemma. An attempt to assail the pro-censorship New Right among feminists by using Old Right imagery, with its accompanying racist associations, must sit in relation to renewed activism on the part of the National Front in Europe, and the political implications of the Asylum Bill for example. Perhaps we should ask how the depiction of lesbian sexual fantasy alongside Nazi symbolism rests in a cultural climate where the appropriated imagery refers not only to Hitler's Germany, but a much more recent climate of renewed racist abuse and legislatory oppression.[14]

Nazi symbolism? Perhaps I had missed a swastika tattoo? Damn! That meant I had to go back and gaze at every inch of flesh again. In the line of duty I did, and found linked women's symbols, a horseshoe, a galloping horse and a unicorn. Yes, it was that peaked cap ... again. Is it cynical of me to suggest that there are better ways to fight European fascism than attacking your fellow lesbians for wearing peaked caps? And am I being obtruse when I suggest that Nazi symbolism means something quite specific, whereas peaked caps in fact carry quite a wide set of codes (admittedly, some of them troublesome)? If Grace's models were draped in double-headed eagles, swastikas and iron crosses, I would question the use of Nazi symbolism. But they are not, and, given the relationship between this urban lesbian community and the *real* fascists who harrass and threaten them, smearing these women as Nazis is doubly offensive.

There is a sting in the tail of 'The Ceremony' which is generally missed when only one or two images are reproduced in isolation: the final shot shows the re-butching of the 'bride' as, in leather jacket and bowler hat, she delivers a mock uppercut to the butch, now altogether less macho in tail coat and crownless hat. This image, owing more to Laurel and Hardy than anything else, transforms the meaning of the entire sequence. It also comments in a very interesting way on the whole symbolic lexicon of masculinity and male bonding, with its elaborate costumes and play-fighting. It is here, in fact, that the key to understanding Grace's work lies. It is not sex or sexuality *per se* that interests Grace, it is *gender*. In particular, the gendering of the sexual.

The sequence in *Love Bites* which caused most controversy is the five-image photo-story 'Ruff Sex', in which two butch dykes – one of whom is the groom from 'The Ceremony' – concentrate their attentions on a leather-slut femme. Two shots show the femme lying on her stomach across a wooden stool (covered with a leather jacket), being fucked from behind by a dildo-packing leather dyke, while her head is held by the erstwhile 'groom'. Critics complained that this was lesbians imitating heterosex at its worst, that the scene simply replicated rape and violent assault. Even positive accounts of the sequence begin with an uneasy reference to the appearance of rape:

> 'Ruff Sex' seems to be a gang bang. But the rapist wears a dildo, the victim seems in sexual ecstasy and the minder cradles her head with tenderness.[35]

> On first view the image invoked a gang rape to me. I saw the blonde woman being restrained, her mouth swollen and open as though she had been beaten about the face. But then I noticed that the rapist is wearing nail polish. The accomplice is smiling rather tenderly. This dimension made the photo even more disconcerting ... [36]

In one of the photographs, Grace highlights the contradictory femme accoutrements of the scene by careful hand-tinting. The femme and the 'accomplice' have pink-tinted lips, but the big daddy butch dyke who is actually doing the fucking (and whose legs and arms are all we can see) has her nail varnish highlighted in the same pink, and the hundreds of little plastic beads in her bracelets have been picked out in red, yellow, blue, white and green. This (feminine?) fussy attention to detail foregrounds the fact that these are three women. Nevertheless, these two images could still, possibly, be interpreted as images of abuse. Again, the meaning is located in the sequence. It opens with the femme standing proprietorially behind 'her' butch, who turns her head to one side, evading our gaze. The femme, on the other hand, confronts the camera with a direct, challenging gaze of her own. This image utterly undermines the monolithic male-subject/woman-object binary of heterosexual archetype.

The two fucking scenes follow, and then a shot in which the dildo-wearing butch bends forward into the picture frame to bury her face between the femme's buttocks. The 'accomplice' leans over the femme, offering a finger to be licked. Both butches are re-femmed in this shot: the dildo-wearer is now wearing strings of beads around her ankle as well as her wrists, and is clearly servicing the femme; and the accomplice's left breast hangs, vulnerable and sharply outlined against shadow, over the femme's head lying in her lap.

In the final shot, 'Be My Bitch', the 'accomplice' kneels at the feet of the femme, hands secured behind her back, gazing up into the femme's face submissively, with a chain hanging from the corner of her mouth like a dog wanting to be taken for a walk. The femme's thigh-booted foot is wedged firmly against the butch's crotch and she holds the other woman's face in her gloved hand, appraisingly. The power dynamic has reversed. Far from being a slavish imitation of heterosexual power relations, this sequence in fact insists on the fluidity and instability of the power relations available in lesbian sex. It represents, in other words, the *difference* which lesbian sex makes.

Following the publication of *Love Bites*, Della went on to become more queer, playing with different ways of destabilizing gender using the sign 'Lesbian'. In a photo-essay published in *Quim*, 'Daddy Boy Dykes', two young white dykes, Skeeter and Aphra, play the part of two gay leathermen involved in a sexual encounter. Dressed as men, right down to stick-on clone moustaches, the women are initially 'read' as gay men. As more and more female flesh gradually appears out of the leather and denim shells – a woman's back, a softly rounded buttock, a breast casting its unmistakable shadow on leather or skin – these gay men hatch into lesbians. This playful (and erotic) series of images is positively stuffed with queer readings. They may be read in various ways: about how masculinity *always* suppresses and disavows the feminine, whether in men or women; about the cultural masculinization of lesbians and the feminization of gay men, and the instability of that straight 'mistake'; about the coding of sexual agency as male and the need for *all* people, male or female, to position themselves as male in order to achieve and express sexual agency; about the *differences* between lesbians and gay men which we may not consciously recognize, but which unexpectedly confront us when the behaviour of these two young women, their body language or gesture does not quite 'fit' the script; about poking fun at those gay men who claim that lesbians aren't a very sexual people; about refusing what Grace calls the 'Lesbian Puritans,' construct of lesbians as 'at the vanguard of angelic sex';[17] about disconcerting the reader; about recognizing the irresistible erotic charge of a body which is *the same as your own*; even about the eroticization of mutuality called for by Sheila Jeffreys and other revolutionary feminists. All these and many other meanings, are densely packed into this sequence of eight photographs.

From *Love Bites* and 'Daddy Boy Dykes', Grace went on to experiment with a more pared-down series of images. The 'Xeno-morphisis' collection consists of one almost abstract series of exquisitely sensual nudes – young, white, shaven-headed women in balletic poses – and another group of shots of three butch women which are less abstract and more theatrical. The first set includes some of the best work Grace has ever produced, in terms of 'art photography'. These are unique. My favourite is 'Triad' (see plate 7), with its intertwined limbs, beautifully tight triangular composition and delightfuly perverse meeting of three sets of lips (referencing a swarm of ideas, from medieval paintings of demons to Luce Irigary's 'two lips' theory of femaleness). Then there is the irresistible 'Pussy-Licking Sodomite', which, with dyke nudity set against socks and Docs, wicked tongues and exquisitely formal composition, is both a dramatic departure from conventional nude photography (and lesbian erotica, for that matter) and as queer as all get out. The baldness of the models, the sensual lighting and the dense, black formless space they occupy combine to play strange games with the ways in which we 'read' the women's bodies. Sometimes soft, almost foetal, sometimes sinewy and powerful, sometimes maternal, at others mischievously sexual, this series manages to resist comfortable readings.

The other series is more confrontational. In pictures such as 'Three Butches', 'Three Graces' and 'The Gatekeeper', the three models – wearing leather-belted shorts or naked (except for socks and Docs) – present an assertive eroticism which stands very firmly on its own territory and on its own terms. These pictures both celebrate and create a space for butch lesbian desire. Parveen Adams, in a thoughtful essay on 'Three Graces', suggests that Grace has succeeded in developing an entirely new space in the representation of women. 'These women', she writes, 'are beyond recognition. For it is within the space of recognition that the representation of women is played out.'[38]

In the final issue of *Quim*, Della published some of her 'boudoir photographs'. In these, she works with couples, individuals or groups of people to construct erotic scenarios according to their wishes. The sequence, in reference to Foucault's notion of the 'ars erotica' (the art of the sexual) is titled 'Ars Poetica' (the art of the poetic), and the five images depict one lesbian couple, two shots of one man and two women, one shot of one man and two women, and a final *pièce de résistance* with three men and one woman. But it is all very queer, to the extent that I cannot quite convince myself that the 'man' in amorous play with the two very femme women *is* a man. Is that 'his' cock he is holding, or is 'he' a third woman with a dildo? It *seems* to be the ultimate straight man's fantasy, being sandwiched between two women, but Della has fucked around in my head and I no longer want to put money on it.

In the final two shots, however, there is absolutely no mistaking the *sex* of the participants. There is too much nudity for mistakes to be made. But the question of sexual orientation is another matter. Surely, with those boots, that leather, those hairstyles, they are all queer? And yet ... here again we have a man sandwiched between two women. Only he is a *gay* man, and those are lesbians. Here is Della Grace, queer photographer, recording (and doubtless aiding and abetting) the queering of sexual categories. I don't like it, because it doesn't address my sexual fantasies. But I am not about to dismiss it as unimportant or politically incorrect.

I don't know what the end result of queer will be: will it turn out to have been a radical turning point, that moment when the first sexual couplings between lesbians and gay men were talked about, or will we look back and groan, 'How could we have been so naff?' Only time will tell. Meanwhile, Della is recording this historical moment in her queer community, and continuing her personal project of ensuring that we are no longer confident about what's a boy and what's a girl, who's straight and who's queer. She writes about her 'Xenomorphisis' series:

> These photographs seek to visually deconstruct our notions of Woman, of Lesbian and of Perversion in order to create a space for the exploration and celebration of diversity and desire. I call this xenomorphisis.[39] Xenomorphisis means to embrace that which is Other within yourself. Xenomorphisis is a gestation period in queer culture.[40]

And Grace is certainly one of the most important (if not the most important) photographers of queer culture. She has also, among the mundane, the self-conscious and the simply clichéd, managed to produce some masterly images of stunning eroticism. If she were a man, she would undoubtedly be taken more seriously as a photographer, and treated less as a titillating eccentric. There is also the very real issue that far too many critics are straight, and that can lead to problems. For example, Sarah Kent writes that, 'Della has been nicknamed "Disgrace" by the lesbian community for contravening moral codes'.[41] This simplistic outsider's view of our communities all too often rides on the back of commentary about Grace's work. Nobody in any lesbian community I've had anything to do with refers to Della as 'Disgrace', and the notion that the lesbian community has some set of 'moral codes' which may be contravened is pure nonsense. If Grace has to collude with such ignorant heterosexist games in order to gain notoriety, she risks being dismissed as a passing fad. And it certainly will not benefit our communities (hands up the dyke who wants to be associated with the idea that there is one true lesbian community with a set of 'moral codes' ...). We need lesbian critics to take lesbian photographers seriously, and this is particularly true of someone like Della, whose hunger for attention could mean that eventually her work is relegated to second place in favour of her desire to shock. We get the photographers we deserve.

Words and pictures: Tee Corinne

Tee Corinne is that rare thing, a politically correct pornographer!

Thoroughly grounded in the American mainstream lesbian-feminist tradition, her work is widely accepted by those lesbian feminists who would not be seen dead with a copy of *Quim* in their hands. Yet this acceptance is in some ways contradictory. For, whereas Della Grace is primarily interested in *gender*, and concerned to deconstruct it and its relationship to sexuality – all of which are true of feminism – Corinne is primarily interested in *sex*, and in sexual pleasure – which is certainly *not* the case for feminism.

Tee Corinne does not play with ideas of masculinity and femininity, she does not deconstruct the cultural construction of 'lesbian', she does not attempt to disengage gender from sexuality or to engage with theoretical questions of the male gaze or the masculinizing of the sexual subject. Her concern is with lesbians and sex, pure and simple, and she sees sex as central to lesbian identity and community: 'As lesbians, our sexuality binds us together. It creates ties of friendship between former lovers and electrical currents between would be, present and future lovers. It is not irrelevant. It is central.'[42]

She not only takes photographs of lesbian sex, she also writes stories and makes drawings about lesbian sex. Although her explorations of the sexual and her creativity in making erotica are both firmly sited within feminism, she does not adhere to any narrow party line about proper feminist sex. Nor is she in any sense pro-censorship. Yet she does propose a spiritual, almost mystical, account of lesbian sexuality which is shaped very directly by a particular political vision of woman-identification. She writes, in the introduction to a collection of her erotic stories:

> This book ... grew out of my interest in the function of erotic writing; in how we, as lesbians, explore sexual issues, learn to grow within long-term relationships, share with new lovers, and use sexual energy as a healing force in our lives.[43]

This may lead the wary reader to anticipate pages of politically pure sex, penetration-free and purged of male-identified behaviours such as the sexual objectification of other women. Yet Corinne, despite her feminist roots, does not fit easily into any stereotypical slot. In her introduction to *Lovers,* she lists several books which have contributed to a growth in the availability of lesbian erotica, and includes Pat Califia's *Macho Sluts* with the straightforward description, 'for lesbians interested in s/m.'[44] She makes no attempt to discredit or demonize Califia or lesbian s/m. Further on, she discusses lesbian-authored accounts of casual sex, butt-fucking and fisting, all in the context of drawing attention to – and celebrating – the breadth of lesbian sex writing:

> From the density and complex levels of caring in Joan Nestle's 'Esther' (*A Restricted Country*) to the structured sex education of JoAnn Loulan's *Lesbian Sex* and Pat Califia's *Sapphistry*, lesbians are making language and meaning work together to facilitate a literature the likes of which has never existed before.[45]

Corinne's own stories include accounts of threesomes, masturbation with carrots, butch/femme dynamics and voyeurism, as well as incorporating traditional lesbian-feminist concerns such as childhood sex abuse, attempted rape, bereavement and substance abuse. They tend to be short and to the point – flipping through a Tee Corinne book looking for the action is more rewarding than doing the same with most other collections of lesbian erotica!

Because Corinne has been involved with lesbian feminism in the USA since the early days of the WLM – it was she who produced the famous *Cunt Coloring Book* – she has made space within the lesbian-feminist political mainstream for sex-positive explorations of the erotic. So her photographs are to be found in Julia Penelope and Susan Wolfe's edited collection *Lesbian Culture*, a book which reflects a very specific lesbian-feminist/political-lesbian account of lesbianism, and also in Tessa Boffin and Jean Fraser's book *Stolen Glances: Lesbians Take Photographs*, which represents a more queer-nuanced, pluralist lesbian perspective. It might be said that her erotica has achieved 'cross-over success'.

Corinne's photography is characterized by technical manipulation. Her subject matter is often overtly located in a feminist political agenda – woman as nature, celebrating the sexuality of fat women or disabled women – but the complexities of the presentation and the explicit nature of the sexual imagery she uses make her work appealing on many additional levels. Sometimes she uses composite imagery: 'Isis in the Woods' is a landscape showing sunlight outside a darkened wood, but in the foreground what briefly appeared to be a branch lying in the grass surrounded by leaf mould is suddenly transformed into a woman's labia and pubic hair. It is too simple to see this as just another image of woman-as-landscape, in the familiar male photographic tradition. It is true that pictures of nude women as landscape are ten-a-penny, but male photographers generally confine this romanticizing genre to coding buttocks/breasts/belly as curving hills, or the nude female trunk as the torso of a tree. It is only when confronted with the shocking fact that Corinne's trick makes the viewer look closely at a woman's *cunt* that we realize how invisible this part of women's bodies has been within the pseudo-romantic male fantasy typical of the genre. Corinne's celebration of woman in the woodland focuses on women's sexuality, the seat of female sexual pleasure. In other words, precisely what is most often erased in the woman-as-landscape genre.

She also uses solarization and negative printing, techniques which distance the viewer, disrupt the fantasy that the photograph is a 'slice of life', and help to protect the identity of her models. This is an important theme in her work, and indicates, as Jan Zita Grover notes, the extent to which the sexuality Corinne represents remains dangerous, at risk:

> Th[e] deliberate obscuring arises out of her concern for 'afford(ing) my models some measure of privacy' rather than prurience ... Corinne's subjects are acting out their personal life, which is paradoxically more in need of protection than the public behaviour of models. ... These heavily manipulated images function not only as protection for the individual model's identity, but also as a correlative for the status of the public lesbian, present yet hidden ... provocative yet in need of protection.[46]

In 'The Three Graces' (called 'Dyke Trilogy' in *Lesbian Culture*), three fat lesbians stand, naked, in the classical pose of the three Graces from Western art. The central figure faces us, her gaze returning ours from behind the lenses of her spectacles. On either side, two women stand with their backs to us, the three linked by a loose embrace. Again, this is a comment on, and a resistance to, a male tradition. The pose – two women with their backs to the viewer flanking one in full face – is entirely traditional;[47] the stance of the three women is not. Whereas in traditional painting and sculpture the three women would be positioned to display their charms to best advantage for the male gaze, with a tantalizing element of Sapphic body contact thrown in for good measure, these three stand firmly on the ground, and their contact with each other excludes, rather than entices, the interloping gaze. Moreover, whereas paintings of the three Graces have traditionally conformed to dominant ideals of female beauty current at the time, these three women do not. In a culture which values thinness in women, these women are fat. Corinne's picture dramatically reverses all the iconographic traditions which her title 'The Three Graces' calls up.

A photograph taken for the cover of *Sinister Wisdom* (No. 3) in 1977 shows two women having sex. One is lying back in the arms of her lover, who is finger-fucking her. Yet the combination of negative printing and lyrical composition – the two could be mother and child or pietà – contrive to make this explicit image appear romantic and aesthetically delightful, without detracting from its frank eroticism. A later image, 'A Woman's Touch No. 7' (part of which is reproduced in *Lesbian Culture* as 'Dykes Kissing'), shows two naked women, one of whom is in a wheelchair, kissing. A composite panel below, in the style of the 'reredos' of early altarpieces, repeats the close-up of their two faces. Again, negative printing affords a degree of privacy, and distances the viewer. The distancing lends a universalism which is often hard to signify in photography: these are not just two particular individuals kissing, they stand for a relationship between lesbian sexuality and disability.

In the 1980s, Corinne began to compose multiple-image prints using reversed negatives and solarization. The 'Yantras of Womanlove' (see plate 8) produced in this way are complex, kaleidoscopic images which reference Tantric religious paintings and look, at first glance, merely pretty. Yet they actually depict, explicitly, women having sex with each other. Corinne's intention was to produce 'images complex enough that people would want to stay with them for a long time, puzzle them out',[48] and this is certainly part of the pleasure of these intriguing photographs. They can be, at the same time, secret and overt, concealed and explicit. A powerful metaphor for lesbian sex indeed! Corinne writes: 'I understand what I am doing as contributing to a kind of sanity, a witnessing, an affirmation of the fleshy side of lesbianism with more than a whiff of the transcendent. That is, when I'm successful.'[49]

One of the reasons for the success of her work with such a wide range of lesbians probably lies in her consciously romantic approach. Here is lesbian sex presented as simultaneously hot and delightful, as beautiful, transcendent and raunchy. In contrast to the work of someone like Della Grace, whose sexual explicitness goes hand in hand with a celebration of perversity, of deviance, of decadence, Corinne's 'Yantras' assert that you can be a nice, gentle, sweet person and *still* have ecstatic, outrageous sex. It is a very appealing vision, especially to feminists who want to steer the difficult line between enjoying sex and turning into a male-identified patriarchal power fiend. Corinne's strategy is quite conscious:

> I have been accused of romanticizing lovemaking between women, of leaving out the times one kicked one's lover accidentally, in the head while turning over. It's true. Lesbians have often been portrayed negatively. And I decided that it was not my inclination to do this. In making my audience what Barbara Greir has called the 'Garden Variety Lesbian', I turned away from the theorists who defined cutting-edge work as necessarily deconstructionist or sado-masochistic.[50]

It's good, wholesome sex, it's lovingly and wittily presented for our delight, it's a beautiful object to hang on your wall, it romanticizes lesbian sex but does not distort it or lie about it in order to do so, and it's hot. What more could a girl want?

Up and coming dyke photographer: Laurence Jaugey-Paget

Della Grace was not the only lesbian sex photographer to contribute to *Quim* on a regular basis. Any afficionado of the magazine cannot have failed to notice the work of Laurence Jaugey-Paget, whose luscious photographs for Pandora's lesbian sex coffee-table book *Making Out* have brought her to prominence as a photographer of lesbian sex.

Unlike Della Grace or Tee Corinne, Laurence Jaugey-Paget rarely uses technical manipulation in her photographs. Nor does she present a theoretical concern with issues such as gender, or attempt to challenge or subvert dominant representations of the female body. She just takes photographs of women having sex. Her chief concern is with the models and what they are doing, rather than with aesthetics of the shot. This means that there is little sense in her work of ideas undergoing a process of development, or of a particular 'eye' at work. Whereas it is often possible to tell that a particular photograph is by Della or Tee Corinne, Laurence has no recognizable style as such, no wider vision which informs her pictures and marks them as hers. This means that her published work is very patchy; although much is decidedly stylish and highly erotic, some is frankly weak. When the photographer has no driving vision, much depends on the models. In some of her sequences – especially those published in *Quim* – the women appear to be really having sex, and there is a raw excitement which makes up for the lack of 'artistic' awareness. In others, especially many of the sequences for *Making Out*, the action appears much more staged, and it becomes hard to 'read' the intention behind the photographs. Are they theatrical scenarios along the lines of much of Grace's work, or can they be read as adopting the classic 'naive' approach (on which so much traditional heterosexual porn depends) of pretending to give us privileged access to something 'real'?

Laurence's use of colour in *Making Out* adds a further dimension of uncertainty. Her most successful work tends to be in black and white, and she can do lovely things with sensual, deep blacks and high-contrast whites produced with a skilful use of lighting and flash. Although she is clearly a very good photographer and takes clear, crisp colour photographs, she is not a colour photographer as such; she does not make the colour work hard enough for her. This means that the use of colour tends to add to the 'illusion-of-reality' effect of some of the shots.

Her subject matter, although never moving into the darker reaches of sex, is broad and varied. *Making Out*, for example, contains a lovely sequence showing two black women, one of them heavily pregnant, playing affectionately together in a shower and a jacuzzi. In presenting beautiful, positive images of black lesbians, *and* in asserting the sexuality (what is more, the *lesbian* sexuality) of a mother, this sequence breaks new ground in the representation of women and of lesbians. Living in the UK – a society which has passed legislation stating that lesbian families are 'pretend', and which generally holds that lesbians are unfit to mother *because* of our sexuality – Jaugey-Paget's sequence is powerfully affirmative, and prepares the ground for an oppositional representational practice.

Less effective is the photo-story illustrating the 'Sex Gear' section of *Making Out*, which shows a fantasy scenario of the seduction of a woman welder by a trash-femme housewife on her kitchen work surface. There is just too much going on. At one point the intent seems to be to parody 1950s American spanking porn à la Betty Page, at another a cigar butt suddenly appears (perhaps a reference to the famous cigar-eating scene between Susan Hampshire and Beryl Reed in *The Killing of Sister George*?). The two women, having established a butch/femme dynamic, switch clothes so that the erstwhile 'welder' dons the slinky satin petticoat and the bleached femme the welder's boiler suit. There is even one shot in the early part of the sequence where the 'welder' sprouts a black silicone cock, which the femme somewhat tentatively fingers. Not sufficiently confident with gender-fuck to carry it through a lengthy fantasy scenario, Laurence is at her best constructing the illusion of voyeurism, taking photographs of ordinary lesbians having ordinary sex, seemingly in their 'natural habitat' – snogging in the cinema or the front seat of a soft-top car, or apparently overwhelmed by desire during a woodland walk.

Not an 'art' photographer like Della Grace or Tee Corinne, both of whom have a clear idea about what they want to say, and who use their models to put their ideas into practice, Jaugey-Paget's skill lies in giving us what appears to be a privileged glimpse of 'real' lesbians having 'real' sexual encounters. This makes her the ideal photographer to illustrate a dyke sex manual. For, in the classic strategy of erotica, her photographs offer a space for the fantasy participation of the viewer. It is difficult, looking at Grace's entwined bald nudes or Corinne's kaleidoscope 'Yantras', to imaginatively insert oneself into the action. That is not what the work is 'about'. Looking at a sequence by Laurence Jaugey-Paget – when they work – the lesbian viewer can fantasize that she is participating, either as one of the women represented or as an onlooker. A budding lesbian, whether baby-dyke or just coming-out older woman, is offered a wide range of possibilities to experiment with and a wide range of protagonists with whom she can identify. Because this is the case, it also opens *Making Out* up for a very specific set of criticisms, which would simply be inappropriate in the context of Grace's or Corinne's work. Although Laurence's body of work represents women from a broad range of ethnic backgrounds, there is a much narrower range when it comes to age, and no attempt to include fat or disabled lesbians. Since her work presents itself as 'reflecting' what happens in lesbian communities, it seems important that lesbians who are excluded from significant areas of lesbian life are not excluded from the sexual fantasy world which Jaugey-Paget's work offers.

Kisses, tongues and telling: Kiss and Tell

Kiss and Tell are a trio of Canadian sex artists – Persimmon Black-bridge, Lizard Jones and Susan Stewart – who use photography as a way of stretching the bounds of the pornography debate, of exploring the representation of lesbian sexuality, and of encouraging a more adventurous and honest approach to speaking about lesbian sex. All three started out in the feminist anti-pornography movement only to became dissatisfied with it. As a consequence, they have developed a critique of sexualized representation which is both grounded in feminist politics and theory and at the same time critical of the direction which pro-censorship feminists have chosen. They are, in particular, deeply alarmed by the alliance between feminists and the legislature, pointing out that while vocal criticism is one thing, the legal power of censorship is quite another:

> when a lesbian group in Northampton, Massachusetts protested against DRAWING THE LINE, saying it promoted violence against women, they had neither the power of the state nor the power of social sanction to use against us. They were angry, they were protesting, but they were not censors.[51]

Their first intervention into the porn wars was to organize an exhibition, *Drawing the Line*, which toured Canada, Australia and the USA in the late 1980s and early 1990s. The exhibition contained photographs of lesbian sex, ranging from the most tender, mild and romantic to more troubling representations dealing with s/m and with the abuse of power in lesbian sex. At each venue, marker pens were made available, and women were invited to write comments on the walls of the galleries (men were asked to write their comments in a book). Thus, the exhibition itself *became a conversation* between the artists and the viewers, and among the viewers. The next step was to select forty of the photographs and publish them as a postcard book, so that they could be distributed to yet more people, and to incorporate into the postcard book a card addressed to the publisher, with space for more comment from the reader (see plate 10). Thus, even lesbians who never got to see the exhibition were included in the conversation about sex which Kiss and Tell had started. Moreover, each postcard carries a selection of comments made by viewers about the exhibition, enabling *their* voices to be widely heard. This represents an extraordinarily powerful opening-up of community discourse on lesbian sex, and an effective challenge to homophobic censorship:

The right wing has its own agenda, which is very different from the feminist debates on porn. In this context, *Drawing the Line* is a refusal to be shoved back into the closet. Lesbians aren't going to stop arguing, exploring, questioning and enjoying our sexuality.[33]

If it achieved nothing else, *Drawing the Line* certainly tapped into a strongly felt and dramatically contradictory set of debates within the lesbian communities where it was shown, as these comments on one image suggest:

This touches me the most intensely because it looks like my experience of real live lesbian sex. It is also the hardest to look at. (San Francisco)

Looks like straight women in porn films. (San Francisco)

Like most lesbian sex in art, this has too much politics and not enough sex. (San Francisco)

These comments, written by women whose readings of the same photograph are almost irreconcilably different, demonstrate vividly that the meaning of images is located in their reception, their reading, rather than in their content or intent. This is an important issue, one which complicates the whole debate about porno/graphy versus erotica, and which no lesbian theory of representation has yet adequately engaged with. By confronting difficult issues such as this, Kiss and Tell are taking the theory and practice of lesbian sexualized representation to a more sophisticated and politically developed level.

Their way of working also challenges traditional 'art' practice. Susan Stewart is the photographer, and Lizard and Persimmon are the models (see plate 11), although Susan does appear in front of the camera in some shots. Because the entire enterprise is a collaboration, Kiss and Tell breaks away from the traditional artist/model relationship, with all its associated problems of power/powerlessness, control, exploitation and authorial 'voice'. By using the same women's bodies in every shot, they avoid the troublesome question of representativeness – clearly it is not possible for two women to 'represent' the entire lesbian community in all its plurality – and reinforce the idea that what you do in bed does not define who you are. After all, if the same two women are seen taking part in a whole continuum of sexual activities, from the vanilla to the sadomasochistic, the notion that what you do determines who you are is revealed as an inadequate fiction. Certainly, the audience seized the opportunity to break down some restricting labels, as these reactions to another photograph suggest:

Drive it in hard.

Sounds like sexism to me. (Vancouver)

Role playing = power = men = boring. (Melbourne)

Where are the lesbian feminists?

Lesbian feminists like to fuck hard. (San Francisco)

After *Drawing the Line*, Kiss and Tell developed a performance piece, incorporating video sequences, photography and live action, which they called *True Inversions*. True to their philosophy of making their work accessible to as many women as possible, they then published *Her Tongue on My Theory*, a book containing essays on the censorship debate, photographs from *True Inversions*, discussion of their working practices and erotic fantasies. The essays in the book set out the theoretical and political position which informs their work. They argue that women's sexual speech has been silenced for too long, and that breaking that silence is a political act: 'Women as self-defining sexual subjects have been invisible or punished in Euro-American culture. There's a lot of scope for a search for truth here'.[53] Importantly, what distinguishes their call for a lesbian speaking about sex from (for example) Celia and Jenny Kitzingers' is their insistence that, far from being intrinsically 'nice' and politically pure, lesbian sexuality is complex and may contain disturbing elements which must be recognized. They also resolutely refuse to absolve abusive *men* of the responsibility for their actions, in a way which is (ironically) unusual in feminist debates on pornography:

Women's truth-seeking is inhibited if we deny that *some* women *do* love to be hurt, that they are *aroused* by rape fantasies, *enjoy* acts that in other contexts would be abuse. We need to look at where we really are, in all its complexity, not pretend that we're all too nice to have these feelings. The fear seems to be that if we talk about it (write about it, makes images of it), some men will take that as license to hurt, rape, and abuse women. I expect men to know the difference between fantasy and reality.[14]

All this theory and politics is all very well, I hear you say, but what about the photographs. Are they good? Are they hot? Do they live up to the theoretical demands which Kiss and Tell make of them? Yes to all that! The photographs, as a body of work, may be located somewhere between the theatricality of Della Grace and the illusion of realism constructed by Laurence Jaugey-Paget. Although clearly staged, the 'spark' which Persimmon describes between herself and Lizard (they are not off-camera lovers), and the trust they have in each other and in Stewart as photographer, informs every image. As in Laurence's sex-manual work, there is a range of sexual games on offer, from passionate embraces in the bath to staged scenarios in a studio setting. Unlike Laurence, however, the aim is to question rather than simply to represent, which (perhaps ironically) gives Kiss and Tell's work an additional level of engagement. Whether it comes from the theory, the strange *ménage à trois* of models and photographer, or from Stewart's technical skill in composing a shot, the photographs carry a more powerful sexual charge than most other lesbian sex photography. It is an irony worthy of further exploration that some of the hottest lesbian erotica around is being produced by three women who started out on the other side of the porn wars!

Conclusion

Lesbian sexuality has, until very recently, been erased, denied or exploited by men. Because representational practices help to construct our sense of self, our sense of community and our ideas about how the world works, the representation of lesbian sex in straight men's porno/graphy, combined with its invisibility in other arenas, has serious implications for lesbians and lesbian sexuality. We are unimaginably lucky to live at a time, and in a place, where it is possible for lesbians to represent lesbian sex for other lesbians. The differences between Grace, Corinne, Jaugey-Paget and Kiss and Tell give some indication of the rich vein of lesbian creativity which is now, for the first time in history, able to explore the representation of lesbian sex and its interplay with complex questions of gender, desire and power. Any attempt to stifle or direct this newly emergent voice, whether in the name of protecting the heterosexual family, defending religious dogma or keeping women to the feminist straight and narrow, is an anti-lesbian and anti-feminist act.

Notes

1. Cited in Cherry Smyth, *Lesbians Talk Queer Notions* (London: Scarlet Press, 1992), p. 40.
2. *Quim*, Issue 3, Winter 1991, p. 5.
3. Cited in Smyth, *Queer Notions*, p. 27.
4. *Ibid.*
5. *Ibid.*, p. 12.
6. Jenny Kitzinger and Celia Kitzinger, '"Doing It": Representations of Lesbian Sex' in Gabrielle Griffin (ed.) *Outwrite: Lesbianism and Popular Culture* (London: Pluto Press, 1993), p. 19.
7. *Ibid.*, pp. 20–21.
8. The phrase 'reproduces Grace's photographs' implies that *Quim* merely recycles the photographs from *Love Bites*. This is not the case. Despite the superficial public interest in lesbian sex and/or 'perverse' images more generally, it is far from easy for lesbian photographers of the erotic to get their work published – especially in a context where they will be available to their intended audience, other lesbians. *Quim* in fact published photographs by Della Grace which are not easily available elsewhere, and allowed her a degree of editorial control which mainstream journals simply don't give their photographers.
9. Kitzinger and Kitzinger, '"Doing It"', p. 21.
10. *Ibid.*
11. Leonore Tiefer, *Sex is not a Natural Act and Other Essays* (Oxford: Westview Press, 1995), p. 114.
12. *Ibid.*, pp.130–1
13. Kitzinger and Kitzinger, '"Doing It"', pp. 9–10.
14. Kiss and Tell, *Her Tongue on My Theory: Images, Essays and Fantasies* (Vancouver: Press Gang, 1994), p. 1.
15. *Ibid.*, p. 2.
16. Cindy Patton, 'Unmediated Lust? The Improbable Space of Lesbian Desires' in Tessa Boffin and Jean Fraser (eds.), *Stolen Glances: Lesbians Take Photographs* (London: Pandora, 1991), p. 239.
17. Kiss and Tell, *Her Tongue on My Theory*, pp. 52–3.
18. Patton, 'Unmediated Lust', p. 238.
19. For a detailed discussion of the shifting meanings of the word 'lesbian', see Tamsin Wilton *Lesbian Studies: Setting an Agenda* (London: Routledge, 1995).
20. Kiss and Tell, *Her Tongue on My Theory*, p. 53.
21. There were instances where privileged lesbians with the freedom and economic resources to do as they pleased were able to produce some (limited) lesbian imagery. This was the case with the small group of lesbian expatriates who lived in Paris before the Second World War – women such as Djuna Barnes, Gertrude Stein and Natalie Barney. However, these are rare exceptions.
22. Kiss and Tell, *Her Tongue on My Theory*, p. 51.
23. Cheryl Wiesenfeld, Yvonne Kalmus, Sonia Katchian and Rikki Ripp (eds.), *Women See Women*, (New York: Thomas Y. Crowell, 1976); Cynthia MacAdams, *Emergence*, (New York: Chelsea House, 1977).
24. Cynthia MacAdams, *Rising Goddess* (New York: Morgan and Morgan, 1983).
25. I don't think this is just personal

preference. Yes, *Rising Goddess* turns me on and *Love Bites* doesn't, but I think this has got far more to do with the contrived and stage-managed nature of Grace's approach than with my own personal sexual 'programming'.

26. Kiss and Tell, *Her Tongue on My Theory*, p. 54.

27. Della Grace, 'Xenomorphisis', *New Formations*, No. 19 Spring 1993, p. 123.

28. *Ibid.*

29. Deborah Orr, 'Say Grace', *Weekend Guardian*, 22 July 1995, p. 12.

30. Sarah Kent, 'Photosensitive', *Time Out*, 12-19 June 1991, pp. 18–19. I am not sure what Kent means by her remark that the lesbian subculture (as if there was only one!) 'legally does not exist'. I must assume that she is referring to the old idea that the law (which criminalizes some forms of gay male sex) does not recognize lesbians. However, this article was written in 1991, well after the passage into law of the notorious Section 28 of the 1988 Local Government Act, and bang in the middle of legal wrangling about lesbian access to fertility clinics, adoption and fostering, etc., when the law most certainly *did* recognize that lesbians exist.

31. *Ibid.*, p. 18.

32. Orr, 'Say Grace' p. 14.

33. Wilton, *Lesbian Studies* p. 147.

34. Louise Allen, 'Looking Good, Feeling Queer: Queer Theory and Lesbian Representation', *New Formations* No. 19 p. 146.

35. Kent, 'Photosensitive', p. 18.

36. Sarah Schulman, 'Della Grace: Photos on the Margins of the Lesbian Community', introduction to Della Grace, *Love Bites*, (London: Gay Men's Press, 1991), p. 5.

37. Kent, 'Photosensitive' p. 19.

38. Parveen Adams, 'The Three (Dis)Graces', *New Formations*, No. 19 Spring 1993, p. 131. This is one of the best theoretical assessments of Grace's work that I have read, and is very positive.

39. For a fuller explanation of 'xenomorphisis', see Grace's article of that name in *New Formations*, No. 19.

40. *Quim*, Issue 4, 1992.

41. Kent, 'Photosensitive', p. 18.

42. Tee A. Corinne, *Lovers: Love and Sex Stories* (Austin, Tex.: Banned Books, 1989), p. 1.

43. *Ibid.*, p. 1.

44. *Ibid.*, p. 2.

45. *Ibid.*, p. 7.

46. In Boffin and Fraser (eds.), *Stolen Glances*, p. 228.

47. The central figure is traditionally full-frontal and most exposed to the gaze of the viewer. The two lesser beauties show us their backs!

48. In Boffin and Frazer (eds.), *Stolen Glances*, p. 228.

49. Tee A. Corinne, 'Art Essay: Artist's Statement on Sexual Art, *Feminist Studies*, Vol. 19 No. 2, p. 370.

50. *Ibid.*

51. Persimmon Blackbridge in Kiss and Tell, *Her Tongue on My Theory*, p. 95. Readers interested in finding out more about the work of this group are recommended to get hold of this book and/or their postcard book *Drawing the Line* (Vancouver: Press Gang, 1991).

52. Kiss and Tell, *Drawing the Line*, Introduction.

53. Kiss and Tell, *Her Tongue on My Theory*, p. 81.

54. *Ibid.*, p. 82.

7

Into the Male/Strom
Dildos and All that Boy Stuff

One question which percolates through much of the literature about lesbians and lesbianism concerns the troubled relationship which lesbian sexuality has with the phallus. This question often takes the form of attending to butch/femme role-play and to dildos,[1] and is located in various strands of feminist discourse, sexological, medical and historical attempts to account for lesbian desire and pleasure, psychoanalysis (including psychoanalytic film theory) and queer theory among others. It is important to clarify that the phallus is not the same as a penis (or even *the* penis). Whereas a penis is a particular genital organ usually attached to people designated 'male',[2] the phallus is a purely imaginary fiction which symbolizes 'pure' male power (sexual, political, intellectual and social), or which signifies, in Lacanian terms, entry to the symbolic order which structures civilization.

Theories of gender or of sexuality which are rooted in psychoanalysis tend to suggest that women cannot ever *have* the phallus, but that they may *be* the phallus and, indeed, that men frequently position women as the phallus in order to deflect the anxiety about castration which the (always already castrated) female body arouses in the fragile male psyche. This (straight) line of thought is of course resolutely and unreflexively heterosexist, as is all mainstream psychoanalytic thinking, but queerying it has given lesbian theorists like Parveen Adams and Teresa de Lauretis plenty to chew on.[3] De Lauretis, for example, comments that

> nearly everyone fails to note that the Lacanian framing of the question in terms of having or being the phallus is set in the perspective of normative heterosexuality (which indeed both psychoanalytic practice and theory strive to retrieve or induce in their subjects) with the sexual difference of man and woman clearly mapped out and the act of reproductive copulation firmly in place.[4]

The centrality of the phallus to psychoanalytic theories means that, when theorists such as de Lauretis attempt to make sense of lesbian desire, much attention is paid to the dildo. (It sometimes seems to me that more hours of lesbian energy are spent theorizing and writing about dildos than fucking with them.) So how should we regard the lesbian dildo? Is it a tool for the radical disruption of heterosexist gender norms and the subversion of male power – a lesbian seizing of the phallus – or is it, as the pro-censorship and revolutionary feminists would argue, a reactionary indicator of the worst form of male-identification? Is the new lesbian sex toy cottage industry an inspirational separatist strategy which nourishes the sisters of the lesbian nation, or is it a depressing sign of the degree to which lesbian energy is co-opted by the patriarchy? Watch this space!

Arguments about the role of gender in lesbian sex do not only coalesce around the question of dildos. What of butch and femme 'roles'? Are they expressions of a core lesbian disobedience to the regulation of gender, or do they merely replicate heterosexual power play? What is 'masculinity' anyway, and what is its relationship to lesbian sex and sexuality? Is playing with codes of *homo*masculinity any different from playing with heteromasculinity, or might we paraphrase Gertrude Stein and insist that 'dick is a dick is a dick'? And, since the question of lesbian 'masculinity' cannot be asked without reference to femininity, what of lesbian femininity, especially in the context of mothering? It is clear that the relationship between gender and sexuality is complex, and that the whole issue of reproduction and parenting, which is generally segregated from the erotic with some anxiety, makes it still more complex. I suggest that the figure of the lesbian occupies a particularly powerful position in the midst of all this complexity. Indeed, the lesbian might be said to occupy the very heart of a maelstrom (male/strom?) of conflicting beliefs about gender and sex. Which may be an exciting and exhilarating place to be, but may nevertheless also lead to personal pain, to a degree of hostility which queer communities can ill afford, and to lesbians trashing other lesbians.

Dykes with dicks: the disputed dildo

'Real lesbians, according to some feminists,' writes Cherry Smyth, 'apparently do not use dildos, yet they appear with remarkable regularity in American lesbian porn.'⁵ This strange phenomenon of the simultaneously erased-yet-visible dildo points to a series of confusions and contradictions within (and between) lesbians and lesbian feminism. Lesbian cartoonist Alison Bechdel sums up the complex history of the dildo in twentieth-century lesbian feminism in the cartoon for November in her 1994 *Dykes to Watch Out For* calendar.⁶ The theme for the cartoon is 'Simpler Times', and what Bechdel is discussing are the transformations in lesbian community mores which have taken place as 'our culture is undergoing change at an exponential pace'. One frame shows two women in bed together, one of whom is reading aloud from a book entitled *The Orthodox Joy of Lesbian Sex*. 'Hey listen to this! "Dildoes are purely a male fantasy. *Real* lesbians have never even *seen* one."' To which her lover, wearing an empty dildo harness and idly playing with a knobbly dildo, comments, 'Hah! That old book of my mom's is so *quaint.*'

This cartoon neatly encapsulates the shift which seems to have taken place in lesbian-feminist culture with regard to dildos. From disavowing them as symptomatic of the patriarchal, phallocentric construct of sex, lesbians seem to have shifted to reclaiming them as instruments of lesbian sexual pleasure which, while not *necessary* to that pleasure, are certainly an optional 'extra'. The current climate in lesbian culture is summed up for me by a full-page advert in the Australian dyke sex magazine, *Wicked Women*,⁷ for '*Non phallic* silicone dildos, made in Australia, by Women, for Women', (my italics) and which proclaims, 'At last toys that don't assume all women suffer from penis envy'. This advert engages in a very direct way with what appears to be the central problem of dildos for lesbians, namely that using a dildo seems to reaffirm the idea of the lesbian as a deficient man, and of lesbian sex as unreal and inadequate because of the lack of a penis.

For pro-censorship and revolutionary feminists, using a dildo is unambiguously reactionary and plays into male fantasies of the supremacy of the penis. As Margaret Hunt comments:

> revolutionary feminists are better at saying what lesbian physicality is not than what it is. Pure lesbian sexuality is not lesbianism infected with phallocentric fantasies or phallic objects (e.g. dildoes). ... Some consider vibrators acceptable as long as they are not the elongated type which you can insert.⁸

In her research into lesbian sexual attitudes published in 1974, Dolores Klaich found many women disapproved of their use (although others were less judgemental). Here are a few typical responses:

> I think they're an invention of male novelists – especially the 18th and 19th century pornographers.

> I feel that only those women with hangups about their sexual identity and desire to be as much a 'man' as possible use them consistently.

> I think men are the ones who commonly suppose this – they can't conceive of how a woman can have sexual satisfaction without a penis or at least a penis substitute.[9]

Clearly, dildos were at this time associated with phallocentric *male* fantasies about lesbian sex. This association dominated 1970s lesbian feminism, but continues to this day. A lesbian responding to a *Quim* survey about dildo use commented that 'a dildo seems to suggest that a woman is not enough', and most writers agree that, indeed, 'Porno-graphic fiction is full of dildoes.'[10] The general interpretation of the profligate representation of dildos in heteromale porn is that the dildo reinscribes male phallic power onto an erotic scene which excludes men. Klaich cites psychologists Phyllis and Eberhard Kronhausen, whose systematic examination of erotic fiction turned up many accounts of dildo-wielding dykes:

> The Kronhausens theorize that the frequency of the use of dildoes in such fiction might be explained by the fact that the heterosexual male author or reader 'projects himself through fantasy into the lesbian situation'. ... He cannot appear penis-less, so one of the lesbians is 'transformed into a male or, at least, into a phallic female.[11]

But this careless elision misses the point. A 'phallic female' is not at all the same thing as a man. The history of sex between women leads us to recognize both that the dildo has an important place in the historical development of lesbian culture and lesbian identity and that *men's* relationship to the lesbian dildo is far more insecure and complex than any oversimplistic Freudian notion of castration and penis envy can enable us to comprehend. For it is from Freud that we may date the belief that women suffer from penis envy, that lesbians want to be men and that, in consequence, the lesbian who uses a dildo is expressing her own *lack* of the phallus (the artificial penis being a pathetic attempt to compensate for that lack) and her own failure to achieve masculinity. 'Freud attributes lesbianism not to woman's own specifically female desires but to her desire to be a man. The lesbian is the woman who has never relinquished, or seeks to recover, her repressed phallic sexuality.'[12] This Freudian position, as Barbara Creed suggests, inevitably leads to the belief that the 'phallic sexuality' of the lesbian dildo marks the dyke as the inevitable loser in the contest between straight men and deviant women for sexual access to (real) women's bodies:

> the lesbian is deemed ultimately as incapable of even assuming a pseudo-male position because, like all women, she signifies an irremediable lack ... she signifies only castration and lack. Her lack, however, can be overcome artificially by the use of a dildo – a popular male fantasy about lesbian sexual practices.[13]

But this model of lesbian sexuality, which seems so powerfully to reaffirm male (hetero)sexual power, is relatively recent. The Freudian model of sexual difference, which has so successfully saturated contemporary notions of gender and the erotic, was not based on empirical evidence and carries the traces of a *political* response to the relations between the sexes of Freud's own day. As Creed goes on to point out:

> Not only Freud ... feared the active woman. Bram Dijkstra points out that at the time there were a number of popular beliefs in circulation about the dangers of the active, masculine woman who threatened to destroy the fragile boundaries which kept the sexes separate.[14]

Freud's response to what seems to have been a fairly general fear of the 'active woman' was to develop a sequence of *sui generis* theories which attempted once and for all to nail the penis to the masthead as the most important organ in human society. Castration anxiety, penis envy, the Oedipus and Electra complexes: the whole body of Freudian theory may be read without too much difficulty as an anxious attempt to insist – in the teeth of a steadily mounting feminist challenge to male power – that having a penis is what counts.

Dispensing with Freud and returning to pre-Freudian history, it is clear the reality is far more complex. Randolph Trumbach points out that in seventeenth-century Europe (and in the colonies) sexual penetration was the prerogative of men, and was jealously guarded as such. The legislative control of sexuality was far less concerned with the genders of sexual partners than with whether or not penetration took place, and with who penetrated whom: 'Women had sex with females, but without penetration. Sodomitical acts contravened the gender system only when they violated the patriarchal code, that is when adult men allowed themselves to be penetrated and when women penetrated women.'[15] The historical research by Trumbach and other scholars highlights the use of dildos by some women whom we would now call 'lesbians' (although the word is, strictly speaking, anachronistic in this context) and by 'passing women' or 'female husbands', women who successfully passed as men, often apparently deceiving even their wives. Trumbach tells us that, 'The author of the 1718 *Treatise of Hermaphrodites* had mentioned that some women used dildoes', and recounts the court case of one female husband who was 'brought to trial when her last wife's relatives found in her trunk "something of too vile, wicked and scandalous a nature"', namely a dildo.[16]

Emma Donoghue has found that dildos were fairly widely available in the UK during the seventeenth and eighteenth centuries, and that men's response to them was not clear cut. For while some texts of the time refer to the dildo 'as a feeble phallic substitute', it may also be 'a way for women to give each other pleasure which is so mysterious and powerful that (in an enduring fantasy) men disguise their penises as dildos'.[17] As Donoghue comments, such a fantasy suggests 'male satisfaction in ... tricking lesbians *whose use of a dildo threatens male power*'(my italics).[18] Far from confirming that lesbians are simply failed men, the dildo in fact may equally well suggest that men are simply inadequate dildos!

In contrast to penises, which come attached to male people and demonstrate a troublesome tendency to resist both the burden of phallic power (they may become soft and flaccid at the most inconvenient moments) and the imposition of disciplinary power (they are not easily controlled or directed by their 'owner'), it is not hard to see that dildos may be perceived as superior. Moreover, a cultural construct of masculinity which depends on sexual difference and which privileges phallic power as the mark and expression of masculinity is utterly undone by lesbians using dildos to give each other sexual pleasure. As

Cindy Patton suggests, 'Paradoxically, macho dykes in leather have undone the phallus with their collections of dildos.' She goes on to say, 'Lesbian erotic imagery must now subvert femininity by ... That remains to be seen.'[19] But, of course, if the dildos collected by the 'macho dykes in leather' have 'undone the phallus', the very plasticity of the lesbian phallus/dildo means that it may undo femininity *as well*. Cherry Smyth describes a lesbian porn video *Clips*, in which a dildo is used in ways which utterly resist its interpretation as an agent of hetero-sexuality. Far from being the phallic tool used by a butch on a femme, this dildo is used by the femme to assert autoerotic self-sufficiency:

> The femme fingers a large, clear dildo. ... Close-ups of the butch undoing her shirt and the femme's heaving chest draw the viewer into the promise of eventual fucking. However, the femme comes single-handed ... then fucks herself with the dildo, discreetly closing her legs to the camera and the viewer.[20]

Not only is the femme here claiming so-called 'masculine' sexual power for herself but she is also concealing the evidence of her penetrated self both from the so-called 'masculine' gaze of her butch and from the conventionally masculinized 'gaze' of the camera and the audience. This makes a mockery, fairly effortlessly, of heterosexual gender/erotic codes. For unless we claim that the femme, in fucking *herself* with the dildo, is enacting a kind of one-person heterosex, this sexual encounter simply cannot be squeezed into the male-active/female-passive framework. Moreover, as Smyth suggests, the whole system of gender stops making sense when confronted with a self-penetrating phallic femme:

> In lesbian porn the presence of the dildo can subvert the potency of the penis by reasserting women's sexual sufficiency and proving that the woman lover is more powerful than any male rival. ... The dildo signifies the lack of fixity of gender, emphasizing that there is always a potential split between the sexual object and the sexual aim, between subject and object of desire.[21]

As Judith Butler points out, the very fact that a penis can never be 'the phallus' – for it can never measure up to the fantasy ideal – means that, far from having a natural biological advantage over lesbians when it comes to fucking women, men are at a *disadvantage*, insofar as they are obliged constantly to put their 'manhood' to the test:

Indeed, if men are said to 'have' the phallus symbolically, their anatomy is also a site marked by having lost it, the anatomical part is never commensurable with the phallus itself. In this sense, men might be understood to be both castrated (already) and driven by penis envy (more properly understood as phallus envy).[22]

For Butler, the lesbian 'phallus' – and by this she means not *just* dildos, but lesbian sexual desire, agency, initiative – is repudiated not only by men anxious to reclaim male power from lesbians but also by 'feminist orthodoxy'. She does not specify what she means here, but it is clear from the context that she is referring to pro-censorship revolutionary feminism, the kind of feminist orthodoxy described by Smyth as 'a moralistic feminist separatism that declared that the further women got from the penis, the better lesbians they became'.[23] Butler's language is notoriously dense and difficult, but her argument is clear: this brand of feminism acts in much the same way as the traditional patriarchal repression of lesbianism to stuff the troublesome business of lesbian desire and lesbian sex back into the container of heterosexuality:

If the phallus is that which is excommunicated from the feminist orthodoxy on lesbian sexuality as well as the 'missing part', the sign of an inevitable dissatisfaction that is lesbianism in homophobic and misogynist constructions, then the admission of the phallus into that exchange faces two convergent prohibitions: first, the phallus signifies the persistence of the 'straight mind', a masculinist or heterosexist identification and, hence, the defilement or betrayal of lesbian specificity; secondly, the phallus signifies the insuperability of heterosexuality and constitutes lesbianism as a vain and/or pathetic effort to mime the real thing.[24]

Both heterosexism and feminism claim that the 'lesbian phallus' (which we may interpret for our purposes here quite straightforwardly as the lesbian dildo) makes lesbian sex a sham. For heterosexuals, using a dildo means that lesbian sex is not 'real' sex, that it depends on a pretend penis for gratification (although, as I hope I have shown, it is in fact more complicated that that!). For feminists, using a dildo means that lesbian sex is not 'really' lesbian, because it becomes a copy of heterosex. Butler recognizes that these two claims exert a pressure on lesbian sexuality, but insists that they are both mistaken, and that lesbians who assert phallic power are able to destroy the link between biological masculinity and the phallus: 'precisely *because* it is an idealization, one which no body can adequately approximate, the phallus is a transferable phantasm, and its naturalized link to masculine morphology can be called into question through an aggressive reterritorialization.'[25] In other words, by claiming the phallus as *lesbian territory*, dykes are forcing men to confront the fragile and artificial nature of male power. The dildo-wielding dyke strikes a blow for feminism! Parveen Adams agrees, and writes more explicitly about the dildo as agent of this feminist achievement: 'What is a dildo? ... Why is it difficult to answer? Perhaps by not being a version of the penis or phallus, it shows ... that there is a gap, a gap there, where penis and phallus are not the same thing at all.'[26]

Certainly, the dildo has become much more prominent in representations of lesbian sex in the last few years. For example, Della Grace has published several photographs of lesbians with dildos, Jennifer Saunders was taken to court for using a dildo to have sex with underage young women,[27] and lesbian sex magazine *On Our Backs* ran into trouble with their printers who refused to print shots of a woman licking the tip of a dildo and holding her labia open to it. There is a growing trend for lesbian-owned sex-toy catalogues featuring a range of dildos, including some shaped like dolphins, crystals, fingers or diving women,[28] in addition to the traditional penis-shape, and the annual Lesbian and Gay Pride fair in London now features a dildo and harness stall alongside the T-shirts, books and badges. For those who continue to object that one woman fucking another woman with a dildo represents a heterosexual inequality of power, the double-ended dildo offers the ultimate in the eroticization of mutuality. As Della Grace comments, 'some of us are more confident and able to play with notions of gender. We are not afraid that if we use a dildo we are aping heterosexual sex.'[29] Of course, lesbian culture is not at all the same thing as lesbian-*feminist* culture, and no doubt lesbians would be playing with dildos whether or not it were a politically 'correct' thing to do. But there is no doubt in my mind that, far from being a lesbian heresy, the use of dildos for lesbian sexual pleasure is politically and culturally empowering.[30] I will leave the last word on lesbian dildos to Cindy Patton:

Working through the existing discursive spaces of masculine presence and feminine absence (although not *lack* as lesbians' reclaiming and possession of dildos shows), changes the unconscious interpretive erotics so that even the most recalcitrant heterosexual male cannot help but be disturbed by his exclusion from lesbian-produced representations.[31]

Although I would add that the *really* phallic dyke doesn't give a damn what the 'recalcitrant heterosexual male' thinks.

Clothes make (the woman) the man: butch and femme again

It is not, of course, only by using dildos that lesbians lay claim to the phallus. By performing butch, a dyke insists on her right to erotic self-determination, sexual agency, the desiring gaze, all the 'properties' of phallic sexuality. For the traditional pro-censorship feminist, this appropriation of the phallus is no more than male-identification and, as such, suspect and politically reactionary or counter-revolutionary. Moreover, butch/femme couplings are 'read' from this feminist position as a mimicry of heterosexuality. Since, for revolutionary feminists, heterosexuality represents the expression and the agent of women's subordination and male supremacy, any lesbian who reaffirms the dominance of heterosexuality in this way is a traitor to the feminist cause. There was a powerful rejection of butch/femme during the 1970s, during the most activist phase of the WLM, as one of the respondent's to Klaich's lesbian sex questionnaire makes clear: '[Butch and femme] exists among unevolved women. With evolved women the roles ... are shared.'[32] Thus, butch and femme was regarded as something to grow out of!

Moreover, to the early lesbian movement, which was primarily assimilationist in character, the butch lesbian was an embarrassing anathema. The editors of a recent book about butch lesbians recall anti-butch hostility in the 1950s lesbian community: 'Consider these letters to *The Ladder*: "The kids in flyfront pants and mannish manner are the worst publicity that we can get".'[33] They go on to point out that such attitudes have not changed much since then, and that fear of a hostile reaction prevented many women from contributing to their book: 'fear is still responsible for what's missing from these pages. ... We're so vulnerable in our lives that pinning ourselves to a page is terrifying.'[34]

Rejected by feminists as an imitation of heterosex, and by the assimilationist lesbian movement as too overt and too different, butch and femme roles nevertheless formed an important part of lesbian culture before the WLM, and have been reclaimed by many lesbians today. However, the butch and femme roles of today's queer scene are not at all the same thing as the roles of 1950s lesbian culture. Although there is an interesting discussion going on in the lesbian community concerning butch and femme as expressions of felt realities – the extent to which one woman may be more or less butch *and* more or less femme – the dress codes and performative identities of butch and femme are more casually adopted and discarded by the new generation of queer girls (and lesbian boys).

So, is it true to say that butch and femme roles simply mirror the oppressive relations of heterosex? The only people who think so are revolutionary feminists who don't perform butch/femme. Theorists, both feminist and queer, and lesbians who do identify as butch or femme, all disagree. Sandy Stone writes that 'The lesbian butch or femme both recall the heterosexual scene but simultaneously displace it. The idea that butch and femme are "replicas" ... of heterosexual exchange under-estimates the erotic power of their internal dissonance.'[35] In other words, the erotic attraction of a butch lies not in her 'masculinity', but in the dissonance between her masculine persona and her female self and body. Similarly, the erotic attraction of the femme lies in the undeniable fact that, by choosing to be a femme and by choosing another woman as her lover, she is expressing a sexual self-determination which contradicts her 'feminine' persona. The femme has the phallus!

Sue-Ellen Case also regards butch and femme as breaking out of – and hence posing a challenge to – the heterosexual economy of desire. She suggests that because butch/femme roles 'are played in signs themselves and not in ontologies' (in other words, because they are self-consciously symbolic), then the butch/femme subject occupies a politically powerful position 'outside the ideology of sexual difference and thus the social institution of heterosexuality.'[36] In other words, butch/femme lesbians, far from reproducing heterosexual supremacy, are the *only* subjects who are able to escape from the structural imperative of heterosex.

Some suggest that it is the butch lesbian who poses the most direct threat to patriarchal power, while others maintain that it is the femme.

JoAnn Loulan, for example, believes that 'It's really a mistake to link butches with heterosexual males', although she goes on to say that 'butch lesbians are competition for straight men.'[37] The subversive power of the femme, however, lies in the fact that although she *appears* to be playing the part of traditional heterosexual femininity, she is in fact in possession of sexual agency, an agency denied to women in the heterosexual model. Barbara Creed points out that the very existence of lesbians threatens 'the active/passive dualism, a dichotomy which is crucial to the definition of gender in patriarchal culture',[38] and it is not difficult to see that an active, desiring *femme* is an especially troublesome creature from this perspective. Ardill and O'Sullivan indeed wonder:

> Is the new embrace of 'femmeness' subversive in the same way the clone look was for gay men a decade ago – so that femininity is no longer essentially a position in relation to men: you can be a lesbian *and* a 'real' woman.[39]

Butch/femme has clearly undergone a major historical shift, one which we do not as yet fully understand. The history of female husbands and 'passing women' indicates that some form of what we now think of as butch/femme (although care must be taken when applying what is essentially contemporary terminology to earlier historical moments) was important to the development of lesbian identity, as historians Rudolf Dekker and Lotte van de Pol make clear:

> Before the end of the eighteenth century the expression of love between two women usually took the form of the imitation of a normal, often even married heterosexual couple. Female cross-dressing has therefore been an important stage in the development of female homosexuality.[40]

As the modern lesbian identity as we know it evolved, and as lesbian culture developed, butch and femme were important survival strategies, clearly functioning as crucial markers and anchors of a sexual identity which was otherwise socially invisible.[41] With the new queer culture and a highly politicized approach to gender by queer and feminist communities alike, butch/femme has shifted gear. Now it is possible to see it, as Joan Nestle does, as 'a lesbian-specific way of deconstructing gender that radically reclaims women's erotic energy', and to celebrate butches and femmes alike as 'gender pioneers with a knack for alchemy.'[42] With the eyes of a queer feminist, the intrinsic gender-fuck in the details of butch and femme life leap into sharp focus. It becomes beautifully queer that American butches in the 1950s and 1960s used rolled up Kotex as makeshift dildos when packing,[43] or that a butch can proclaim that 'this short haircut, because it's mine, is a woman's hairstyle.'[44]

Yet butch/femme has been universally castigated. Joan Nestle sums up the history of hostility expressed against butch/femme lesbians, often by those very groups who might have been expected to show a greater degree of insight:

> Everyone has taken a turn at denigrating the butch-femme couple, from the sexologist at the turn of the century who spoke about the predatory masculine invert and the child woman who most easily fell her victim, to the early homophile activists of the fifties who pleaded with these 'obvious' women to tone down their style of self-presentation, to the lesbian-feminists of the seventies who cried 'traitor' into the faces of the few butch-femme couples who did not cross over into the new world of cultural feminism.[45]

The lack of understanding and respect which lesbian feminism showed to butch/femme culture was fairly typical of their approach to traditional lesbian culture generally. It joins the disrespectful feminist dismissal of sadomasochism, lesbian erotica and many other aspects of lesbian erotic culture. For many lesbians, feminism became as rigid and repressive as the homophobic wider culture. As one lesbian remembers, 'the burgeoning lesbian movement [of the 1970s] was horrible. You had to dress exactly right, more rigid than the dress codes in high school, talk exactly right, eat exactly right, act exactly right and fuck exactly right.'[46]

It is important to recognize that this is not simply a question of a sophisticated sexual-political critique confronting an unsophisticated, apolitical community. There are also many issues to do with class and race embedded in this conflict. There was no attempt on the part of the mostly white, mostly educated middle-class feminists who made up the majority of the WLM to understand the importance of butch/femme for black and minority lesbians, or for working-class lesbians. Today, it is the 'bad' lesbians – supporters of butch/femme such as Joan Nestle, producers of pornography such as the editors of *Quim* – who pay most attention to questions of race and class in their discussions of lesbian sex. From this perspective, the orthodox lesbian-feminist attack on butch/femme looks like nothing more than cultural imperialism – the attempted by 'evolved' (generally white, generally class-privileged) lesbians to 'civilize' the 'unevolved', sexually primitive, lesbian savages.

The idea of cultural imperialism is important in this context. For lesbian 'sexual behaviour' is never simply a matter of personal erotic preference. Rather, it expresses and affirms the relationship of individual lesbians to their community, the acceptance or rejection of certain community mores and norms, the development of sexual signs, codes and languages. Sex and sexuality form the bedrock of lesbian *culture*, and must be understood as such. To deal with a particular sexual practice (such as using dildos) or community practice (such as butch/femme dynamics) as if they were significant *only on account of a perceived relationship to mainstream patriarchal culture*, as orthodox lesbian feminism does, is to denigrate lesbian culture and, ironically, to elevate the heterosexual patriarchal mainstream to a position of greater importance. Indeed, political lesbianism always maintained a very uneasy relationship to (real? sexual? pre-feminist? non-political? traditional?) lesbianism. Anna Livia suggests that lesbianism remains as powerfully erased and uncomfortable within orthodox lesbian feminism as it does within the homophobic mainstream, and interprets the trivialization of butch/femme as symptomatic of that:

> I wonder whether lesbian resistance to taking the idea of butch and femme seriously, or even talking seriously about them is partly because it is a purely lesbian issue – while age, disability, race and class can be discussed as human issues.[47]

This desire on the part of feminists to control the unruly lesbian, the troublesome sexy sister, is beautifully encapsulated by Joan Nestle's suggestion that

> the word 'Lesbian-feminist' is a butch/femme relationship (as it has been judged, not as it is) with 'Lesbian' bearing the emotional weight the butch does in modern judgement and 'feminist' becoming the equivalent of the sterotyped femme, the image that can stand the light of day.[48]

A strange pattern begins to emerge during the discussion of lesbian sex and feminism, with 'lesbian' being butch and 'feminist' being femme, or with (as I suggest) 'feminist' being sadist/top and 'lesbian' being masochist/bottom. Certainly, it is easy to argue that the pro-censorship feminist gaze 'pornographizes' lesbian erotic imagery. The ways in which revolutionary feminists/political lesbians/pro-censorship feminists have chosen to mess around with lesbian sexuality begin to look quite suspect.

In the time of AIDS: a reflection on dykes and gay men

I would like to conclude this chapter and book by moving away from a focus on feminism, and back to a consideration of the dynamics within my queer community. From a queer vantage point, it is both impossible and immoral to ignore the effect of the HIV pandemic on queer (lesbian *and* gay) sexuality, and I think that gender performance is probably a significant issue here. There is no doubt that lesbians have, of late, been exploring the eroticism of gay men in a new way. Some lesbians have been having sex with gay men, and much lesbian erotica makes use of gay male characters or plays with the codes of gay male sexuality. In Smyth's words, 'In the past two years more lesbians have been discussing their erotic responses to gay male pornography and incorporating gay male sexual iconography into their fantasies, sex play and cultural representations',[49] a move which is clearly mirrored on the other side of the Atlantic, where 'For the last few years the lesbian sex magazines have been quite openly playing with the (gay) boys.'[50] Phenomena such as 'Drag King' shows, lesbian boys and the 'Daddy Boy Dykes' represented in Della Grace's photographs speak of a *lesbian* incorporation of some aspects of gay male sexuality.

Such playing around with gay male signs and signifiers forms part of the deconstructive manipulation of gender regulations so characteristic of queer activism. In this context, it is not masculinity *per se* which is significant, but the performance of *gay* masculinity by *lesbians*, by those women whose own relationship to both masculinity and femininity is as complex as that of gay men. Essentially, 'the butch daddy dyke and lesbian boy ... appropriate masculine codes without denying the femaleness of their protagonists',[51] thus manipulating gay male sexual codes in the same way as they subverted heterosexual codes by means of the dildo. Just as the flexible nature of the dildo – which may be used by both 'butch' and 'femme' lesbians – highlights the distance between the fleshly penis and the phallic power which it supposedly represents, so the adoption of the gay male masquerade by lesbians emphasizes the artifice of gay men's gender roles and hence *all* gender roles. 'Lesbian "maleness" may be a "gay maleness" – not a re-enactment of fixed gender roles, but an exploration of the very signs "male" and "female".'[52]

But it is unlikely that lesbians have suddenly started dressing up as gay men *just* for the high-theory buzz of deconstructing artifice and masquerade. This is a description of the implications of such acts, not an explanation. My (tentative) suggestion, based on my own shifting relationship to the gay men in my life, is that this might have a lot to do with AIDS. It is a very strange and distressing business being a lesbian member of a lesbian and gay community at the century's end. During the time I have been writing this book I have learned of the death from AIDS of yet another gay man who had been a much-liked and respected colleague. His name has been added to the list of gay men whose illness and death I mourn. It is not simply personal friends whom I grieve for (although personal losses are, of course, the sharpest), but also those whom I never met but whose work has been important to my life. My gay friends have become immensely precious to me. Each one of them appears so terrifyingly vulnerable – are those shadows under his eyes due to overwork, or is he, too, about to go beyond reach? If I don't see an expected face at a conference or party, there is always the fear that I may never see it again. The cumulative effect of loss and grief is almost unbearable, and I am not by any means at the epicentre of the epidemic. The number of my losses is (for the moment) relatively few.

Other lesbians are beginning to speak of the sadness and strangeness of being part of queer communities where the numbers of men are shrinking. Jewelle Gomez writes:

> Although few talk easily about this, it will be a long while before we fully appreciate the extent of the losses the lesbian/gay community has suffered. First, expressly through the HIV-related deaths, we have lost the larger part of a community of men, from all age groups. Gone are men who made possible Castro and Christopher Streets, haute couture, camp, some of the finest literature, theater, and visual art of our generation.[53]

Truly, it feels like a war. The experience of watching HIV steal away so many gay men does not eradicate the political differences within queer communities, it does not make gay men into saints overnight, it does not take away my anger at the misogyny of so many of them, and at the refusal of many others to recognize their race or gender privilege. But it does put all that into perspective. Frustrations engendered by regular political disagreements with gay friends seem very different when I know my time with those friends may be limited. In this dreadful moment, the culture of gay men, with its rich variety, its outrageousness, its wild, creative chutzpah, its many elements simply incomprehensible to me, seems to be running away like a handful of water.

Is this why so many dykes are celebrating gay male sexual culture? Is this why so many of us are setting aside simple lesbian 'butch' in favour of masquerading as gay boys? Are the daddy boy dykes, the lesbian boys, the queer women passing in order to cruise gay men or packing in order to cruise lesbians *as if* they were gay men perhaps expressing a response to AIDS which cannot be put into words? It seems almost as if some lesbians among us are reaching out to carry the banner of gay men's sexual defiance, or as if we are transforming ourselves into the boys that have gone, because we cannot bear the empty space that they have left. Just a thought.

Whatever its relationship with HIV/AIDS, the boisterous new queer culture has not died the easy death which everyone was foretelling at the time of its birth. Something about queer is clearly speaking to this historical moment. Perhaps this is not surprising. For, after all, as an anonymous leafleteer declared, 'Queer means to fuck with gender.'[54] These six words have a double meaning. Not only does queer 'fuck with gender' in the sense of mucking around with it, disobeying its codes, transgressing its rules, refusing its regulation, but it also literally fucks *with* gender – in other words, incorporating a lively awareness of gender, and of the artifice of gender, into sex play and sexual acts, into fucking.

Radical-feminist deconstructions of gender are, of course, a very important influence on the development of the new queer activism (as well as of Queer Theory); but so too are the rich lesbian cultural traditions of butch and femme, of packing dildos and conjuring the phallus out of menstrual protection, of bull daggers who 'conquered masculinity as secret agents of lesbian desire',[55] of femmes who paraded the incomprehensible spectacle of the phallic feminine. Slavish imitations of oppressive heterosexuality? Far from it.

Conclusion

This brief foray into lesbian sex has travelled from dildos to porn, from butch and femme to s/m, from hair-combing in fields of daisies to fucking and fisting. Throughout, the ghost of pro-censorship revolutionary-feminist orthodoxy has been hissing maledictions at various lesbian sexual behaviours, while our queer community is constantly shaken by unbearable grief for those we continue to lose to AIDS, and by anger at the savagery of the homophobic religious and political right.

Lesbian sexual desire and pleasure are everywhere silenced, denied, belittled, misrepresented and suppressed by those who would eradicate us. Among them we must count some who should be our friends, our allies, our supporters. It is especially ironic, and particularly distressing, that the radical political activism which is feminism should be exploited in order to repress lesbian sex and sexuality. Yet in this moment, in the social and cultural context of such unrelenting hostility, lesbian sexual culture is blooming as never before. The energetic catalyst of queer activism and of AIDS activism, and the need to resist the efforts made to stamp out lesbian sex, have prompted the development of a lively, inventive and sophisticated lesbian sexual culture. Despite the weariness of continual struggle, we are confident, voluble and active as never before. This is a unique historical moment – there has never been a better time and place to be a dyke.

Of course, our own privilege should not make us unwilling or unable to recognize the enormous difficulties facing lesbians in other places – especially in the 'third world' and in countries where fundamentalist religions dominate. Nor should we lose sight of the social and political problems which structure our own lesbian communities: the racism, the ageism, the continuing exclusion of disabled lesbians, the failure to recognize lesbian poverty. Yet, it is also commonplace now for women to live as lesbians, celebrating their lesbian desire, building queer families and communities and making a lesbian sexual culture. The power of this should not be underestimated. Lesbian sex is an agent of transformation, of queer power, of feminist revolution. Some of us also suspect (although the empirical evidence is probably inadmissable) that it is simply the best sex possible – finger-licking good. Enjoy!

Notes

1. Some writers use 'dildoes' as the plural, others 'dildos'. I choose 'dildos' in the interests of minimising the strain on my fingers – and is this not, after all, what dildos are for?

2. Although, since even biological sex is far more complex than is generally supposed, the relationship between penises and 'male' babies is not always straightforward. See, for example, Gisela Kaplan and Lesley Rogers, 'The Definition of Male and Female: Biological Reductionism and the Sanctions of Normality' in Sneja Gunew (ed.), *Feminist Knowledge, Critique and Construct* (London: Routledge, 1990).

3. Parveen Adams, 'The Three (Dis)Graces', *New Formations,* No. 19, Spring 1993 pp. 131–38, and Teresa de Lauretis, *The Practice of Love: Lesbian Sexuality and Perverse Desire* (Bloomington and Indianapolis: Indiana University Press, 1994) are good examples for readers who wish to pursue the dykely queering of psychoanalysis.

4. De Lauretis, *The Practice of Love,* p. 220.

5. Cherry Smyth, 'The Pleasure Threshold: Looking at Lesbian Pornography on Film', *Feminist Review,* Spring 1990, No. 34, p. 157.

6. Alison Bechdel, *Dykes to Watch Out For* calendar (Ithaca NY: Firebrand Books, 1994).

7. *Wicked Women: A Magazine of Lesbian Sex and Sexuality* (Strawberry Hills, Australia) No. 25, 1995, p. 50.

8. Margaret Hunt, 'The De-Eroticization of Women's Liberation: Social Purity Movements and the Revolutionary Feminism of Sheila Jeffreys', *Feminist Review,* No. 34, Spring 1990, p. 38.

9. Dolores Klaich, *Woman Plus Woman* (Talahassee, FL: Naiad, 1974), pp. 49–50.

10. *Ibid.,* p. 50.

11. *Ibid.,* p. 51.

12. Barbara Creed, 'Lesbian Bodies: Tribades, Tomboys and Tarts' in Elizabeth Grosz and Elspeth Probyn (eds.), *Sexy Bodies: The Strange Carnalities of Feminism* (London: Routledge, 1995), p. 94.

13. *Ibid.,* pp.93–94.

14. *Ibid.,* p. 95.

15. Randolph Trumbach, 'London's Sapphists: From Three Sexes to Four Genders in the Making of Modern Culture' in Julia Epstein and Kristina Straub (eds.) *Body Guards: The Cultural Politics of Gender Ambiguity* (London: Routledge, 1991), p. 114.

16. *Ibid.,* p. 128.

17. Emma Donoghue, *Passions Between Women: British Lesbian Culture 1668-1801* (London, Scarlet Press, 1993), p. 184

18. *Ibid.,* p. 208.

19. Cindy Patton, 'Unmediated Lust? The Improbable Space of Lesbian Desires' in Tessa Boffin and Jean Fraser (eds.), *Stolen Glances: Lesbians Take Photographs* (London: Pandora, 1991), p. 239.

20. Smyth, 'The Pleasure Threshold, p. 155.

21. *Ibid.,* p.157.

22. Judith Butler, *Bodies that Matter:*

On the Discursive Limits of 'Sex' (London: Routledge, 1993), p. 85.

23. Cherry Smyth, *Lesbians Talk Queer Notions* (London: Scarlet Press, 1992), p. 36.

24. Butler, *Bodies that Matter*, pp. 85–6.

25. *Ibid.*, p. 86.

26. Adams, 'The Three (Dis)Graces', p. 136.

27. Julie Wheelwright, 'Girls will be boys', *Guardian*, 24 September 1991. Wheelwright manages to get through her entire article on the Saunders case without once mentioning that Saunders is a lesbian; indeed, the 'L' word remains entirely absent!

28. A pleasing pun on 'muff-diving', a slang term for cunnilingus.

29. Cited in Smyth, *Queer Notions*, p. 43.

30. And pleasurable of course ... although clearly not all women enjoy using dildos, and far be it from me to insist that all lesbians begin using them simply in the cause of overthrowing the patriarchy!

31. Patton, 'Unmediated Lust?', p. 238.

32. Klaich, Woman Plus Woman, p. 241.

33. Lily Burana, Roxxie and Linnea Due (eds), *Dagger: On Butch Women* (San Francisco: Cleis Press, 1994), p. 9.

34. *Ibid.*

35. Sandy Stone, 'The Empire Strikes Back: A Posttranssexual Manifesto' in Epstein and Straub (eds.) *Body Guards*, p. 296.

36. Sue-Ellen Case, 'Towards a Butch-Femme Aesthetic', *Discourse*, vol. 11, No. 1, 1989, pp. 70 and 56.

37. In Burana *et al.* (eds.), *Dagger*, pp. 94–5.

38. In Grosz and Probyn (eds.), *Sexy Bodies*, p. 93.

39. Susan Ardill and Sue O'Sullivan, 'Butch/Femme obsessions', *Feminist Review*, No. 34, Spring 1990, pp. 79–85.

40. Rudolf Dekker and Lotte van de Pol, *The Tradition of Female Transvestism in Early Modern Europe* (London: Macmillan, 1989), p. 100.

41. See essays in Joan Nestle (ed.), *The Persistent Desire: A Femme-Butch Reader* (Boston: Alyson, 1992).

42. *Ibid.*, p. 14.

43. Burana *et al.* (eds.), *Dagger*, p. 104.

44. Del Martin and Phyllis Lyon, cited in *Quim* No. 3, Winter 1991, p. 15.

45. Nestle (ed.), *The Persistent Desire*, p. 14.

46. Debbie in Burana *et al.* (eds.), *Dagger*, p. 108.

47. Anna Livia, cited in *Quim*, No. 3, Winter 1991, p. 15.

48. Cited in *Quim*, *ibid.*

49. Smyth, *Queer Notions*, p. 42.

50. Patton, 'Unmediated Lust?' p. 238.

51. Smyth, *Queer Notions*, p. 42.

52. Julia Creet, cited in *ibid.*, p. 43.

53. In Jewelle Gomez, Dale Peck, Mab Segrest and David Deitcher (eds.), *Over the Rainbow: Lesbian and Gay Politics in America since Stonewall* (London: Boxtree/Channel 4, 1995), p. 55.

54. In Smyth, *Queer Notions*, p. 17.

55. Cindy Patton in Boffin and Fraser (eds.), *Stolen Glances*, p. 238.

Bibliography

Abbott, Sydney, and Barbara, Love. *Sappho Was a Right-On Woman: A Liberated View of Lesbianism*. New York: Stein & Day, 1972.

Allison, Dorothy. *Skin: Talking about Sex, Class and Literature*: London, Pandora, 1995.

Baker, Roger. *Drag: A History of Female Impersonation in the Performing Arts*. London: Cassell, 1994.

Barrington, Judith (ed.). *An Intimate Wilderness: Lesbian Writers on Sexuality*. Portland, Oreg.: Eighth Mountain Press, 1991.

Boffin, Tessa, and Jean Fraser, (eds.), *Stolen Glances: Lesbians Take Photographs*. London: Pandora, 1991.

Bright, Susie. *Susie Sexpert's Lesbian Sex World*. San Francisco: Cleis Press, 1990.

Bright, Susie. *Susie Bright's Sexual Reality: A Virtual Sex World Reader*. San Francisco: Cleis Press, 1992.

Burana, Lily, and Roxxie and Linnea Due, (eds.). *Dagger: On Butch Women*. San Francisco: Cleis Press, 1994.

Butler, Judith. *Bodies that Matter: On the Discursive Limits of 'Sex'*. London: Routledge, 1993.

Califia, Pat. *Sapphistry: The Book of Lesbian Sexuality*. Tallahassee, FL: Naiad, 1988.

Califia, Pat. *Macho Sluts*. Boston: Alyson, 1988.

Califia, Pat. *The Advocate Adviser*. Boston: Alyson, 1991.

Card, Claudia (ed.). *Adventures in Lesbian Philosophy*. Bloomington and Indianapolis: Indiana University Press, 1994.

Card, Claudia. *Lesbian Choices*. New York: Columbia University Press, 1995.

Cartledge, Sue, and Joanna Ryan, (eds.). *Sex and Love: New Thoughts on Old Contradictions*. London: The Women's Press, 1983.

Cole, Susan. *Pornography and the Sex Crisis*. Toronto: Amanita, 1989.

Cooper, Emmanuel. *The Sexual Perspective: Homosexuality and Art in the Last 100 Years in the West*, 2nd edn. London: Routledge, 1994.

Corinne, Tee A.. *Lovers: Love and Sex Stories*. Austin, Tex.: Banned Books, 1989.

Crane, Paul. *Gays and the Law*. London: Pluto Press, 1981.

Cruikshank, Margaret. *The Gay and Lesbian Liberation Movement*. London: Routledge, 1992.

Daly, Mary. *Pure Lust: Elemental Feminist Philosophy*. London: The Women's Press, 1984.

Daly, Mary and Jane Caputi. *Webster's First New Intergalactic Wickedary of the English Language*. London: The Women's Press, 1987.

Darty, Trudy, and Sandee Potter, (eds.). *Woman-Identified Woman*. Palo Alto: Mayfield, 1984.

Dekker, Rudolf and Lotte van de Pol. *The Tradition of Female Transvestism in Early Modern Europe*. London: Macmillan, 1989.

Delacoste, Frédérique, and Priscilla Alexander (eds.). *Sex Work: Writings by Women in the Sex Industry*. London: Virago, 1988.

Donoghue, Emma. *Passions Between Women: British Lesbian Culture 1668–1801*. London: Scarlet Press, 1993.

Douglas, Carol Anne. *Love and Politics: Radical Feminist and Lesbian Theories*. San Francisco: ism press, 1990.

Doyal, Lesley. *What Makes Women Sick? Gender and the Political Economy of Health*. London: Macmillan, 1995.

Duberman, Martin, Martha Vicinus,

and George Chauncey, (eds.). *Hidden from History: Reclaiming the Gay and Lesbian Past*. Harmondsworth: Penguin, 1989.

Dworkin, Andrea. *Pornography: Men Possessing Women*. London: The Women's Press, 1981.

Dworkin, Andrea. *Letters from a War Zone: Writings 1976–1987*. London: Secker and Warburg, 1988.

Edwards, Tim. *Erotics and Politics: Gay Male Sexuality, Masculinity and Feminism*. London: Routledge, 1994.

Epstein, Julia and Kristina Straub, (eds.). *Body Guards: The Cultural Politics of Gender Ambiguity*. London: Routledge, 1991.

Faderman, Lillian. *Surpassing the Love of Men*. London: The Women's Press, 1981.

Foucault, Michel. *The History of Sexuality: Vol. 1: An Introduction*. Harmondsworth: Penguin, 1976 (this trans. 1979).

French, Marilyn. *The War Against Women*. London: Hamish Hamilton, 1992.

Freud, Sigmund. *On Sexuality*. Harmondsworth: Penguin, 1905.

Garber, Marjorie. *Vested Interests: Cross-Dressing and Cultural Anxiety*. Harmondsworth: Penguin, 1992.

Gilbert, Harriett. *The Sexual Imagination from Acker to Zola: A Feminist Companion*. London: Jonathan Cape, 1993.

Gomez, Jewelle, Dale Peck, Mab Segrest, and David Deitcher, (eds.). *Over the Rainbow: Lesbian and Gay Politics in America since Stonewall*. London: Boxtree/Channel 4, 1995.

Grace, Della. *Love Bites*. London: Gay Men's Press, 1991.

Grant, Michael. *Erotic Art in Pompeii*. London: Octopus, 1975.

Greer, Germaine. *The Female Eunuch*. London: Granada, 1970.

Grier, Barbara and Coletta Reid, (eds.). *The Lavender Herring: Essays from 'The Ladder'*. Baltimore: Diana Press, 1976.

Griffin, Gabrielle (ed.). *Outwrite: Lesbianism and Popular Culture*. London: Pluto Press, 1993.

Grosz, Elizabeth, and Elspeth Probyn, (eds.). *Sexy Bodies: The Strange Carnalities of Feminism*. London: Routledge, 1995.

Gunew, Sneja. *Feminist Knowledge, Critique and Construct*. London: Routledge, 1990.

Gurley Brown, Helen. *Sex and the Single Girl*. New York: Bernard Geiss, 1962.

Harriss, Kathryn. *What Is this Big Fuss about Lesbian Sadomasochism? Lesbian Sexuality and the Women's Liberation Movement*. University of Kent at Canterbury, Women's Studies Occasional Papers, 1988.

Harvard Law Review, editors of, *Sexual Orientation and the Law*. Cambridge, Mass.: Harvard University Press, 1990.

Hellman, Harald, and Burkhard Reimschneider. *Betty Page: Queen of Pin-Up*. Cologne: Benedikt Taschen, 1987.

Hepburn, Cuca, and Bonnie Gutierrez, (eds.). *Alive and Well: A Lesbian Health Guide*. Freedom, CA: The Crossing Press, 1988.

Hirsch, Marianne, and Evelyn Fox Keller, (eds.). *Conflicts in Feminism*. London: Routledge, 1990.

Hoagland, Sarah Lucia. *Lesbian Ethics: Towards New Values*. Palo Alto: Institute of Lesbian Studies, 1988.

Hoagland, Sarah Lucia, and Julia Penelope, (eds.). *For Lesbians Only: A Separatist Anthology*. London: Onlywomen Press, 1988.

Hubback, Judith. *Wives Who Went to College*. London: William Heinemann, 1957.

Jay, Karla (ed.). *Lesbian Erotics*. New York: New York University Press, 1995.

Jeffreys, Sheila. *The Spinster and Her Enemies: Feminism and Sexuality 1880–1930*. London: Pandora, 1985.

Jeffreys, Sheila. *Anticlimax: A Feminist Perspective on the Sexual Revolution*.

London: The Women's Press, 1990.

Jeffreys, Sheila. *The Lesbian Heresy: A Feminist Perspective on the Lesbian Sexual Revolution*. Melbourne: Spinifex Press, 1993.

Kappeler, Susan. *The Pornography of Representation*. Cambridge: Polity Press, 1986.

Kennedy, Mary, Cathy Lubelska, and Val Walsh, (eds.). *Making Connections: Women's Studies, Women's Movements, Women's Lives*. London: Taylor & Francis, 1993.

Kiss and Tell. *Drawing the Line*. Vancouver: Press Gang, 1991.

Kiss and Tell. *Her Tongue on My Theory: Images, Essays and Fantasies*. Vancouver: Press Gang, 1994.

Klaich, Dolores. *Woman Plus Woman*. Tallahassee, FL: Naiad, 1974.

Klein, Renate, and Deborah Steinberg, (eds.). *Radical Voices: A Decade of Resistance from Women's Studies International Forum*. Oxford: Pergamon Press, 1989.

Krafft-Ebing, Richard von (trans. by M. E. Wedneck). *Psychopathia Sexualis*. New York: Putnams, 1882, reprinted 1965.

De Lauretis, Teresa. *The Practice of Love: Lesbian Sexuality and Perverse Desire*. Bloomington and Indianapolis: Indiana University Press, 1994.

Linden, Robin, Darlene Pagano, Diana Russell, and Susan Leigh Starr, (eds.). *Against Sadomasochism: A Radical Feminist Analysis*. San Francisco: Frog in the Well Press, 1982.

Lorde, Audre. *Sister Outsider: Essays and Speeches*. New York: The Crossing Press, 1984.

Loulan, JoAnn. *Lesbian Sex*. San Francisco: Spinsters Ink/Aunt Lute, 1984.

Loulan, JoAnn. *Lesbian Passion: Loving Ourselves and Each Other*. San Francisco: Spinsters Ink/Aunt Lute, 1987.

MacAdams, Cynthia. *Emergence*. New York: Chelsea House, 1977.

MacAdams, Cynthia. *Rising Goddess*. New York: Morgan and Morgan, 1983.

Martin, Del and Phyllis Lyon. *Lesbian/Woman*. New York: Bantam Books, 1972 (reprinted 1995).

McEwen, Christian, and Sue O'Sullivan, (eds.). *Out the Other Side: Contemporary Lesbian Writing*. London: Virago, 1988.

Masson, Jeffrey. *Against Therapy*. London: Fortuna, 1990.

Merck, Mandy. *Perversions: Deviant Readings*. London: Virago, 1993.

Meyer, Moe (ed.). *The Politics and Poetics of Camp*. London: Routledge, 1994.

Miles, Robert. *Racism*. London: Routledge 1989.

Morgan, Robin (ed.). *Sisterhood is Global: The International Women's Movement Anthology*. Harmondsworth: Penguin, 1984.

Muirhead-Gould, John (ed.). *The Kama Sutra of Vatsyayana* (trans. by Sir Richard Burton and F. F. Arbuthnot). London: Panther Books, 1963.

Nestle, Joan., *A Restricted Country: Essays and Short Stories*. London: Sheba, 1987.

Nestle, Joan (ed.). *The Persistent Desire: A Femme-Butch Reader*. Boston: Alyson, 1992.

Oikawa, Mona, Dianne Falconer, and Ann Decter, (eds.). *Resist! Essays Against a Homophobic Culture*. Toronto: The Women's Press, 1994.

Onlywomen Press (ed.). *Love Your Enemy? The Debate Between Heterosexual Feminism and Political Lesbianism*. London: Onlywomen Press, 1981.

Penelope, Julia. *Call Me Lesbian: Lesbian Lives, Lesbian Theory*. Freedom, CA: The Crossing Press, 1992.

Plummer, Ken. *Modern Homosexualities: Fragments of Lesbian and Gay Experience*.

London: Routledge, 1992.

Reuben, David. *Everything You Always Wanted to Know about Sex*. New York: Bantam, 1969.

Rich, Adrienne. *Blood, Bread and Poetry: Selected Prose 1979–1985* London: Virago, 1987.

Richardson, Diane (ed.). *Telling It Straight: Theorizing Heterosexuality*. London: Macmillan, 1996.

SAMOIS (eds.). *Coming to Power: Writings and Graphics on Lesbian S/M* 3rd edn. Boston: Alyson, 1987.

Schramm-Evans, Zoe. *Making Out: The Book of Lesbian Sex and Sexuality*. London: Pandora, 1995.

Scruton, Roger. *Sexual Desire: A Philosophical Investigation*. London: Weidenfeld & Nicolson, 1986.

Seager, Joni, and Ann Olson. *Women in the World: An International Atlas*. London: Pluto Press, 1986.

Sedgwick, Eve Kosofsky. *Epistemology of the Closet*. Hemel Hempstead: Harvester Wheatsheaf, 1991.

Segal, Lynne. *Straight Sex: The Politics of Pleasure*. London: Virago, 1994.

Segal, Lynne, and Mary McIntosh, (eds.). *Sex Exposed: Sexuality and the Pornography Debate*. London: Virago, 1992.

Sheba Collective (eds.). *Serious Pleasure: Lesbian Erotic Stories and Poetry*. London: Sheba, 1989.

Shepherd, Simon, and Mick Wallis, (eds.). *Coming On Strong: Gay Politics and Culture*. London: Unwin Hyman, 1989.

Signorile, Michelangelo. *Queer in America: Sex, the Media and the Closets of Power*. London: Abacus, 1993.

Smyth, Cherry. *Lesbians Talk Queer Notions*. London: Scarlet Press, 1992.

Snitow, Ann, Christine Stansell, and Sharon Thompson, (eds.). *Desire: The Politics of Sexuality*. London: Virago, 1983.

Stein, Arlene. *Sisters, Sexperts, Queers: Beyond the Lesbian Nation*. Harmondsworth: Penguin, 1993.

Stoltenberg, John. *Refusing to Be a Man*. London: Fontana/Coliins, 1989.

Storr, Anthony. *Sexual Deviation*. Harmondsworth: Penguin, 1964.

Tatchell, Peter. *Out in Europe: A Guide to Lesbian and Gay Rights in 30 European Countries*. London: Channel 4/Rouge Magazine, 1990.

Thompson, Bill. *Sadomasochism: Painful Perversion or Pleasurable Play?* London: Cassell, 1994.

Tiefer, Leonore. *Sex Is Not a Natural Act and Other Essays*. Oxford: Westview Press, 1995.

Vance, Carole (ed.). *Pleasure and Danger: Exploring Female Sexuality*. London: Pandora, 1985.

Vida, Ginny (ed.). *Our Right to Love: A Lesbian Resource Book*. Englewood Cliffs, NJ: Prentice Hall, 1978.

Walker, Alice, and Pratibha Parmar, *Warrior Marks: Female Genital Mutilation and the Sexual Blinding of Women*. London: Jonathan Cape, 1993.

Watney, Simon. *Policing Desire: Pornography, AIDS and the Media*. London: Methuen, 1987.

White, Edmund. *The Burning Library: Writing on Art, Politics and Sexuality 1969–1993*. London: Picador, 1994.

Wiesenfeld, Cheryl, Yvonne Kalmus, Sonia Katchian, and Rikki Ripp, (eds.). *Women See Women*. New York: Thomas Y. Crowell, 1976.

Wilton, Tamsin. *Lesbian Studies: Setting an Agenda*. London: Routledge, 1995.

Wilton, Tamsin. (ed.). *Immortal, Invisible: Lesbians and the Moving Image*. London: Routledge, 1995.

Wilton, Tamsin. *En/Gendering AIDS: Sex, Texts, Epidemic* (forthcoming).

Winship, Janice. *Inside Women's Magazines*. London: Pandora, 1987.

Index